E. M. Forster

E. M. Forster

A Critical Study

by Laurence Brander

Lewisburg
Bucknell University Press

© Laurence Brander 1968
First American edition published 1970
by Associated University Presses, Inc.,
Cranbury, New Jersey 08512

Library of Congress Catalogue Card Number: 78-123431

ISBN 0 8387 7743 0

Printed in Great Britain

to Ahmed Ali

I wish to acknowledge the generosity of
Mr Forster and his American publishers in
the matter of quotations. Acknowledgment is
made to Alfred A. Knopf, Inc. for permission
to quote from the following copyrighted
works of E. M. Forster: *Where Angels Fear
to Tread*, *A Room With a View*, *The Longest
Journey*, *Howards End*, and *The Collected
Tales of E. M. Forster*; thanks also go to
Harcourt Brace & World for their kind
permission to quote from the works that they
publish. I have debts to Mrs Molly Dickins,
who read the typescript; to T. O. Beachcroft,
who led me to the Kipling comparison with
the Caves episode; and to Oliver Warner for
much genial encouragement.

Among the books I have a special debt to
Miss Kirkpatrick's *Soho Bibliography*, which
has transformed Forster studies, and among
many things gave me the clues to the
development of thought from *Alexandria* to
A Passage to India.

Contents

1*

Introduction

FORSTER'S NOVELS ARE Edwardian, even the Indian one, and they describe a world which existed bèfore the breaking of Europe and which has altogether gone. They have become part of that rich history of our island which has been told for two hundred years in novel form. They are vividly alive because the writing has what he calls 'the magic' in it and, because he described things so accurately as well as so amusingly, they are social history as well as studies of the Edwardian mind. The writer was a young man who was twenty-one on the first day of this century.

The chief character in any novel, and often the most interesting, is the writer of it, and we may meet this Edwardian novelist most easily by approaching him through the later books, which are written by a man who lived through all our political and social crises. He has felt our wars and revolutions acutely and he has set an example of stoical steadiness all the time. But he has never lost the sense of gaiety which so often saves us and he will lead us back to the Edwardian world in which this young genius wrote. So we begin with the biographies, which all have an autobiographical strain in them, and then come the Alexandrian writings which help us so much to understand *A Passage to India*, and after that the book on the novel, which leads directly to the creative writing. The short stories are typical Edwardian fantasies, escapes from a society that at times looked too solid and secure. And after the creative writing, the essays, the conversations with the reader which took the place of storytelling in a shattered world that would come breaking in.

As in the case of Orwell, his writing on public affairs was done before we had lived through our despair, before we realized in England—the French were so much quicker—that we were part of what could be an evolution into a new world from which the secular pain and stress of humanity could be in great part removed. Without that prophetic vision, he could only seek to conserve the freedoms man had gained through the centuries and he spoke all through the years of the breaking of Europe, especially for the freedom to think and the freedom to speak so that human societies can one day rise out of their muddles. He tilts at muddles with the devotion of a Don Quixote tilting at a windmill. He is a humanist and, as humanists will, he became obsessed for a time in studying religious beliefs until they became a main theme in his greatest novel. He cares passionately for the intelligence and has seen how it is abused in revolutionary times. Proudly liberal, he has not been able to enjoy the revolutions of the western world. He has always sought the Stoic steadiness. Our own shuffling revolution must have been particularly tedious; it has what he calls a sausage and mash quality he could not approve. In these sixty years of change and shifting values during which he wrote, he has clung to friendship as the only reliably secure thing left and some of his best writing has been in celebration of friends, a friend in Cambridge, one in India and the old lady, a great-aunt, who left him enough money to keep him until his writings supported him.

He has never had to work for a living and so has been free to work hard at what he lived for. He never had to sell writing quickly to get money. It could lie maturing for years until it was fresh enough to live for many years. Until it had 'the magic' in it.

He is a traditionalist, born into the tradition of English writing and when he wrote in parallel with that firm traditionalist T. S. Eliot, it was easy to see who was the Englishman so much in the tradition that he could neglect it or adapt it to a farther stage of usefulness. He is of the tradition which includes Milton, sternly and rigidly incorruptible for truth. Of the tradition of Keats, who spoke for 'the holiness of the heart's affection'. Of the eccentric English travellers: 'For four hours yesterday evening I walked barefoot in petticoats through the streets with black and red powders smeared over my forehead, cheeks and nose.' Of the tradition of Hardy, 'the work of Hardy is my home', and the writing about the English heart with the feeling that goes away back to the people of the great rings in Wiltshire. When he wrote the biographies he was writing not only about friends but about the places that have meant most to him, Cambridge and India and London with the countryside around it where the commuters live, but where also the great houses stand from Tudor times, reminding us that until recently, and perhaps even now, the strength of London comes from the earth of the Home Counties.

All the essential English things are his inheritance and many of the paradoxes. His creed is personal relations and he enjoys the society of the elect, but he has the preacher's itch, the English puritan disease, inherited both from the Forsters and the Claphamite Thorntons. Tolerance is one of his golden virtues, but it is difficult to be tolerant of Sawston and the bureaucrats and the Foreign Office and Scott's novels. He sees that the wholehearted nature of communist rule is as desirable in our present discontents as the Christian brotherhood and charity in that creed, but it can be very upsetting and charity can produce a great deal of harm. A democracy of aristocrats is preferable.

He is naturally a liberal, but in an age of wars and revolutions he has spent his time conserving what he cared passionately about saving. He felt as another great liberal, Benedetto Croce, felt at that time: 'surely nobody would complain of those who try to conserve intellectual vigour, artistic sensibility, moral insight or love of liberty; for, in these cases, "conservatism" means hoarding our resources and equipping ourselves to fulfil our functions and to advance in the struggle of life.'

To the Edwardians Forster was an interesting novelist and short story-teller of no very great importance. In the ebullient twenties, his reputation as a novelist soared and everyone enjoyed the latest novel about India which was a lively study of comparative religion and foretold that all our professional cadres would be cleared out of India—to give our traders greater scope. As the twenties faded into the haunted thirties, in that nightmare decade Forster became the embodiment of the liberal man of letters, precociously a grand old man, because he was free and ready to take up good causes, to speak and write for freedom of expression. This was his greatest decade as a social influence; in a decade of Leaders, he led our young writers, a humanist in a world of idealist communists and High Churchmen.

The books came more slowly. He had published four novels and a dozen short stories between 1905 and 1910, all clearly under the influence of Cambridge, that most tender nurse. Apart from *A Passage to India,* written in great part soon afterwards and before the first war interrupted all writing, his creative period was over. His themes would have been English or European themes. With Europe smashed up, prophecy was impossible and preaching could be done in more direct ways.

He found himself in Alexandria during the first war with enough leisure to do a good deal of journalism and to write a *Guide* to the city with a brilliant historical introduction. The stream of journalism continued when he returned home after the war. A small output for a professional journalist, but as usual he was free to write only when he liked. The material gradually mounted up and he collected some of it in a small paperback volume, *Pharos and Pharillon,* which covered much of the ground in the historical introduction to the *Guide.* Then the second visit to India, which gave him the ending to his novel, more journalism and many years later a biography of an Indian friend. Next, the invitation to give the Clark lectures canalized his energies and gave us a book on the novel which tells us much about his favourite novels and more about his own.

Pious duty some years later inspired the first biography, a book of Cambridge and one of its amiable sons. Soon afterwards, the first big collection of essays, *Abinger Harvest,* going back to his first appearance in print, in journals edited by Cambridge friends, and covering all his interests as creative writer and scholar for three decades. The second large collection of essays carries us on to 1950 and we are thirsty for the third, which we know will be equally fascinating. But Forster has never hurried into print.

Two more biographies complete the tally of volumes, fourteen in all. Not an excessive output, and not a dull book among them. That is the secret. Everything he has written is still full of life. Books so easily grow dull or dated. A man who writes much must sometimes write dully. But the Horatian who has let his work mature and confined his energies to the subjects where his heart lies has written books that will always be refreshing for those of us who enjoy intelligence and gaiety.

Goldie

BEGIN WITH THE nonsense: 'nonsense is too seldom recorded. Wit and humour get put into a biography, foolery is missed out. It is so evanescent.' Lowes Dickinson the boy, listening to Derwent Coleridge preaching his annual sermon which began: 'Reading Plato the other night...' The old don cooking himself in Gibbs's Building: 'The atmosphere was hot: gas, electricity, cosy-stoves, valor-perfection lamps, sizzled and roared.' Then into the open air. He visited Forster's garden at an unfortunate moment, a moment when there was too much pink: 'I don't like pink. I did speak to God about it; however some people do, and anyhow it can't be helped.' Best of all, nonsense in India, where Forster was usually gay and happy like a man just come home from wandering, so that there were many 'little glints of nonsense, like flying fish'. There was the deplorable Indian servant (so untypical of a great company) 'who wailed "this is no proper arrangement" as soon as he had to do any work', Dickinson's apology for keeping an elephant waiting and the monumental reply: 'elephants sometimes wait four hours.' The comment of the Maharajah's Private Secretary: 'The padre sahib is a very nice man indeed, he has no interest whatever in religion, and that is suitable for a clergyman.' There is so often an edge to Cambridge nonsense, the lighter criticism of life. There is more in this last example, Dickinson dining in an English army Mess in Peshawar, sitting afterwards with the colonel, while the young men 'got rather drunk in exquisite style' and were charming to him and made him swallow prairie oysters. In that gay moment, the gaiety providing common ground between the don and the soldiers, between the solid figure and the young men: 'I see him there for the first time as a solid figure, who has won his own place in the world, and holds it firmly.' Forster, the affectionate spectator, as in another moment in India, years later, as he watched his Maharajah dancing himself into a religious ecstasy at a Hindu festival.

The nonsense is no more than a trace element, a tiny essential ingredient in what is rather like a twentieth century prose Lycidas, a series of elegaic themes which resolve into what Forster wanted in celebrating his friend. 'I should like to make him live for people who never met him in the flesh.' That comes from the Epilogue and echoes the Preface where he says that Dickinson 'admired a biography not when it treated its subject in a reverent spirit but when it made it come alive. I should like to adopt his own standard here.'

He begins at the beginning and at once he notes that the schoolboy had 'the feeling that he was alien...the rest of the dormitory belonged to another world'. Dickinson in old age admitted: 'I have never lost this feeling. Indeed in my old age I feel it as never before. Men become to me simply unintelligible', a saying that will be echoed in many ageing hearts. It would have been easy for him to become a recluse in his college, but the memoir is a celebration of the College and of Cambridge, which gave him the strength and independence to go into the world and help found the League of Nations.

The Memoir centres on the achievement, the writing and the public work in time of war, so the early years are dealt with faithfully but briefly. 'And there were anemones and bluebells in spring, but he couldn't feel they belonged to him, for he did not yet belong to himself. In this dim and unsatisfactory way, the years wore away...' Life, the suggestion is, really begins in college. In a famous passage, the first in which we are shown the close sympathy between biographer and subject, Forster celebrates the joyous release of college after school:

> He had no idea what Cambridge meant — and I remember having the same lack of comprehension about the place myself, when my own turn came to go up there. It seems too good to be real. That the public school is not infinite and eternal, that there is something more compelling in life than team-work and more vital than cricket, that firmness, self-complacency and fatuity do not between them compose the whole armour of man, that lessons may have to do with leisure and grammar with literature — it is difficult for an inexperienced boy to grasp truths so revolutionary, or to realize that freedom can sometimes be gained by walking through an open door.

This illustrates the apparent impossibility of discussing Forster's writings without copious quotation. He always has the inevitable word and phrase, and 'the magic', as here for a kind of schooling that no longer exists in the great schools and as in this animated description of the setting in which Dickinson spent most of his life:

> To the north of the front court of King's rises a precipitous wall of stone and glass: Henry VI's chapel, tending by its very size to nullify itself when it has become familiar and to enter but little into the general consciousness of the college. On the south of the court the chapel is acknowledged by some presentable buildings of the Gothic revival, containing the Hall, lecture rooms, the undergraduates' reading room, the dons' combination rooms and so on. Westward, the eighteenth century speaks; Gibbs's Building, or Fellows' Buildings, almost closes that side of the court: a solid three-storey block, graceful, grave, and grouping with its precipitous and perpendicular neighbour into a harmony peculiar to England. There are compliments outside the rules of etiquette, and perhaps they are the only compliments worth receiving. Gibbs is pierced midway by a cavernous entry, known to initiates as Jumbo House, in whose sombre recesses are usually found a ladder, a handcart, and a small heap of sand. These too are peculiar to England. The range from them to the soaring chapel-buttresses, pinnacled in the intense inane, is the range of the English mind.

Match these words with other celebrations of Cambridge courts

down the centuries and you are fortunate. They are a good intro-
ductory sample of the quality of the technique which Forster
brought to his task of making Goldie 'live for people who never met
him'. He poses the problem in the Preface: 'He was not merely
intelligent, affectionate, charming, remarkable; he was unique. But
how is this to be conveyed?' He responds to his question in the
Epilogue, using a favourite device, the echo. Mephistopheles 'who
should inhabit a cranny in every biography' poses the question: 'is
there nothing which will survive when all of you also have vanished?'

Forster feels that the bleak question is pressed and he gives way
on point after point. Dickinson's life was externally dull, it cannot
be said he was a good writer, the League of Nations failed, so it
would be difficult to maintain that Dickinson achieved much for his
fellowmen in that field and lastly he cannot be classed with McTaggart or Bertrand Russell as a philosopher and 'takes no place in the
philosophic hierarchy of the past'. Then we hear the echo: Dickinson was 'beloved, affectionate, unselfish, intelligent, witty, charming'
and these qualities were fused so that he was 'an indescribably rare
being...in the only direction which seems to be infinite: the
direction of the Chorus Mysticus. He did not merely increase our
experience: he left us more alert for what has not yet been experienced and more hopeful about other men because he had lived.'

Contact with such a man is indeed invaluable and the biographer
realizes that if he can bring Dickinson alive for those who could
not otherwise have met him ('turn the passing into the everlasting')
he will have succeeded. That was the literary challenge which
'lured me on' and the reader will acknowledge gratefully his success.
It is the challenge which all university biographers accept. To get at
the essence of a quiet life. A. E. Housman acknowledged defeat at
the end of a brief and fine piece on Arthur Platt: 'Yet what most
eludes description is not the excellence of his gifts but the singu-
larity of his essential being, his utter unlikeness to any other creature
in the world.' Forster had space and time and the will to achieve
success and he has brought alive a man with rare qualities invaluable
in any human society, and an independent mind with standards
based confidently on those of his friends in a college community, a
man whose life was devoted to serving others.

The service a man can give is dictated by the times in which he lives and in Europe in this century much of his time must have been given to ameliorating the consequences of the political lunacy which surged right across the continent. Dickinson was in his maturity when the first war came and spent his war years in the painful isolation of a man who works for sanity when all around him are earnestly insane. When the war was over he gave his energies to trying to prevent the next. By that time his biographer too had reached maturity and worked for sanity while the majority lapsed again.

There is another service an intelligent European has been able to offer all through this century, the positive service of helping men to assimilate the incredible amount of new knowledge made available to European societies. There has been nothing like it for hundreds of years and Cambridge has played a special part in disseminating the knowledge in digestible form. Men bred in the classical discipline would seem to play no part here, and that seeming has led to the heresy of the two cultures. Heresies are noisy and the quiet answer is found before the heresy was formulated in the work of men like Dickinson and in this quiet narrative of his useful life.

It is the quiet men, often the quite unknown and unremembered men who carry any human society along. They are independent and do not compromise, unlike all men in public life who are ready to traffic daily with the devil. They are independent but it is in their nature to involve themselves in the perpetual struggle in all human societies against the erosion of moral and intellectual values. The most difficult years in England for such a man in this century were the years of the first war, 1914–1918. It was bad enough in the second war but there was not the same obsessed animal hounding of anyone who would not career along with the herd in lunatic unison. Dickinson became lonely even in his college and his one protection, as we shall see, was to isolate himself even from some of his close friends. He was forced back on the discipline in which he had been bred, the Greek discipline, and we remember that the Greeks too had to cope with an explosion of scientific knowledge.

The preoccupation with the Greeks brings amusing overtones to the biography, for Dickinson obviously leaned heavily on the

Socrates created by Plato, one of the great resurrections of one
intellectual by another. But there are things about that resurrected
character Forster cannot bear: 'to a Goth like myself he seems much
more Socratic than Socrates. Socrates...would have emptied any
modern room at once. Dickinson kept every room full, never
nagging, never setting traps, never reducing the company to
silence while he demonstrated the supremacy of his intellect, the
justness of his opinions, the aptness of his wit, the profundity of his
vision.'

There is imperfect sympathy also in Dickinson's reliance on
Plato, Goethe and Shelley. Dickinson approached Plato through
esoteric Buddhism so 'it is natural that he should be involved in
Plotinus'. As for Goethe, 'he was soon confronted with the immense
boringness of Goethe'. And 'few of us have felt Shelley's fascination
as he did, or we should have outgrown it and taken to "business or
Keats".' Shelley's influence, he says, was immediate and turned
Dickinson to politics and schemes of social reform. We may note
that all three were greatly attracted to science, as Dickinson was and
as Forster never was. At the end of the passage Forster offers a
sympathetic description of their influence. ' "Books" is an inade-
quate word to use in so personal a connection. It was rather that
three people who knew his language proved willing to speak to him
in it and to say sentences which he could not have framed for himself. He entered a world which was an extension of his own heart.'

This is quite early in the book, while Forster is still concerned to
revive for us the ambience in which his subject was growing. It is
done unobtrusively, as the narrative of Dickinson's development
proceeds. A word for King's: 'Brains are not everything, as we all
keep telling one another, still they do counteract social silliness.'
And the word for Cambridge is associated with Forster's regular
theme of personal relations: 'As Cambridge filled up with friends,
it acquired a magic quality...People and books reinforced one
another, intelligence joined hands with affection, speculation became
a passion, and discussion was made profound by love.' Here most
of us become outsiders. We cannot follow these sensitive spirits
into their order of affection. We can respond when Keats speaks
of 'the holiness of the heart's affection' for that describes the

privacy of the heart. We appreciate bachelors of either sex, for they can be always at the service of their friends, they are not tied conjugally in emergency. But this hint of closer relationships, which can bridge the generations so readily, is something we must respect though we cannot share. They are part of the infinite delicacy of nature. Forster says of Dickinson: 'He believed, furthermore, in something more definite, in love between two individuals.' It involves revulsion from the physical, mentioned here, as Forster never shirks what must be said, but mentioned as 'a uniform orgy where anything is everything, and blackberries and pismires are indistinguishable from Socrates.' It is a revulsion from Pan and we feel it strongly in the character of Caroline Abbott thirty years before.

Back to the public aspects of our existence. It is noted that Dickinson 'loved humanity—as far as that phrase has any meaning; and it still has some meaning, though not so much as it promised in the nineteenth century' and a little later the heaviness of social duty is hinted: 'even when he was afraid of human beings, as at school, or bewildered by them, as in the War, he refused to escape from them.'

There is a momentary easing of the tension in this exploration of a personality, nicely calculated, when Goldie works on a co-operative farm and then becomes a University Extension lecturer. 'Goldie had no turn for manual labour, and only a theoretical affection for the working classes.' It did not take him long to discover that in the country animals are all right but human beings sometimes are. He was 'endowed with a sense of humour rather than a zest for comedy' which did not help him when he was pigging it with the peasantry. Idealism had dictated the experiment: 'All through his life Dickinson had this hope that, at a touch, the world of matter would be— not annihilated but transformed.'

Then come the Extension lectures and the narrative quickens, the sentences scintillate. It is exactly the contrast later between the account of Dickinson's visit to China and to India. In the one case Forster was plodding through narrative, in the other describing the familiar and enjoyable. So when it comes to telling how Dickinson lectured under the University Extension Scheme, the sun of his wit shines. 'His idea was that he should reveal [the beauties of recent writers] to enthusiastic working men, who would be grateful for any crumbs from the academic banquet. It is an idea which other extension lecturers have shared, and it even seems to have flitted through the minds of the organizers of the scheme. His audiences were actually composed of women of the middle classes.' He gave 'terrific offence' when he quoted Emerson: 'The ladies of Chester were prepared to hear about Emerson, but not what Emerson said.' Then we catch the personal experience which lighted up the account: thirty years later there was the case of 'a lecturer upon Euripides at Weybridge having to defend himself against the charge of condoning the conduct of the Bacchae'.

Peasant farming was out, extension lecturing was out, and Goldie next tried to be a doctor, a sympathetic decision, for anyone who wishes to excuse his existence by serving his fellowmen had better take to medicine. When Goldie gave up after two years he said: 'I still think that that profession is the best, and does combine the possibilities of that combination of learning and life which I wanted then and want now.' Forster quotes his subject so well, a natural obligation in a biographer which this subject makes easy.

He returned at last to Cambridge. He had made honest but abortive efforts to make his way in the world and he returns home. So again we have celebrations of Cambridge, as this one about discussion societies:

> The young men seek truth rather than victory, they do not try to score off one another, they do not feel diffidence too high a price to pay for integrity; and according to some observers that is why Cambridge has played, comparatively speaking, so small a part in the control of world affairs. Certainly these societies represent the very antithesis of the rotarian spirit...There is nothing specially academic about them, they exist in other places where intelligent youths are allowed to gather together unregimented, but in Cambridge they seem to generate a peculiar white light of their own which can remain serviceable right on into middle age.

From the general to the particular, to the great theme, personal relations. Goldie's especial friends were Fry, the artist and McTaggart, the philosopher. Wedd, who was Forster's tutor: 'When I was at King's, Wedd taught me classics...Wedd was then cynical, aggressive, Mephistophelian, wore a red tie, blasphemed, and taught Dickinson how to swear too—always a desirable accomplishment for a high-minded young don, though fewer steps need be taken about it now.' The other great friend was Schiller: 'He stands apart from the rest and he was to occupy the supreme position in Dickinson's life.' The ultimate word on personal relationships comes a little later: 'It is the experience of most of us that personal relations are never perfect, but that when they are intense, they hint at perfection.'

We are in the late '80s now and there is just a decade until the biographer says: 'This is the moment when I want to introduce myself.' It is a decade of great general interest, for in it Dickinson becomes a very successful lecturer, 'accurate, well-informed, polite, dignified, clear, punctual'. The list can be commended to lecturers everywhere, since the medieval business of lecturing, so often a medieval torture, is likely to go on. Dickinson lectured on history, particularly political history and he was not like so many historians, who use the past as an escape from the present and the future. 'Knowledge of the past will help us to control the future, and unless we control the future our happiness, private and public, is at the mercy of chance.' The words are Forster's, himself a student of history, who might have been one of our great historians. In these few words he describes the human dilemma which has sharpened since then into a choice between control or annihilation and, apart from that ultimate threat, has taken sharper meaning as we have contracted our world by the efficiency of our communications.

Dickinson, pursuing the logic of control, was later to suggest the League of Nations, almost as soon as the 1914 War began, but meanwhile, back in the '80s, he is concerned with our domestic revolution and the diseases of the state common at that time. 'The worst of these diseases—international war—had not yet expanded in his consciousness, it too lay folded up like a flower. He was rather occupied with such problems as forms of government, social distinctions, the distribution of wealth, the franchise.' They are all aspects of the revolution which will go on for a hundred years and the reactions of subject and biographer are not surprising. Dickinson wrote to Fry: 'We're really in a revolution without knowing it, and how dull it is! . . . As soon as the working classes begin to *get* their bread and butter they show up as a new and equally dreary bourgeoisie.' And Forster adds: 'He might have written "an even drearier", for when Labour gets thoroughly respectable, and is stimulated neither by danger nor by art, it does seem to acquire a sausage-and-mash quality unknown to suburbia.' All of which, as we shall see, was made plain in *Howards End*.

The human being exists because it is so difficult to discourage him and Dickinson, though he saw our revolution plain, continued to preach his Utopia, which was that he: 'wanted a democracy where everyone would be an aristocrat.' It would seem to us today to be democracy's only hope. In the 1930s, Forster's comment was the comment of the artist: 'He feared that there would be a levelling down, instead of a levelling up, and that the Many, in the process of making themselves comfortable, would throw away the pearl of great price which has been handed down to them by the Few. Art, literature, music, culture are not external decorations, but age-long secretions in the soul of man, and one of the problems of our revolution is to prevent man from despising or forgetting his own past.'

Dickinson describes himself at this time, when he was writing his 'Development of Parliament in the nineteenth century' as a 'kind of socialist Tory' and when that book was published in French a decade later he has discovered something about democracy which echoes in our minds today: 'He says that further study of democracy, especially in the United States, has convinced him that it is a menace to the poor rather than to the rich, because the rich have the intelligence and the leisure to manipulate the political machine, whereas the poor are too inexperienced and too much occupied in the struggle for existence.' Today we might argue that the professional classes have turned out to be the greatest sufferers for just that reason, that they have the sense of responsibility to keep them at their work while others play political economics.

The essential and insoluble problem of democracy remains the same as that in any form of rule of great masses. Crowds have to be swayed and we can still sympathize with Dickinson: 'when two or three hundred are gathered together, he felt too sure it was in the name of the devil.' And in his belief that 'it is impossible to touch men to fineness when they are gathered into anything so clumsy as a mass'. From this he proceeds to argue that the 'House of Commons can only express the forces which excite the nation, whereas national wisdom is expressed in the House of Lords'. It is natural for the individualist to think so and certainly the record of the House of Lords continues to be a finer one than the record of the Commons, but how are the mass of people to be helped now and touched into the fineness which will give us all that touch of the aristocratic so essential for the success of democracy? Dickinson was dedicated to the pursuit of reason in human affairs and there is always the hope that education one day will spread about enough reason to leaven the democratic lump.

There is an interval before the biographer continues the discussion of politics, an interval for personal matters and for Cambridge. It begins with Forster introducing himself and it is an invaluable *locus* for all who wish to understand his academic antecedents. The third biography will tell us about his family, this about his intellectual familiars. 'I met him first in 1898…We had Winchester cutlets, a sort of elongated rissole to which he was then addicted,' a form of gastronomic oddity to be classed with Brown Windsor soup. Those who despair of progress will do well to remember that these dreadful twice baked meats are much less used in England now. The same paragraph offers us one of these exquisite flashes of life which are the special quality of this biography. In these moments he brings his subject alive. Not only that, he brings back the young Forster we should never otherwise meet: 'A few weeks later I asked him to lend me a play which had a great vogue among my fellow freshmen. I forget its name. He handed it to me gloomily, and asked when I brought it back what I thought of it. I replied nervously that I was afraid I didn't think it so very good. His face lit up.'

This, to his friends, was the outward and visible evidence of Dickinson's charm, which was not merely a decoration: 'Charm in Dickinson was structural. It penetrated and upheld everything that he did, it remained into old age, and I saw it first that afternoon at the end of the last century, when he was only thirty-five, and when I kindled him by managing to be honest over a trifle.' The prose takes on the beat which Thackeray used when he was searching back through time to great feeling. It continues through two more sentences to the end of the paragraph and we hear in it the fineness of this elegaic celebration of friendship. 'The "lighting up" really belonged to a greater occasion than this—to the entrance into the room of a friend. Then he would emerge from his inner life with a smile, which made him for the moment indescribably beautiful.' It is at moments like these that biography challenges the supremacy of prose fiction.

From the personal back to the place and almost immediately there is choric utterance on Cambridge: 'the undergraduate is the true owner of the university and the dons exist for the purpose of inducting him into his kingdom...Cambridge shared with Ancient Athens the maieutic power which brings such minds into light...Ancient and modern unite through the magic of youth.' Then the condemnation 'of the organizing and researching don. Stuffy yet raw, parochial yet colourless—what a city this was! What a hole! Schoolmasters paraded its streets, specialists riddled its walls, governesses, married to either, held their lugubrious courts in its suburbs.' Forster's honesty bids him name 'a third Cambridge whose existence he forgot', the Cambridge of that formidable creature, the Cambridge philistine, whose influence in public life has been so very vexatious, for: 'silly and idle young men did not come his way, no more did hearties and toughs unless they had intellectual leanings.' Then the typical annotation: 'he loathed [the world's] brutality and bullying—with them there was no compromise; his objection to rowdiness was not its noise but its inability to flourish without a victim.'

Dickinson hated pain, as we all do. 'There's no getting round the toothache' is Forster's plain way with the subject, and Dickinson hated it as Shelley did, so that: 'His knowledge that people suffer pain, his belief that suffering can be cured, are the two foundation stones of his political life.' That burden, at any rate, we are reducing now, thanks to the chemists, but as Forster describes the brisk years in Dickinson's life round the turn of the century we are reminded that the birthright of each generation is the failure of the last. The more life changes the more it remains the same. 'It seems impossible to go into active life of any kind without being ready to kill, to lie or to cheat.' So Dickinson in his *Modern Symposium* in 1905, and he says he wrote the book 'to raise the mind above the fighting attitude'. But the Englishman seems to be unable to think of political life as anything but a fight and like Dickinson we must all give attention to politics if we are ever to raise its level to reason and truth. We cannot opt out, for politics 'represent the attempt of Man to adapt himself to his environment and control his future'. In these pre-occupations we see Dickinson leading as if guided by fate to his function in the 1914 War, his efforts to found the League of Nations. Forster, perhaps warned by the ill success of that effort and very much by the changed circumstances of the totalitarian approach to the next war, concentrated in these years on an effort to preserve the ideas of individuality and truth when their very existence seemed under threat.

It is in this spirit (and Forster was writing his book when we were just beginning to realize the nature of the totalitarian threat to the human spirit) that he discusses Dickinson's views on religion. The discussion can be read as an apology for humanism. Authority is rejected, ritual mistrusted and the specifically religious virtue of humility is condemned. The profounder humanists understand 'the importance and the unimportance of reason' and they can hope for immortality without having great faith in it. In Dickinson's case, there was an obligation to sift all the evidence, even the claims of psychical research, 'that dustbin of the spirit'. Dickinson 'had the religious temperament, but he hated all religious weapons'. ' "God" and "Jesus" and "Krishna"...He saw at the end of these famous short words, which boom like a gong out of darkest night—he saw not light, but more darkness, mass-psychology, crowd-cruelty.' For him the intellect must be the guide, 'which anyhow sheds less blood'. To give the intellect its full scope, we must 'link up within us such gifts as we have'. This, too, Dickinson had achieved, for he was 'a person who had allowed no internal barrier to survive, so that whatever side one touched him there was the same impression of unity'. Which is exactly the harmony of a religious spirit, so there is more than one way to the quietness of unity, and those who enjoy it are content to see others take their own way.

From these private cogitations we are taken out into the winds of the world, to visit America and then India and China. Forster went to India with Dickinson but he had not been to America at that time and never went to China. So it is in the Indian descriptions that we get the intimate things, including the nonsense which is so revealing, for in India Forster was at home. The American tour was hardly a success: 'His real objection to the country was the absence of personal relationships as conceived in Cambridge discussion societies and indeed in England generally. So much cordiality, so little intimacy.' A sad judgement on the friendliest people on earth. At the other extreme stood China. 'He came to her as a lover, who had worshipped from afar for years. In a life which contained much illusion, China never never failed him. She stood firm as the one decent civilization, and when he mourned over her it was not because she had disappointed him but because he had lived to see her destroyed by the violence and vulgarity of Europe...If China could have been saved, he would have been persuaded that humanism is indestructible.' That was before the world fell to pieces and the long business of putting it together again began.

Dickinson approached India with quizzical curiosity and his reaction to what he found is summarized in that glimpse of him which Forster gives here and again when he was introducing the *Letters from John Chinaman:* 'cowering under the great sandstone portal of a temple, repelled by the monstrosity of its forms.' For India is the home of religions and the humanist could only be depressed. But not Forster. He scintillates, for he is among friends who understand and exploit the whole art of personal relationships, and only in the background is the 'boum' which is Krishna, or the 'boum' of the Marabar caves, or the claims of the muezzin quavering from the minarets. It was in India that Forster could have written what Dickinson wrote in China: 'I have had one of the great days which come now and again.'

What is left of the biography divides into the two great themes, the 1914 War and the last portrait of his subject. It was the portrait of a sensitive European who had gone through the first European madness of this century and, like all who had to go through it, had never completely recovered. If historians survive to chronicle this half century they will have far more evidence of the effect of the breaking of nations on sensitive men than has ever been left before. Goldie was already too old to be caught up by the military machine. He stayed at home and just by keeping his head and seeing truly what was going on, spent years of great pain. His biographer celebrates the courage of a man 'who was condemned to follow the intellect in a world which had become emotional', a man of uncompromising uprightness who could not seek shelter in silence. He celebrates the effect on one man of that catastrophe for European civilization: 'The shock broke something in him which was never mended.' King's and Cambridge became unfamiliar, unfriendly, in the ambience of war. 'Cambridge only increased his sadness. All that he had cared for and worked for had vanished and a grim obscene power took its place.' Bertrand Russell was another victim of what we now call war hysteria and lost his lectureship at Trinity.[1] Friendships were often strained. Rupert Brooke represented the young men who went to war with pride: 'I wish everyone I knew were fighting', he wrote to Dickinson, probably realizing the mental tortures his friend was enduring, for, as Forster records: 'He could not take the war lightly and quietly, even for a weekend. His moral earnestness forbade him, just as his intellect forbade him to seek the solace either of patriotism or anti-patriotism or religion.'

This is the saddest elegaic strain in the book and it ends on this note, which introduces Dickinson's great public work for peace, helping to found the League of Nations. 'He had shirked the horrors of crowd psychology, and Cambridge was now compelling him to view them in surroundings where he thought they could not occur.' It was one of the many frightening discoveries of the war that our European culture was still so frail that masses of people could still be carried away, so far away from reason and for so long. Despite these disturbing and humiliating developments, Dickinson 'never abandoned his fundamental hope for humanity. He fought, all through the war, for the spirit of reason in human affairs.' As far ahead as we can see, honest men of intelligence may have to stand

---

[1] Bernard Shaw was practically ostracized after publishing his *Common Sense about the War*. This is well described in Hesketh Pearson's book, in the chapter 'The War to End Shaw'.

against the crowd, and this biography tells them what the cost can be.

It is the benefit of the generations that mankind can recover so resiliently, so innocently, from unbelievable crimes. But the aftermath of the first European War was so terrible that it led to the second. So the League of Nations, brought into being so that reason should order human affairs, was doomed to failure by the wrath and retribution which grew up beside it. Forster describes the atmosphere in which the League was created and in which it declined. His account is all the more interesting because it was in this part of the biography that he was most tempted to accept help. The decision that he should write everything himself was based on Dickinson's experience in writing the McTaggart biography: 'Various friends contributed chapters or paragraphs at his request, and these, however excellent in themselves, blurred the main outline.' Forster's judgement on the McTaggart performance is: 'Biographically speaking, such a man needs rather ruthless handling if he is to come alive.' That is Forster's test; to bring the man alive. Dickinson failed because he 'only brought sensitiveness and piety'. As we should put it, because he could not write well enough, while Forster had 'the magic of words', and the wit which is an essential trace element in all his successful writing. As in that phrase about the delegation of the Henry Ford Peace Expedition in 1916, 'who had just been over to Europe to ask the war to stop. The war had made no reply.'

The description of Dickinson's part in founding the League of Nations offered few opportunities for Forster's special gifts and we get the impression that Forster carried out his task dutifully. While he was writing it, the League was failing as hard as it could. The narrative reminds us of the difficulties in getting any international group to agree usefully on any subject and in the fewest number of words we get the impression of argument and suspicion and cynicism which delay useful human association. Dickinson's part is soon told. He sketched out the idea before anyone else.[1] As early as March 1915 he saw the futility of crushing the other side. He was active in the founding of it and he withdrew as soon as it was

[1] For a different view of the founding of the League of Nations and of Lowes Dickinson, see Leonard Woolf's *Beginning Again*, 1964, p. 190 ff.

sufficiently well launched for the public figures to come crowding in. He knew by that time that the first war and its aftermath made the prelude to the second and when all around him were gladly returning to their normal lives he continued to brood over the problems of peace and war. 'He felt more and more that civilization must hasten if it wants to be saved.' He asked himself all the bitter questions about the League and especially if it would work quickly enough. 'I should not mind the League moving slowly if events didn't move fast.' The narrative is another elegiac theme, the birth and death of man's first effort to cope with the smallness and irritability of our world and the apparently ineradicable pugnacity of man.

What could a private don do for sanity in human affairs? He had retired from Geneva and its committees because he saw there was no longer a place for him. He had urged that Germany must be present and when she was not admitted he was left 'with the suspicion that ill-faith, as well as timidity, lay entrenched at Geneva'. The diplomats had taken over and when he spoke urgently: 'Unable to silence him, the committee became every inch a committee.' The don did what he could: 'He established a truce in his own heart. He could do no more against the powers of evil.' He felt that if he went on in public work for peace 'he would become mechanical, hysterical...shrieking peace, peace through a megaphone.' He surveyed his powers 'with merciless honesty...In his old age he forced tragedy into the background because he could not handle it fruitfully any more.'

This was in 1926, the year of the publication of the book which was his final effort for peace, *The International Anarchy*. It was a massive final effort, a three volume book which demonstrated that traditional diplomacy leads to war and would produce war again. A simple and obvious theme not yet learned. 'He has written a book which he knows to be good and which might save Europe if its lessons were heeded, and under a thousand copies of it have been sold...Practical men don't want him. He retires without bitterness.' All through this account of the war and the squandering of the peace, we find only one moment of gaiety; when they first met when the fighting was over. 'I stopped with him at Lyme Regis in the spring of 1919. We had not met for three years, so there was much

2

to say. He was looking old and worn, but he was gay and chirpy, we took long walks, played chess at the same level of badness and piquet under conflicting rules.'

Grace and gaiety return in the description of the last years. Dickinson is safely back in Cambridge, back in King's, in 'the most beautiful college set I know as well as the best beloved'. A secure refuge from a silly and a naughty world. 'He was determined to get comfortable, why not?...He succeeded. There was even a bath, which had, in the end, no need to be filled with kettles off the ring: there was even that rarest of all academic birds, a w.c.'

At the end: 'He was chiefly occupied in saving us trouble and in sparing our feelings. Oddly enough he succeeded...There was no self-consciousness or cynicism in his departure, no sentimentality, and no "message", it called for no special tone of voice because he had never used one. It did not suggest that he had become one with the universe or that he had gone forever.' It is the final elegaic strain, a note so gentle that it does not carry a sigh.

In the Epilogue the intelligence sharpens. He poses the question why a biography of Dickinson should have been written. One reason after another is put forward to be rejected. He did none of the things which are accepted as making excited reading, no adventures, 'never starved or penniless', or went to prison, he was not a great writer or a great thinker, his one public effort failed and since it failed 'he will join Shelley and the other ghosts who have protested against the course of doom and fate'.

In the last sentence of the book Forster tells us what lured him on to write the life story. It was the desire to keep his friend alive: 'a biography of him, if it succeeded, would resemble him, it would achieve the unattainable, express the inexpressible, turn the passing into the everlasting.' It would seem to us to have its origin in pious duty, which the writer turned into a creative achievement. The preacher had his opportunities and we enjoy them when he was discussing the writings and the one essay into political life. But the achievement is the celebration of the friend and the college and Cambridge, not as A. E. Housman celebrated Arthur Platt but as Milton celebrated his 'learned friend' in Lycidas. Once again Forster's prose has found the magic quality of great verse.

The Hill of Devi

THE BEST PORTRAIT is of Forster in 1921 and it is an unexpected
one. Enjoy some glimpses. 'Imagine me inspecting garages!': 'To
check the idleness, incompetence and extravagance is quite beyond
me': 'I am rather good at getting hold of money—the coins lie in a
heap in the courtyard': 'For four hours yesterday I walked barefoot
in petticoats through the streets with black and red powder smeared
over my head, cheeks and nose': 'I revisited the Taj...After all
the mess and confusion of Gokul Ashtami where nothing ever
stopped or need ever have begun, it was like standing on a mountain.'
The Edwardian novelist has become the Georgian traveller in a little
Indian State which frequently reminded him of the eighteenth
century and sometimes of the fourteenth. He had advantages. 'My
deepest wish was to be alone with them': 'I reflected with pleasure
that there was not another European within a radius of twenty
miles.' He was in Indian India, remote from the oppressive suburbanism which the memsahibs imposed on civilian English communities in British India. Nor was he in English-Indian society in
which the norms of behaviour were English. He was in exclusively
Indian India and Maratha at that. The court at Dewas Senior was
vulgar and extravagant, it was saturated with intrigue and that most
usual obsession among Indian rulers, a fear of being poisoned.

Forster was there because the Maharajah was lonely and 'needed some friend who stood outside the court and its intrigues'. In that way his visit was a great success. Life at court was not easy for him. 'You would weep at the destruction, expense and hideousness'. As for his personal life, there was no privacy: 'it was not very private, but what was? We all lived in a passage, the ruler included' and later: 'I cannot get over the constant publicity', a public existence conducted amid tawdry furnishings and tinsel decorations. It affected him so much that he could fall into a generalization: 'I am coming round a little to your view of the...Hindu character—that it is unaesthetic.' He was in a small State of a military race and he felt 'starved by the absence of thought' whereas in so many other places he visited in India he would have cried out opposite conclusions.

The immediate contrast is with Chhatarpur which he visited with Goldie in 1912 and again during this second visit. Again and again in the description of Dewas the contrast is with this other little State: 'Ridiculous magical Chhatarpur! Its perfection will make my own raw, jejune graceless state almost unbearable in comparison.' The earlier visit, in 1912, when Forster was 'touristing' with Lowes Dickinson and R. C. Trevelyan, had been to Chhatarpur rather than to Dewas and here we may notice Forster's chief advantage in writing about India, he never stayed there long. The first visit was a matter of weeks and set him off on *A Passage to India*, the second was for a few months, during which time he was always going off somewhere to rest from the noise and the anxiety and the intrigue. The second visit gave him the ending to *A Passage*. A third visit, which does not come into *Devi*, was only for a week or two, as has become usual in the aeroplane age. If one stayed long in India, it was very difficult not to be overcome by the richness and intensity of life all around, constantly impinging with the effect Forster records in one of his letters: 'The noise, the noise, the noise, the noise which sucks one into a whirlpool, from which there is no re-emerging.'

Forster, as much as anyone in his time, has the writer's eye. He quickly saw what he needed and carried his impressions away. In India, he was the perfect spectator, taking part sometimes but only to be unnoticed: 'I squatted against one of the pillars, occasionally smiling at the Singers, which seemed the proper thing to do': 'I...am ashamed that the good people here should have felt I was so sympathetic. The mere fact that I did not hold aloof seemed enough...' He was altogether sympathetic in the sense that he was prepared to be interested and ready to be persuaded. Another English writer, Somerset Maugham, who visited India briefly a little later, brought nothing away as he was not prepared to compromise his European sophistication. It would have gone against his grain to do so. Aldous Huxley wrote well about India in *Jesting Pilate*, but never for a moment did he compromise his Europeanness or attempt to get beneath the surface of the teeming life around him. J. R. Ackerley, celebrating 'magical Chhaturpur' in *Hindoo Holiday*, is more successful, and his book is the natural comparison with *Devi*. Forster was able to loosen the bonds of his humanist sophistication in an effort to describe an Indian State and to understand the mind of an oriental prince, its ruler. Unlike Ackerley, he allowed himself to become involved. His book is the result of these efforts and this involvement.

The technical interest of *Devi* is that a portrait of a baffling character emerges from three periods of writing. First, the 1912–13 letters, then the 1921 letters, which are much fuller and richer. Forster had been a little overshadowed by his companions in the earlier visit. Now, he is on his own, that much older, and living his subject matter entirely on his own and with plenty of time for observation and long journal letters. These two series of letters are harmonized by the third period of writing, the connecting comments and the brief essays interspersed in the narrative. The writing of the first two periods is immediate, that of the third is historical. Many a novelist, like Thackeray, believes he will come to history when the creative vein has worked out and many novelists in one way or another do come to it. Forster used his visits first in his novel and now for this biography which is a unique little bit of history: 'It is indescribable and unimaginable—really a wonderful experience, for it is the fag-end of a vanished civilization.'

Forster has made a uniquely wonderful description of his experiences, for nothing else in English writing about India evokes that great country so strongly. This is the best travel book in English on India and the most interesting portrait of a Hindu prince in English. It is the best travel book because he lived what he described and he saw things which few Europeans have seen. And for the technical reason we always come back to, he had the magic of words while he wrote. He lived the life of the festival wholeheartedly, for on the plane of physical ribaldry Hindu and humanist can meet happily. Recall his description of a custom followed everywhere during this festival: 'we went under a large black vessel, rather handsome, that was hung up in the aisle, and we banged it with our painted sticks, and the vessel broke and a mass of grain soaked in milk fell down over our heads. We fed each other with it.' Or a more seemly moment in the procession that evening: 'The preacher of the sermon...walked with me, indeed we were hand in hand...I enjoyed the walk...My feet held out well...But my back...I thought it would break. "We are pained to see your pain" remarked the Indore preacher, "but we are greatly pleased by your good nature. We have not met an Englishman like you previously." ' Then the real sympathy comes and this is what is repeated in *A Passage*: 'Only one thing is beautiful; the expression on the faces of the people as they bow to the shrine', which becomes in *A Passage*: 'When the villagers broke cordon for a glimpse of the silver image, a most beautiful and radiant expression came into their faces, a beauty in which there was nothing personal, for it caused them all to resemble one another during the moment of its indwelling, and only when it was withdrawn did they revert to individual clods.' In *Devi*: 'A lady fanatic was in the Dewan's group'; and in *A Passage* she becomes: 'a woman prominent, a wild and beautiful young saint with flowers in her hair...'

It would be an interesting study in the nature of memory to compare what is in the letters and in *A Passage*, what is changed by artistic necessity, what is remembered differently and what is recalled although not previously recorded. Time brings fragments of memory into place and there was also the need to order memory so that the various parts of the festival could alternate equably with the scenes in which Aziz becomes reconciled to his old English

friend again. India, so overpowering in contact, becomes altogether
attractive in recollection.

Forster's book throughout has the two dimensions of immediacy
and recollection and the two coincide most easily in the main purpose, the portrait of his Maharajah. He is the theme of the second
batch of letters and there is natural comparison again with Chhatarpur, the Raja who figures in the earlier letters. Chhatarpur, he says,
did not misgovern his kingdom as Dewas did his: 'He had not the
energy for that. He merely omitted to govern it, and did what the
English told him, lamenting or tittering all the time.' That was the
rub. Dewas was intelligent and in spasms tried to rule. 'He was
certainly a genius, and possibly a saint and he had to be a king.'
What sort of rule did he offer his people, who were an agricultural
peasantry? 'He was part of the military aristocracy of India and
sprung, at a pinch, from the sun.' He was trained for his high duties
by the British ('Politically, we are still living in the fourteenth
century'), who sent young Malcolm Darling, who became one of the
outstanding men of his time in the administrative service. Darling
was interested in agriculture and experiments were attempted and,
as usual, lapsed soon after he had gone. The only other reference in
Devi to Darling's curriculum for a king is in a report Forster sent to
him from Dewas: 'He follows all allusions to Greek mythology, and
he cannot have heard them since your tutorial epoch.'[1]

Darling continued the classical approach by suggesting that
Forster should come out as Private Secretary while the regular
P.S., an ex-colonel in the Indian army, came home on holiday. The
suggestion was apt, for what was needed was friendship. The
Maharajah's marriage had broken down and, as his wife's family
was the most powerful Maratha family, the Maharajah's dream of a
powerful Maratha confederacy possibly under his own leadership,
was smashed. So: 'he certainly felt lonely...he needed some
friend who stood outside the court and its intrigues.' On that plane,
the arrangement was a brilliant success, for this was a matter of
personal relations and Forster found, when he met his Maharajah,
that 'it was possible with him to reach a platform where calculation

[1] Sir Malcolm Darling has now published his own account of these days,
Apprentice to Power (1966).

was unnecessary'. It is typical that he adds: 'It would not have been possible with an Englishman.' The other part of the paradox is stated much later, when Forster describes his Maharajah as 'one of the sweetest and saintliest men I have known...his goodness is not mawkish, but goes with deep insight into character and knowledge of the world. It is very difficult to describe him because he does belong to another civilization in a way that other Indians I have met do not.' In *A Passage*, we may note, there is no attempt to make a full character of the Ruler. He is a shadowy, sick figure, a dying saint. His Highness of Dewas was still alive when the novel was published so there could be no attempt at a portrait and every reason to avoid a likeness. For literary purposes the proportions of the plot kept the story middle class and the religious dancer Professor Godbole.

One of the tensions we remember in *A Passage* is between Aziz and Godbole. In *Devi* it is foreshadowed in Forster's sympathetic comic treatment of the meeting between His Highness and Ross Masood. This was the Cambridge friend who had first interested Forster in India. His descent from the Prophet was more clear than His Highness's descent from the sun, and when Masood came to see Forster in Dewas: 'Two extremes were meeting...There was some nervousness on both sides. On Masood's it took the form of incisiveness and pomposity...H.H. was...extremely courteous, and behaved almost as to a fellow-ruler: there were certain civilities and attentions which Masood had not expected to receive and they gratified him.' But Masood belonged to the twentieth century, so: 'After three days of Hinduism Masood retired...Our incompetence distressed him more than it could me because he saw in it an extreme example of his country's inefficiency.'

There we have the two personal themes of Forster's narrative, his affection for H.H. and his sense of the burden of inefficiency which he was unable to alleviate. 'So long as I am out for enjoyment, all contribute to it, but as soon as I try to serve Bapu Sahib [H.H.] or to make others serve him, I grasp a cloud...ignorant of the language and of administration generally, I could not stop on here permanently. It would not have been fair. To check the idleness, incompetence and extravagance is quite beyond me.' Forster's day to day duties were to look after the 'gardens, tennis courts, motors, Guest House, Electric House. None of these had much to do with reading or writing, my supposed specialities...this did not disturb us.' Precisely the situation of the great Indian administrators.

He rejoiced the court by so obviously enjoying the Maratha sense of fun, so like our own soldierly jokes. It was April Fool's Day: 'But I did drink some whisky-and-salt, to the court's uncategorical delight. Foolery, fun, practical jokes, bawdry—I was to be involved in them all...But gay, gay.' Which echoes so much of Forster's conversation. Not the bawdry; but again and again the word 'gay'. The niceness is expressed later in a letter appropriately to Goldie: 'the tiresome practical jokes, the growing dread of education [that could only let Gandhi's teaching in] the bawdy talk which is subtly wrong' is listed as 'nearly all I don't like about his character.' The tradition of bawdry to amuse rulers is very old in India.

There was another reservation, already mentioned. The doubt in his mind as Forster watched his Maharajah dancing. The humanist spectator of the religious festival noted its sole merit: 'Priests took little part in it, the devout were in direct contact with their God.' Watching his Maharajah, he says: 'I have never seen religious ecstasy before and I don't take to it more than I expected I should, but he manages not to be absurd...*he* is dancing all the time... At the end of his two hours he gets wound up and begins composing poetry...Ten minutes afterwards I saw him as usual, in ordinary life. He...discussed arrangements connected with the motor cars. I cannot see the point of this, or rather in what it differs from ordinary mundane intoxication.' He returns to the problem, fascinated because it is obviously an integral part of the character of H.H. 'He felt as King David and other mystics have felt when they are in the mystic state. He presented well-known characteristics...He was in an abnormal but recognizable state.' His experiences were real.

The religious characteristics which Forster immediately understood were affection and understanding: 'Affection...was the only force to which Bapu Sahib responded...without it nothing worked. Affection and its attendants of human warmth and instinctive courtesy.' This could be weakness. When Forster suggested

2*

that he should receive no salary because he was not earning it, as the work was so much outside his competence (here he parted company with the great administrators) and implied some weakness in the affairs of State: 'As always, he was sweet and understanding, and has promised to reform at some early, but future, date.' At the end of the book Forster has resolved his doubts: 'his religion was the deepest thing in him...He penetrated into rare regions and he was always hoping that others would follow him there. He was hopeful that we should all be recalled to the attention of God.'

India is the country of religions and any sensitive western man who lives there, even for a short time, will ponder these questions again. The one brief note that Forster permits himself on Christianity is best stated, like so many of the good things thrown off in this book, in *A Passage*: 'By sacrificing good taste, this worship achieved what Christianity has shirked: the inclusion of merriment. All spirit as well as all matter must participate in salvation, and if practical jokes are banned, the circle is incomplete.' He had forgotten the Middle Ages, a golden period in European life with which he has always had imperfect sympathies.

At the end of *Devi* we see how Forster has tried to make everyone come well out of his story and that nobody at all seems to come out well. It is written in the blasting honesty of old age which least of all spares the narrator, who fails to provide the miraculous help which alone could have saved his Maharajah, and towards the end even becomes an embarrassment by being so prickly with the wretchedly sick and senile Colonel Wilson. And the pitiful ending. The Maratha chief with kingly blood boiling in his veins ruined by moneylenders and his State with him, and running like a rabbit for a burrow before a pack of avenging bureaucrats. Not an edifying spectacle and without the photographs of the stricken old man after a penitential fast, the philosopher brooding before the lens, to compare with the photographs of the Maharajah amid his courtiers, it is doubtful whether we should feel the tragedy, the fall from power to piteousness, as we should.

Nor can we altogether go along with Forster in his strictures of the bureaucrats, and this is frustrating for any reader. 'The wheels of western righteousness rolled on and crushed him', says Forster.

But what could the bureaucrats do with a ruler who had ruined his people and quarrelled seriously with at least one neighbouring prince? A foolish prince had ruined all his people and most Claphamites would agree that he should be called to account.

We are on easier ground with what we remember most vividly from the book, the Edwardian novelist becoming a Georgian traveller. We can search all our travel books of Arabia, so much our best travel books, and find nothing more bizarre, nothing that more becomes the great gallery of English eccentric travellers. How very little good writing we have had from all the generations of the English who lived in India. They were not the writing sort, professional men and business men, all of them with full lives. There was the occasional diarist, Hickey, whom Forster celebrated, Bishop Heber, Macaulay. Then each generation had its books about gardening and pets and wild beasts and hunting, and fun about domestic life, like Fanny Parkes. There were children's books, often written by those memsahibs with whom Forster never got on, and some of them have regular appearances in nurseries still. And the travel books, with a history away back to the early 1800s, and a selection from them would offer a fascinating picture of the ordinary life-sufferings of young exiles of Empire for a hundred and fifty years. What is difficult to find is any book that gets below the surface of any human life in India, whether Hindu, Muslim or English. Among the best writing was Richard Burton's, who wrote his excellent sketchbooks, *Scinde* and *Goa* in his early twenties; and Kipling's *From Sea to Sea* which penetrates the surface as we shall see in discussing *A Passage*.

But they were written very long ago and latterly it has been a matter of our own feeling about India, which changed after we had won a war and lost our imperial confidence for ever. The difference between Kipling's book and, say, Ackerley's, is as total as can be. Ackerley's appalling truthfulness in retailing what his Rajah said and what a memsahib said would have been unthinkable twenty years earlier. Orwell's *Burmese Days* had the same artistic integrity in his descriptions of seedy English philistines in Burma with no concession (except in portraying an administrator) to the necessity to conceal these things if imperial rule was to go on. We had lost our will to rule and it helped in opting out to look at the cheap and nasty side of imperial drudgery.

Among all these books, *Devi* is in a class of its own, for it is a unique effort to paint a portrait of a Hindu in English. Nothing could be more difficult, and affection as much as the technical brilliance of the management of the material gave it a wonderful measure of success. As in the Goldie portrait, Forster's chief concern was to bring his subject alive. He does so, with a character of baffling intricacy and foreignness.

Marianne Thornton

'AND THERE HE was sitting on his Throne with his King's Crown on, his robes scarlet velvet and ermine, held his speech written out for him just what he had to say. But Oh dear he stood up and made a bow and began "My Lords and Peacocks".' It is an account of George III opening Parliament in 1804, a mad old king enjoying a flicker of disdainful sanity, and the story is told in the 1880s by an old woman writing a letter to her great-nephew, Morgan Forster, then four or five. A year or two later she has to rebuke him about his attitude to royalty: 'that reminds me that I heard you do not like the Queen—but I think that must be because you do not know her, neither do I as an acquaintance, but I do know she is the best Queen or King we have ever had…she is the only King or Queen who has been saving—always paying everybody all she owes them—and she is so kind and full of pity for those who are ill and in trouble.' Alas, the appeal fell on deaf young ears, and only police intervention prevented a republican display by young Forster when he first saw the Queen. It was in the Jubilee year, 1887, and she was driving to Hatfield House to see Lord Salisbury. Along with other children the boy sat on a wall to see her pass. Their legs hung outside, and the policeman, every inch a Victorian, made them for propriety hang them inside. 'I boiled with rage and I determined that I would not take off my sailor hat and wave it, nor would I cheer. At the critical moment, though, I thought the policeman was looking at me, and before I knew what I was doing my hat was off, and my lungs were squeaking.'

Marianne writes beautifully to the child (despite that odd hiatus in the first sentence) but then she was experienced in that sort of thing for she had produced more than one series of educational Readers. She was born in 1797, the eldest child of Henry Thornton, banker and member of Parliament, and the elder sister of Laura, Forster's grandmother. The Thorntons lived in a great house near Clapham Common called Battersea Rise, where the family and its retainers lived in 'a blend of feudal loyalty and eighteenth-century enlightenment'. Among their neighbours were the Wilberforces, the Stephens and the Macaulays, the families which formed the Clapham Circle. 'Two things are notable about it. The first is its homogeneity. With the exception of the Macaulays, all its members were wealthy, and all of them without exception were devoted to good works, and were intelligent rather than artistic.' By Thornton standards Marianne was not well off. She left £20,000, eight of them to Forster. 'The interest was to be devoted to my education and when I was twenty-five I was to receive the capital. This £8,000 has been the financial saving of my life.'

So in this third biography Forster is celebrating not so much someone he loved as someone who loved him. Again he brings his subject alive and again he is working on a very considerable personality. While he brings her alive he transforms the Claphamites from figures into living people. Once again, he is offering unique background material. In Goldie, Cambridge, in *Devi,* an Indian Native State under the Raj, and now the Claphamites. Marianne has herself some cogent remarks to offer on biography. Young Wilberforce was writing the life of his father and she says: 'as to thinking such a creature as that can appreciate or describe that winged being and all his airy flight—why you might as well put a mole to talk about an eagle.' And when her beloved Hannah More was 'menaced by one of those Lives that might be called Deaths' as Forster puts it, and the writer bowdlerizes some of her best sayings, Marianne cries out: 'if such an oaf as that will write a book at least he should be honest.' This time, as we know, the old lady's great nephew listened usefully to what she had to say.

Forster never had more material from which to produce the miracle of life. He tells us in the Preface that he had sixteen manuscript books and 'Various letters, MS brochures, diaries, notes, etc, dating from about 1750 to 1900. Originally they filled ten tin boxes, which have been reduced in the course of the years to the Sibylline number of three.' He revels in his task. He quotes, deliciously; he comments, wittily; he provides narrative that is as lively as anything he ever wrote and all this at the age of seventy-five and more. We are growing accustomed to our writers giving of their best after their allotted span of three score and ten, but nowhere in contemporary writing shall we find more genially warm October sunshine than in this biography of a daughter of the Claphamites.

Her span alone was tremendous. As a little girl she was afraid of Napoleon because he was going to invade England and Battersea Rise to cut down her favourite tulip tree. In her teens she was doing good works in the aura of the rich Wilberforces and Wedgwoods and the poor Macaulays. In her twenties she stood by her brother Henry while he saved the bank which is William Deacon's Bank today. Later, she turned educationist and at sixty wrote the Recollections which give such strength to the biography. Later still, she became tyrannical and the biography becomes another study by Forster of extreme old age. With him it was a tyranny of affection to which he was schooled to respond. At the very end, as we shall see, she showed great consideration, rather like Goldie, to those who would be left.

As so much of this biography is her own work, something should be said now about her writing. At its best, it is superb. She was fortunate in having Hannah More as a correspondent in her twenties, when so much was happening to the family. Already she has a plain, bare way of writing. But her style matured, as good styles do. Her biographer's first comment on it is about a letter written in her teens: 'Lively and loquacious. Her style has not yet matured, most of her sentences are a couple of clauses too long, and her observations lack the brilliance and precision she was able to give them in later years.' The next comment is on a letter of 1842, twenty-six years later. 'It suffers from volubility, like much of her earlier writing. Later on her style strengthened.' Then we come to a letter of 1865. 'The subject matter is unimportant, but isn't her style improving? Isn't there from the sixties onwards, a terseness and brightness which were lacking in the long leisurely epistles from Battersea Rise?' The last comment on style is about the letter she wrote in the middle eighties to young Morgan about the King opening Parliament. She had said it was dullish and had better end: 'Dull letter? I wish I could get many like it or write any like it!...How much has died with her which, properly evoked, might have lived!'

We find her early manner at its best in the long letters to Hannah More, who lived down in Somerset, about the bank crisis. The letters are printed in full and as an account of a crisis which involved the whole family fortune they could not be bettered. The hero is Henry, aged twenty-five, with only five months' experience as a partner. The year is 1825. The story begins with a run on the bank. The other partners were incapable or absent:

> Henry saw it all lay upon him. Had he believed the House was really insolvent he said he would have stopped instantly sooner than have involved a human being any farther, but he was sure the money was theirs only they could not get at it, and he resolved to fight it out to the last minute, tho' what he endured, knowing that if any *large* Bill was presented they *must* stop— he says he never shall forget.

With an hour to go before the bank closed: 'they would have to pay thirty-three thousand, and they should receive only twelve thousand. This was certain destruction, and he walked out, resolved to try one last resource.' He went to the head of a rival house, who generously helped him out. They held out during that last hour, but the crisis had still to be solved. We are away back in the personal days of banking, when all depended on the good sense and astuteness of the partners. But the personal element meant there could be generosity also and the head of the rival firm who had helped him, John Smith, did not desert the young man:

> I suppose there was something in the sight of so youthful a pilot weathering such a storm, which interested John Smith and one or two old-stagers, who had seen his father act just

like him in olden time, and they told him that the openness
and firmness with which he had acted, made them very desirous
to see whether nothing could be done.

The only institution that could save them was the Bank of England.
Henry could not believe they could hope for help from that quarter.
There was no precedent for it. He went home and 'proceeded to do
two or three things which almost broke my heart. He paid me and
Nurse two or three pounds he owed us, for he said he shouldn't
feel any was his own by Monday.' Marianne sat up with him 'most
of the remainder of the night, for sleep was out of the question. I am
sorry to say I behaved much the worst of the two, for the thought of
their breaking was very intolerable to me.' When he went off next
morning 'he desired me to say nothing to my sisters, or anyone else
of their difficulties, and I had to get through Sunday as well as I
might.' Could Defoe have bettered that bare narrative?

By Sunday night he was back with the wonderful news that the
bank was saved. The letter becomes a success story, rich and rapid
in its style. But the next letter begins: 'I little thought when I closed
my last happy letter to you how soon it would all be reversed—and
that a few hours would realize our worst anticipations.' There was a
run on the country banks associated with Henry's bank. The bank
went down but Henry survived to become a successful banker. His
conduct of the crisis had attracted attention. Henry is the hero of the
story and all goes well with him. He noted one sympathetic thing as
he watched the crisis in which he was so completely involved. He
realized the great and benign power of money as never before: 'I
always loved the character of a City Merchant and Banker, and it is
delightful to see how they unite the powers of a man of business
with the romantic effects of the heroes of fairy tales. I said the other
day that John Smith appeared to me like the beneficent genius in a
fairy tale, he not only promised impossibilities, but he was always
performing them.' Let us enjoy such agreeable glimpses of Regency
capitalists when we may. The next letter gives us another glimpse
of them: 'Alexander Baring says there are two things he hates—an
abolitionist and a saint—and yet he can't help liking that young
Thornton, in proof of which he very carelessly yesterday offered

him £200,000 to begin with, if they were likely to want it.' As
Forster says: 'It is the triumph of youth.'

The next story about Henry is a very unhappy one, but meantime
we have some fascinating glimpses of two great Claphamites,
William Wilberforce and young Tom Macaulay. The 1820s was one
of London's more brilliant decades and we have many glimpses of it,
in Lamb's essays, in the Opium Eater, in Hazlitt and Crabb Robinson and Thomas Hood. Here is a very different part of London in
the same decade, the 'May Meetings' of the evangelicals. Wilberforce was there: 'he was all over the place—fragile, whimsical,
inspired—and would wear himself to death.' By 1825, Marianne
tells us: 'He looks very, very thin and reduced, and walks feebly but
really he is almost a proof already of the immortality of the Soul—
for I never saw him in such spirits—or appear so keenly *alive* upon
all subjects.' That is so well said that Marianne might have been
modelling her writing on *The London* of Elia.

Tom Macaulay made his mark as an orator at the 1824 Week:

> ...when I saw the grave old steady senators all so carried
> away by the eloquence of the youthful orator, that even the
> decorum of the platform were forgotten, and the dignity of the
> Royal Duke compromised, by Mr Wilberforce and Mr Stephen
> catching hold of him as he was going back to his place, and
> keeping him there, each shaking a hand, while the very walls
> seemed to be coming down with the thunders of applause.

The young writer is carried away too and forgot to complete her
sentence. As the decade wore on: 'The meetings had become
fashionable and were attended by persons who were trying to
advertise themselves.' Edward Irving the preacher and the like.

The chapter is a brilliant collaboration between Marianne and
Forster, and so is the next, The Marriages. They began with the
strange affair between Forster's grandfather and grandmother,
which did not run quite smoothly, and gave the sisters at Battersea
Rise an opportunity to keep the gallant Forster informed about
Laura's 'state of mind and of his own prospects'. 'He . . . enjoyed
their palpitating missives, and an atmosphere of transferred
amorousness sprang up which I find inelegant.' There are many

more good things in the chapter: 'Aunt Sophy, whom I can just remember, died every inch a countess.' Then there is Henry Thornton's interest in fire, to the delight of the children when he lit a newspaper at the fire, put it on his leather armchair and sat on it: 'The vision of that substantial extinguisher descending cheers me.' Then there was the courting of Aunt Isabella and the Archdeacon, the nub of it all being that Aunt Isabella was forty-five and nobody could tell if the Archdeacon would ever come up to scratch:

> The Archdeacon was a dear little man with a squint who had been hanging round for some time, but no one was sure whether he would come to the point or whether Isabella would accept any one so small. All the day he had been particularly uproarious, had mimicked a Canon singing, had ventured on giving an opinion, which he was not prone to do, and at night when Marianne's hair was being brushed and her feet were already in hot water the news arrived and she had to go down.

And in that fine old feudal home: 'Nurse Hunter was called down too.'

The narrative turns then to Nurse Hunter's death. Forster remembers he has promised he will not describe illness or death at any length but now he will break his promise. It is a promise well broken, for the scene is as wonderful as the letter which describes it: 'The energy expended in writing it is amazing, and she was writing letters of similar diffuseness throughout her life.' The quality of the writing is remarkable also, the Regency diffuseness has gone, it would have been inappropriate. The tone and movement of the sentences in this long, spontaneous utterance is exactly right and the quotation ends: 'There is nobody to whom I could, and did, tell everything as I did to her, and there was no one who could give me such good advice.' It comes to mind at once that a few miles away Marx was writing about the class war. The comparison of that piece must be with the directions Marianne wrote decades later about her own ending. The old lady had become very modern in feeling: 'There is generally an interval of twilight as it were during which a painful watch is kept around my bed. I would gladly spare those I loved and who loved me (and they are many) this useless painful scene.'

Victorian glimpses follow: a Lord Mayor's tea in the Guildhall in 1842, a unique fragment of early Victoriana, and the Hereford tea-party, with mechanics, for contrast. For variety, there is a visit to Cambridge, nephews coming over from the Charterhouse, and to round off these glimpses of wonderful source material, a visit to the Exhibition. Can there be many similar hoards of such writing which will never be known to us for lack of nephews with the time and skill to present them?

Now comes the chapter of bitter family calamity, the second long story about her beloved brother Henry: 'Henry announced that he intended to marry Emily although she was his deceased wife's sister, that he was going to get the Law altered in Parliament, and that until it was altered he and she would live abroad.' This meant that Battersea Rise was abandoned, Victorian security was shattered, the family scattered. 'It was the loss of Battersea Rise that distressed them most and exacerbated their genuine moral distress.' There was no question of the sisters recognizing the new wife. Marianne at the age of fifty-five left her home and set up house in a modest way at the other end of the Common. There were squabbles about the furniture she took with her. 'No doubt the exiled pair were in a state of suspicion and irritability and had worked themselves into a panic lest Battersea Rise was being rifled in their absence.' Worse still for Marianne, the children were exiled and their beloved aunt could not see them. They were promised and did not come. 'The very day and hour were fixed, and I spent the whole of it as you will believe at the window.' Nowhere is Forster more sensitively sympathetic:

> Anyone who has waited in vain for a beloved person will understand what she felt. A wound had been inflicted which no subsequent reunion quite heals. The insecurity against which we all struggle has taken charge of us for a moment — for the moment that is eternity. The moment passes, and perhaps the beloved face is seen after all and the form embraced, but the watcher has become aware of the grave.

Everything is in personal relationships. Marianne never lost her poise and she never lost her sympathy with her brother. During that fateful year, 1852, when this family disintegration happened, a year which 'pullulates with correspondence', her letters seek to ameliorate bitterness by their temperate phrases and their charity of mind. This is in strong contrast to the prelates and parliamentarians who betrayed the obstinate bigotry we normally associate with the Victorians. It took fifty-five more years for the law about marrying a deceased wife's sister to be brought into line with sensible thought. Perhaps by that time it was recognized that the dangers of inbreeding which were the prudent concern of the 18th chapter of Leviticus did not arise here.

On this matter of public concern 'yet another example of the cruelty and stupidity of the English Law in matters of sex' Forster is temperate. In the domestic crisis, which is his concern, he is equally temperate. Uncle Henry, the banker, the Claphamite, ran away for love, abandoning all his domestic and social gods in doing so, is dealt with so sympathetically that the obvious description of his action is never even hinted at. The family, 'pullulating with correspondence' is kept in the background and always at the centre of the stage is Marianne, with her sympathy and understanding. 'Looking back at her conduct during that crucial period, I am overwhelmed with admiration. She behaved like a statesman—a stateswoman. She temporized. She would push nothing to a conclusion even in her mind. She was affectionate without weakness and moral without asperity.'

We pass on to a new generation, who knew Darwin and Huxley and Galton, and Forster exploits the historian's gift of showing time passing. A favourite nephew, Inglis Synnot, 'wanted to know how the world was made and why it worked. The Thorntons had never cared to know that; they had confined themselves to being good and doing good, and to being generally intelligent.' Marianne's view of science are shown in this dictum on weather forecasting in a letter to her nephew: 'I think any man's head is wrong, who professes to know anything about the weather. The wind bloweth where *it* listeth, and that is all.' A later letter from Miss Forster to Miss Darwin further explains Marianne's scientific views. She had recommended Galton's *Hereditary Genius* to her although she had not read it herself, 'as it must quite confute the Darwin theory that

we inherited things from animals if F. Galton proved we got them
from our fathers and mothers.' And all this without the advantage
of a formal classical education. A sudden modern note is struck in
1882 when Marianne reports a long conversation with Mr Knowles,
remembered as the founder of the *Nineteenth Century*. It shimmers
with the fourth dimension of time-space.

> Here Mr Knowles has come in, in a perfect storm of terror
> about the tunnel under the channel tell Laura, he is persuaded
> that 20,000 soldiers will be able to force their way through, all
> ours are in Ireland, England is no longer an island, and tho' as
> Britannia able to rule the waves she could not manage the
> tunnels.

If there is anything in Galton's views we see one source of Forster's
talent.

Marianne has moved to her new house, a fragment of 'what was
once a Clapham Palazzo' and she has for immediate neighbour a Dr
Spitta, with whom 'there flickered faint suburban warfare'. Despite
this descent to suburbia Marianne writes bravely of her 'rambling
ragged old house', with its 'four rooms on a floor, opening into each
other'. And it is her great sayings from these rambling rooms that
reverberate through the chapter. She makes a new acquaintance,
Florence Nightingale, who 'went to the Crimea because she was tired
of picking up her mother's spectacles'. The nephew-in-law who was
so big he would make two ordinary men 'but what very ordinary
men they would be'. The biographer does rather well too. 'Isabella
and the Archdeacon adored pottering in and out of the Cathedral; it
stood at the other side of their lawn, a huge booming toy with which
they could not play too much. "Love me, Love my Cathedral." '
And the exquisitely tart tribute to another cousin: 'as Lady of the
Manor she ended her unquiet life. "Requiescat in pace" comes to
one's lips, but she may not have wanted peace.'

It is here too that a future biographer will come to some puzzling,
fascinating material about Forster's father, who followed Thomas
Hardy as an architectural pupil with Blomfield. 'It is one of Life's
Little Ironies that I should have got to know Mr Hardy and stayed
with him at Max Gate, and should never have known my father,

seven years his junior...As an architect he was promising, despite his retarded start and his rather unpractical character, and the only house by him I know has great distinction externally.' The sense of remoteness from this unknown parent is then confirmed: 'He was quick at the uptake, amusing, sarcastic, could always make old Monie laugh, and he had integrity and unselfishness. How these qualities combined to make him a real person I do not know. He has always remained remote to me.'

The chapter on Marianne's educational activities is consoling when we ponder today how much there is to be done, for it reminds us how much has been done. 'The early nineteenth-century scene was of an educational simplicity that we cannot imagine. The carriage stops, the pious occupants get out and teach, and drive on.' We can find there a pleasant impression of an old attitude to learning, something received that is so valuable it must be passed on. Marianne's zeal over education was similarly enlightened. 'First and foremost was her dislike of ignorance and her eighteenth-century faith in reason. If children knew more, they would grow up happier, healthier, and more helpful.' That connects sensibly with the second reason, for 'by "knowing more" she meant fuller knowledge of the way in which to get the best out of their lives. They must therefore...be educated according to their station...she was anxious that education should produce servants and governesses of good quality.' There is a hint of criticism of her views, but surely we have changed only to remain the same. We want happier factory workers and transport men and miners so that everything is made more cheaply for ourselves and others so that we can become independent again.

Marianne lived right on to the days of provincial university education, with every stage in education organized and inspectors to see that the organism was efficient. 'Spectres' she called them and fed them well in the hope of inspiring good reports. She even compiled a series of Readers, her only descent into publishing, her Clapham instincts no doubt impelling her into one of the more lucrative branches of bookmanship. We should have liked to know much more about these things, we are grateful for any historical comparisons which help us in our Sisyphusian efforts to find a way

of educating the masses of our young, but: 'Her business correspondence, unlike her private correspondence, is exiguous.'

We come at last to the time when Forster knew his aunt personally.
Those who are interested in the child being father of the man will
find much comfortable material in the chapter called 'My Recollections'. It is the story of a fatherless boy who was spoilt by being
too much with the servants and by being groomed to be careful
during every moment he was with his ageing great-aunt so that he
would inherit a share of her money. 'I was growing at the rate of a
month a day, she was static in her eighties...I behaved fairly
well, thanks to my mother's admonitions. She would urge me to be
nice before I went in, and she has recorded my attempt to get into
intellectual touch with Aunt Monie, and my dejected expression
when I realized I had failed.'

The visits to Clapham were 'dun-coloured' and the sunshine was
in Hertfordshire, where, on Monie's advice, the young widow had
buried herself to look after a child who was supposed to be delicate.
Now comes the father of the man who wrote *Howards End*: 'The
truth is that she [my mother] and I had fallen in love with our
Hertfordshire home and did not want to leave it...From the time
I entered the house at the age of four...I took it to my heart and
hoped...that I should live and die there.' Then comes the familiar
stark way of recording calamity: 'We were out of it in ten years.'
But these ten years were long enough for an abiding influence: 'The
impressions received there remained and still glow...and have
given me a slant upon society and history. It is a middle-class
slant, atavistic.'

There were so few children about that servants were deputed to
play with him. There was Ansell the garden boy. 'We slid and we
shouted. Ansell hid and left his billycock as a decoy. Not finding
him I jumped on it and stove it in, and this did ruffle him.' A better
side to the medal. He says to the maid: 'Have you heard one of my
long stories about things that have never happened except inside my
head?—I'll tell you one.' And the same voice, seventy years later
briefly relates in a footnote the one about Chattering Hassocks:
'fifty lions and as many unicorns sit upon hassocks, and the lions
put forward a plea for tolerance and for variety of opinions which I

still support.' Education for the garden boy was not neglected either: 'I neglected no one's education. I recounted to him what I had read in *Swiss Family Robinson,* and he retold it to me fairly well.' Not much change in method from Aunt Marianne's forays into education at the same age, but with the rush of progress, extra-mural. All education is in some sort two way and the garden boy 'probably did more than anyone towards armouring me against life. That is why I bring him in.' But Emma the maid may have provided him with the best armour of all, the armour of the comic spirit which is able to see that most things can be seen as nonsense and enjoyed. Forster's mother is writing: 'The way she likes to amuse him is to make some foolish speech over and over again through the entire afternoon and then they both laugh as if they would have fits. The last speech is: 'My name is Sir William Podgkins.' I ask what it means but they can't speak for laughter and then M[organ] manages to say "there is no meaning and that is why we laugh".' So in this biography too the nonsense has not been left out, and it tells us all it should.

We are coming to the end and we arrive there in a little flurry of history, the stories about the mad old king and the Queen in her first Jubilee year with which we began. The book is ending as it opened with greetings from the old to the young and at the very end there is that autobiographical note about the inheritance and he drops a final pious tribute on her grave. He sums up his life, set on its way by the money she left him and he says: 'I am thankful so far, and thankful to Marianne Thornton; for she and no one else made my career as a writer possible, and her love, in a most tangible sense, followed me beyond the grave.'

Alexandria & Pharos and Pharillon

IN THE AUTUMN of 1915 Forster went to Alexandria to serve in the Red Cross. He arrived 'in a slightly heroic mood'. The Turks were expected to invade. They did not do so, but Forster stayed on for three years. He was thirty-six when he arrived and at the height of his powers. His Red Cross work must have become routine and all the Mediterranean lay between him and the European fighting. Gallipoli and Mesopotamia were far away. Alexandria was an oasis in a world conflict, a cosmopolitan city uncommitted to anything but the joy of living in a perfect climate by a warm and tideless sea.

It was natural that he should write. Modern war makes imaginative writing impossible, but there was in Alexandria the spirit of its ancient library and Forster, once the city had taken hold of him, was able to study its history and produce, not a great history, for that too was impossible under the circumstances of his occupation, but a good deal of journalism and a guide book with an historical preface of a hundred pages. He was able, when off duty, to go about in mufti 'and it was then that I apprehended the magic and the antiquity and the complexity of the city, and determined to write about her'. The journalism appeared in *The Egyptian Mail* in 1917 and 1918 (that dread European year 1916 produced nothing) and continued after his return home in *The Athenaeum* with more sophisticated pieces. The *Guide* was printed and published in Alexandria four years after Forster left, in 1922. A fire destroyed most of the copies. Forster was in Alexandria again a few years later (and lost his way almost as soon as he left the railway station: 'What a humiliating experience for the writer of a Guide!'). He inspired another edition during that visit and the fairly extensive revision was undertaken by Alexandrian friends: 'she was still the city of friends who were willing unselfishly to set aside their own work and to work for others.' This appeared in 1938 and again it did not sell well because the next war came. It has never been published in this country but an excellent paperback of the first edition was published in America in 1961 with a new preface by the author.

The historical essay which prefaces the *Guide* is one of the most perfect things Forster has given us. His first attempts as a writer were neat little essays on classical themes, inspired by his desire to make people alive again just as they are alive in that Alexandrian idyll of Theocritus. Now, at the height of his powers, he is able to bring Alexandria alive from its extraordinary birth right through the great days when it tempered Christian teaching to make it acceptable to the western civilized world.

Pharos and Pharillon recalls Theocritus even more strongly. It is a collection of the journalism about Alexandria and Egypt and it covers much of the ground of the *Guide*. Until the American paperback, it had to take the place of the *Guide* in Britain, and it is all we have of the intensity of journalism Forster threw off in these years except one or two pieces in *Abinger Harvest*.

But the *Guide* is the thing. Here the Gibbonian streak in Forster is best developed, and when we want a gloss on the *Guide* we naturally turn to Gibbon's 21st and 47th chapters. The *Guide* stands up to comparison so well that we are bound to wonder what Forster could have given us if he had given his years, after the creative ones, to historical writing. But the historian requires serenity and Forster as much as any of our European writers was agonizingly aware of the shattering of European civilization; the political domination of barbarity, the social domination of vulgarity. That was a later mood. During the first war it was still possible to hope, indeed all our actions then were impelled by the promise of better days to come, and in that spirit Forster wrote his notes on the contemporary Egyptian scene in the Labour Research Department's publication *The Government of Egypt*. He is always incisive and frequently astringent on contemporary affairs and we notice the difference in temperature as soon as we open the *Guide*. Here is the warmth of mental excitement about one source of our western civilization.

He opens with 'The Land and the Waters' just as a few years later in *A Passage*, when again he is going to discuss men and religion, he describes the earth and the rocks and the great river, the soil and the climate out of which, through the minds and spirits of men, these thoughts developed. It is the same feeling for nature which we find in *The Longest Journey* and which is celebrated again in *Howards End*. Historically, he notes it as significant that our first glimpse of the place where Alexandria was to be built was through the eyes of a Greek sailor, Menelaus returning from Troy, for in its greatest years Alexandria was to interpret the Greek spirit and the Hebrew spirit through Greek to the western world.

Then comes the ancient little Egyptian town of Rhakotis, where later the cult of Serapis developed—'Alexandria's great religious effort'. The essay is alive with echoes and cross-references. As usual, they are there for the lively reader to hear as he can and this time more than that, they are the plan on which essay and *Guide* work together. For at the end of each little section of the essay is a list of references in the *Guide*, so that the wanderer in Alexandria, like Forster, can feel ancient presences at every corner. The cult of Serapis is discussed and introduced again as the antagonist against which Christianity had to make its way. The discussion develops the humanist theme that certain ideas appear in most religions and the gods of one religion may be those of another under different names. We shall see in *A Passage to India* how Forster went out of his way to adapt his account of the Gokul Ashtami festival in *Devi* to recall many incidents in the Christian story of the birth of Christ. The humanist becomes the sympathetic spectator of man's capacity for belief, noting that the Alexandrian 'never thought that the gods of his neighbour had no existence, and he was willing to believe that they might be his own gods under another name'.

Forster here displays an equal interest in great men, as good historians should, and in one of these miracles of succinct writing which make up this essay he sketches the idea of Alexander in building his city:

> He needed a capital for his new Egyptian kingdom, and to link it with Macedonia that capital had to be on the coast. Here was the very place — a splendid harbour, a perfect climate, fresh water, limestone quarries, and easy access to the Nile. Here he would perpetuate all that was best in Hellenism, and would create a metropolis for that greater Greece that should consist not of city-states but of kingdoms, and should include the whole inhabited world.

The 'young man hurried on' and soon he had wider ambitions:

> He became an oriental, a cosmopolitan almost, and though he fought in Persia again, it was in a new spirit. He wanted to harmonize the world now, not to Hellenize it, and must have looked back on Alexandria as a creation of his immaturity.

It was Mrs Moore in *A Passage* who was paid the greatest compliment by Aziz: 'You are an oriental.' Echoes will not reach so far, but this view of Alexander is echoed, like so much else, in *Pharos*, where there is sometimes greater acerbity of comment. There, Alexander:

> flung himself again, but in a new spirit, against the might of Persia. He fought her as a lover now. He wanted not to convert but to harmonize, and conceived himself as the divine and impartial ruler beneath whom harmony shall proceed. That way lies madness.

The section in the *Guide* about Alexander is a good example of the historical gift that Forster enjoyed, he could get into the minds of the great ones of the earth. Conqueror, like Alexander or Amr the Arab; saint, like Clement; courtesan, like Cleopatra; he understood them and helps us to understand their quality and their motives. Another gift enjoyed by competent historians is the broad imaginative vision and Forster displays it here. The treatment of the Ptolemaic century which followed the death of Alexander is a good example. We see the character of the dynasty settled and we observe the logic of its peculiarity: 'The royalties of today, for fear of debasing their stock, marry first cousins; the Ptolemies, more logical, tried to propagate within even narrower limits.' Such inbreeding, we now know, favours recessive genes. Physical weaknesses persist and develop. It is apt to produce morons, it may produce a genius. The later Ptolemies grew soft: 'And as the men soften, the women harden. The dynasty is interwoven with terrific queens.' It is all leading to Cleopatra, and the five-page sketch of her career is one of the great enjoyments of the essay.

> She did not differ in character from the other able and unscrupulous queens of her race, but she had one source of power that they denied themselves — the power of the courtesan — and she employed it professionally. Though passionate, she was not the slave of passion, still less of sentimentality. Her safety, and the safety of Egypt were her care; the clumsy and amorous Romans, who menaced both, were her natural prey. In old times, a queen might rule from her throne. Now she must descend and play the woman.

Inset in that portrait is an astringent comment on Octavian, which recalls an essay on 'The Consolations of History' written at that time, which begins: 'It is pleasant to be transferred from an office where one is afraid of a sergeant-major into an office where one can intimidate generals, and perhaps this is why History is so attractive to the more timid amongst us. We can recover confidence by snubbing the dead.' And the snub to Octavian reads thus: 'He is one of the most odious of the world's successful men, and to his cold mind the career of Cleopatra could appear as nothing but a vulgar debauch. Vice, in his opinion, should be furtive.' Then the great sweep over the period which began with Alexander and ended with Cleopatra, and the final word on these two great figures: 'Yet for all their differences, the man who created and the woman who lost Alexandria have one element in common: monumental greatness; and between them is suspended, like a rare and fragile chain, the dynasty of the Ptolemies.'

The plan of the essay is to summarize the political history and then discuss the culture of the period and assess its influence on our western civilization. The discussion of the Ptolemaic Culture which follows naturally stresses the Mouseion and its library, that great alembic through which so much of Greek, Hebrew and Christian thought was to pass and be distilled into a spirit powerfully to affect Mediterranean Europe. In itself, as expressed through its literature, the spirit of the Mouseion was not great: 'It developed when the heroic age of Greece was over, when liberty was lost and possibly honour too. It was disillusioned, and we may be glad it was not embittered also.' In the literature we have the first example of the maturing influence of Alexandria; on a poet, not a culture. Theocritus was 'a genius that Alexandria matured but cannot be said to have formed', and there follows the analysis of the Fifteenth Idyll, more in the spirit of *Pharos* (which it inspired) than in the more remote manner of the historian. The rest of the section reminds us briefly and forcefully of the remarkable advances in many sciences made in this century in this city. In general: 'The Ptolemies were more successful over Science than over Literature…In mathematics there was Euclid, in geography, Eratosthenes, in medicine, Erasistratus.' The description of the work of these men is admirable but the conclusion comes from the literary world: 'It did not bring happiness or wisdom: science never does.'

Then comes the Christian period. When Gibbon deals with Christianity over the same period, he is apparently unbiased, tolerant. When there is irony, it is in the nature of the facts, which are always allowed to speak for themselves. Forster achieves the same historical balance but we see in *Pharos* how difficult it must have been. He begins with the political events of the period, right on until Islam sweeps across Egypt and takes a prize whose value it cannot realize, Alexandria. He covers the centuries in appropriately magnificent style: 'Imperial Rome, who, despite her moments of madness, brought happiness to the Mediterranean world for two hundred years.' 'In about A.D. 250, she [Alexandria] with the rest of the Empire, re-entered trouble. The human race, as if not designed to enjoy happiness, had slipped into a mood of envy and discontent.' The protest against the divinity of the Caesars had come unexpectedly from Alexandria: 'To the absurd spiritual claims of the state, Christianity opposed the claims of the individual conscience, and the conflict was only allayed by the state itself becoming Christian.' The casualties in that war were the martyrs and they died in such numbers that the Egyptian Church 'dates its chronology, not from the birth of Christ but from the "Era of Martyrs" (A.D. 284)'.

Alexandria became the spiritual capital of the Empire for a time, but: 'An age of hatred and misery was approaching', an age of theological disputes. With now familiar clarity and brevity the great dispute between Arius and Athanasius is described. We shall find a parallel description in *Pharos*. We move on to the fourth and fifth centuries and the rule of the monks. 'The monks had not been important as long as each lived alone, but by the fourth century they had gathered into formidable communities, whence they would occasionally make raids on civilization like the Bedouins today.' They are disposed of thus:

> The monks had some knowledge of theology and of decorative craft, but they were averse to culture and incapable of thought. Their heroes were St Ammon who deserted his wife on their wedding eve, or St Antony, who thought bathing sinful and was consequently carried across the canals of the delta by an angel. From the ranks of such men the Patriarchs were recruited.

Gradually the monks became the nucleus of a nationalist movement and were given the name of Copts. So Egypt was held for the Empire only by Greek garrisons 'and consequently when the Arabs came they conquered her at once'.

We are approaching a silence of a thousand years but in this brief description of the clash between Christianity and Islam there are many excitements. Alexandria first fell to Persia and by treachery: 'A foreign student—Peter was his name—got into touch with them.' Later, when the presents are listed which were sent by the Imperial Viceroy of Alexandria to an 'obscure Arab Sheikh named Mohammed, 'the last item is two Coptic maidens' and 'one of the latter, Mary, became the Sheikh's favourite concubine. Amidst such amenities did our intercourse with Mohammedanism begin.' Are we hearing ironic echoes?

There is the description of the Arab general which is a good example of what Forster describes in his 'Consolations of History':

'an indubitable triumph of evolution—oneself, sitting untouched and untouchable in the professorial chair, and giving marks to men.' He gives high marks to Amr. 'He was an administrator, a delightful companion, and a poet—one of the ablest and most charming men that Islam ever produced. He would have been remarkable in any age.' Then comes the prelude to the long silence over Alexandria: 'The Arabs could not realize the value of their prize. They knew that Allah had given them a large and strong city. They could not know that there was no other like it in the world, that the science of Greece had planned it, that it had been the intellectual birthplace of Christianity.'

We have come to the centre and core of the essay, to the description of its spiritual life, which became the city's great contribution to western civilization and in particular its contribution to the spread of Christianity, which began apparently so inauspiciously. For who could have supposed that the eleven followers who were chosen to spread the Word throughout the sophisticated Mediterranean world were likely to be successful propagandists? Forster describes how Alexandria was attracted to the spiritual problems of Christianity as it was attracted by the spiritual problems of the Jews and the Greeks, for they were the same problem and they were trying to 'solve it in the same way'. The problem of finding a bridge between man and his remote God.

First came the Jews, attracted by the 'lucrative and seductive city', where they soon learned Greek and forgot Hebrew and so required the Septuagint, the Greek translation of their scriptures. Then came that fine piece, *The Wisdom of Solomon*, in which wisdom becomes 'a messenger who bridges the gulf and makes us friends of God'. The idea of the anonymous author is developed by Philo, who spoke of the Logos or the Word, as St John was to do later. Then came the Greeks and they contributed Neo-Platonism which has obvious connexions with Hindu thought which Forster was to develop in his last novel a few years later. 'Man's goal is to become actually, as he is potentially, divine' and, for this, rebirth is permitted: 'the whole Universe has an inclination towards good... the Christian promise is that a man shall see God, the Neo-Platonic —like the Indian—that he shall be God.'

3

Then he comes to Christianity and again we see him thinking along lines he followed in *A Passage*: 'Did Christianity borrow from the Osiris cult her doctrines of the Resurrection and Personal Immortality, and her sacrament of the Eucharist? The suggestion has been made.' Then comes the typical Alexandrian contribution. They took over a religion which had been addressed to a 'poor and unfashionable people' and prepared it to dominate the Mediterranean: 'as soon as it reached Alexandria its character altered, the turning point in its worldly career arrived. The Alexandrians were highly cultivated, they had libraries...their faith inevitably took a philosophic form. Occupied by their favourite problem of the relation between God and man, they at once asked the same question of the new religion as they asked the Jews and the Greeks—namely, what is the link? Philo said the Logos, Plotinus the Emanations. The new religion replied "Christ".'

The discussion goes on to Gnosticism and Early Orthodoxy, taught by Clement of Alexandria who appears so persistently in *Pharos*. Here: 'his methods forestall those of the advanced missionary today...he set Christianity upon a path she did not long consent to follow. He raised her from intellectual obscurity, he lent her for a little Hellenic persuasion, and the graciousness of Greece seems in his pages not incompatible with the grace of God.' And in *Pharos*: 'in that curious city, which had never been young and hoped never to grow old, conciliation must have seemed more possible than elsewhere, and the graciousness of Greece not quite incompatible with the Grace of God.'

After that, the theological arguments become barren and at last comes the utterly barren contact with Islam, which 'was the 'one system that the city could not handle. It gave no opening to her manipulations...The physical decay that crept on her in the seventh century had its counterpart in a spiritual decay. Amr and his Arabs instinctively shrank from Alexandria: she seemed to them idolatrous and foolish; and a thousand years of silence succeeded them.'

Recovery came and Alexandria once again is a great city. Napoleon and the French arrived. The English bombarded it in 1882 and occupied Egypt. It is all described astringently, but the essayist's heart is not in it in the same way. It is just a modern city, with none of the greatness or the glory of former times. There is nothing to sustain the great historical manner and the material is more suitable to the little personal essays in *Pharos and Pharillon*.

That little collection has always been the substitute in Britain for the *Guide* until the American edition came. The writing is more relaxed and intimate and we are allowed to see how Alexandria took hold of Forster's imagination during his three years of residence there and how these preoccupations with comparative religion first engrossed him which were to appear so imaginatively in *A Passage*. That these interesting subjects were much in his mind in these years we can see from an essay 'Salute to the Orient' written just before his second visit to India.

> So if we say of the Oriental, firstly, that personal relationship is most important to him, secondly, that it has no transcendental sanction, we shall come as near to a generalization as is safe, and then it will only be safe in the nearer East. Farther afield, in Persia and India, another idea, that of Union with God, becomes prominent, and the human outlook is altered accordingly.

In that case Forster is an oriental, for he consciously cultivates personal relationships and again and again among his essays we find the personal celebration of a friend. As here, in *Pharillon,* which ends with one of the most delightful of them, an appreciation of C. P. Cavafy and his poetry: 'They turn and see a Greek gentleman in a straw hat, standing absolutely motionless at a slight angle to the universe...he may be prevailed upon to begin a sentence—an immensely complicated yet shapely sentence...despite the matured charity of its judgements, one feels that it too stands at a slight angle to the universe; it is the sentence of a poet.'

It is the most attractive piece in *Pharillon,* the second part of the little collection, named after the lesser lighthouse which succeeded Pharos and eventually 'slid unobserved into the Mediterranean'. It begins with a piece on Mrs Eliza Fay, who claimed his attention again in an edition of her letters and in a *Cornhill* article. The essay here foreshadows a technique he was to develop in his biography of Lowes Dickinson and use to the utmost in *Devi* and *Marianne.* The subject is allowed to speak through letters and journals with just enough comment to connect and enliven the original material. It is a modest method and it has modest beginnings here, where the comment is so rich and vivacious. As, for instance, this comment on Suez before the aeroplane age, when the throb of the ship's engine falls almost silent as if in sympathy with the desert silence:

> The beauty of the Gulf of Suez—and surely it is most beautiful —has never received full appreciation from the traveller. He is in too much of a hurry to arrive or to depart, his eyes are too ardently bent on England or on India for him to enjoy that exquisite corridor of tinted mountains and radiant water. He is too much occupied with his own thoughts to realize that here, here and nowhere else, is the vestibule between the Levant and the Tropics.

The echo is in *A Passage:* 'The Mediterranean is the human norm. When men leave that exquisite lake...they approach the monstrous and extraordinary; and the southern exit leads to the strangest experience of all.'

The pieces between Eliza and Cavafy are slight, a description of the Bourse (which is very like the one in Bombay) and of baling cotton, the search for an opium den, about the Rue Rosette, and about the flowers that bloom suddenly and fade as quickly in the country that stretches westward from Lake Mariout. Slight pieces on slight subjects, suitable for the local newspaper, without the weight and quality of the essays in *Pharos* which echo so often in the sections of the *Guide*.

Pharos, we said, was the British substitute for the Guide until the American paperback came. The opening paragraphs are similar and they are the first use of the technique he was to employ with such imaginative effect in *A Passage*. The structure and composition of the earth is the solid stage on which all human action takes place. A commonplace that becomes imaginative excitement. It was implicit in *Howards End* but *Howards End* is about the gentle earth of England. Here, the background is the Mediterranean and the Nile and the desert; and in *A Passage*, the Ganges and the vast plain and the most ancient rocks that rise out of it.

The pieces in *Pharos* which follow are best described in the words of the Conclusion: 'A serious history of Alexandria has yet to be written, and perhaps the foregoing sketches may have indicated how varied, how impressive, such a history might be. After the fashion of a pageant it might marshal the activities of two thousand two hundred and fifty years.' In the *Guide* he puts it thus: 'The "History" attempts (after the fashion of a pageant) to marshal the activities of Alexandria during the two thousand two hundred and fifty years of her experience.' The method of the pageant, the representative incident, is more evident in *Pharos,* where it becomes, it has been said, very like the Idyll of Theocritus celebrated in one of the pieces. The imaginative glimpse is relied on instead of the steady record.

The detachment of the historian is unnecessary and personal quiddities are in order, as in these notes on the Hebrews:

> Meantime the Jews had been attentive. They, too, liked delectable spots. Deeply as they were devoted to Jehovah, they had ever felt it to be their duty to leave his city where they could, and as soon as Alexandria began to develop, they descended upon her markets with polite cries.

As these sketches were written for individual publication it is natural that each should dwell upon an idea more emphatically than the scope and structure of the *Guide* allowed. As in this conception of the Lighthouse, whose structure he describes so vividly:

> Just as the Parthenon had been identified with Athens, and St Peter's was to be identified with Rome, so, to the imagination of contemporaries, 'The Pharos' became Alexandria and Alexandria the Pharos. Never, in the history of architecture, has a secular building been thus worshipped and taken on a spiritual life of its own. It beaconed to the imagination, not only to ships.

The attentive reader may find echoes there from an earlier Claphamite historian whom we meet as young Tom Macaulay in *Marianne.* There is splendid pageantry of the mind of Alexander in the description of his visit to the Oasis at Siwa where he met the priest who hailed him as Son of God. Or did the priest intend to

say 'my child' but his Greek was so poor he got it wrong? And was
Landor right in saying that Alexander got a scare at some moment in
this visit?

> 'A scare he did get—a fright, a psychic experience, a vision, a
> "turn". His development proves it. After his return from Siwa
> his aspirations alter. Never again does he regard Greece as the
> centre of the world.'

The method of the pageant has its own power, as we see when we
turn to the account of the visit in the *History,* where the little incident cannot be allowed to rise (it is too speculative) out of the record
of which it is such a small part:

> His next care was a visit to the temple of Ammon in the Siwan
> Oasis, where the priest saluted him as a god, and henceforward
> his Greek sympathies declined. He became an oriental, a
> cosmopolitan almost, and though he fought Persia again, it was
> in a new spirit.

In *Pharos,* he is able to let us see the whole incident and dwell on it:
'He has caught, by the unintellectual way, a glimpse of something
great, if dangerous, and that glimpse came to him first in the recesses
of the Siwan Oasis.'

Pharos can supplement the *History* in another way. The *History*
has no space for the story of Ptolemy V, the father of Cleopatra, but
Pharos has a vivid little account and altogether ignores Cleopatra,
who is celebrated with such splendour in the *History.* Here, in
'Epiphany', in a word pageant of less than a thousand words, we
have the weakness of the Ptolemies, the fierceness of their wives and
the savage power of the Alexandrian mob:

> ...the wife of the forage contractor who would say to the
> King, 'Here, Daddy, drink this'. The King liked young women
> who called him Daddy; and he drank, and when he had drunk
> enough he would get up and dance, the others danced too, he
> would fall down; it was all delightful.

He died, and the Queen essayed to take charge:

> The old heroic feelings came back to her. Life seemed worth
> living again. She returned to her apartments full of exaltation.

She entered them. As she did so, the curtains, which had been soaked with inflammable oil in her absence, burst into flame. She tried to retire. The doors had been locked behind her, and she was burnt to death.

Rhetoricians will dwell on this management of the short sentence. For fourteen months these deaths were concealed from the people and then misgovernment brought things to a crisis and the Queen's murderers were dealt with: 'All were dragged from their retreats, tortured, and killed, the women being stripped naked first.'

The next little pageant is more farce than melodrama, Caligula fooling the petitioners from Jewish Alexandria. Then come the pieces on Christianity and in the first, on Clement, we get the answer to a question which must have been at the back of our minds all through the discussion in the *History*. Did Forster think that Alexandria did more to spread Christianity than St Paul? Apparently he did:

> And now Clement, taking over the completed conception, raised upon it a storied fabric such as the Alexandrians loved, and ensured that the deity should be at the same time accessible and inaccessible, merciful and just, human and divine...it impressed the passing age; Clement, working in and through Alexandria, did more than even St Paul to recommend Christianity to the Gentiles.

The piece on St Athanasius which follows usefully supplements the *History*. There is a sympathetic sketch of Arius: 'Learned and sincere, tall, simple in his dress, persuasive in his manner', and a brief exposition of Athanasius' reasons for taking the other view. He 'viewed the innovation with an expert eye, saw that while it popularized Christ it isolated God, and raised man no nearer to heaven in the long run. Therefore he fought it.' Then the pageant-master awards the marks:

> ...he had weaned the Church from her tradition of scholarship and tolerance, the tradition of Clement and Origen. Few divines have done more for her, and her gratitude has been both profound and characteristic; she has coupled his name to a Creed with which he had nothing to do—the Athanasian.

The last pageant in *Pharos* is about the rule of the monks, those 'formidable communities' in the *History* which 'would occasionally make raids on civilization'. The pageant is about the Monophysites who founded the Coptic Church and it is a satire which ends in five words that contain more irony than all the rest of the pageants put together:

> ...the curtain may drop now...The Copts still believe, with Timothy the Cat, in the single nature of Christ; the double Nature, upheld by Timothy Whitebonnet, is still maintained by the rest of Christendom and by the reader. The Pharos, the Temple of Serapis; these have perished, being only stones, and sharing the impermanence of material things. It is ideas that live.

In such studies the circumstances of war condemned Forster to spend three years of his prime. They have been neglected or ignored by the critics, which is strange because we have seen how they developed attitudes towards human thinking about religion which are at the centre of his greatest novel, which was completed very soon afterwards. It is likely that, but for the scholarly preoccupations of the war interlude, the powerful development of these ideas in *A Passage* would not have been possible.

Aspects of the Novel

WHEN WE ARE two centuries away from the Edwardians, we may
see that they treated the novel as seriously as the seventeenth century
treated the epic. Forster made his chief contribution to the subject
in the Clark Lectures which he delivered in the spring of 1927. A
course of lectures has the quality of a serial: 'if it is to be more than a
collection of remarks', he says at the opening of his sixth lecture, it
'must have an idea running through it'. Which, as he says, seems
obvious enough. But it is the special pleasure of a lecture series that
everything comes to a point and early lectures echo back with new
meaning as the tempo increases and the idea behind all the lectures
becomes plain and gathers force. Nothing could fit Forster's talent
better and if we think of the circumstances of a lecture, the lonely
distinguished figure providing solo entertainment for at least fifty
minutes once a week with nothing but his voice and his words to
help him, we can feel again the dramatic triumph of the idea being
steadily and ever more perceptibly unfolded.

He is deprecating as usual about his performance and decides not
to edit his text before he prints it: 'They were informal, indeed
talkative, in their tone, and it seemed safer when presenting them in
book form not to mitigate the talk.' Before we finish reading that
note we may recall Virginia Woolf's hint that: 'There is something

73

baffling and evasive in the nature of his gifts' and then go on: 'since the novel is itself often colloquial it may possibly withhold some of its secrets from the graver and grander streams of criticism, and may reveal them to backwaters and shallows.'

What we find, in the end, is an idea of the novel which will stand beside the great celebrations of the epic form. It might have helped if Forster had edited away quotations and discussions of contemporary books now forgotten, if some listener had made notes of the fine things and left the rest, as happened to Aristotle, for then we might have found it easier to realize that here we have one of the great appreciations of the most lively organism in words that genius has developed during the past two hundred years.

We may find something of the spirit in which these novelists approached their craft expressed more directly than Forster would ever have done in an essay on the contemporary novel by another Edwardian novelist, H. G. Wells:

> The success of civilization amounts ultimately to a success of sympathy and understanding. If people cannot be brought to an interest in one another greater than they feel today, to curiosities and criticisms far keener, and co-operation far subtler, than we have now; if class cannot be brought to measure itself against, and interchange experience and sympathy with class, and temperament with temperament, then we shall never struggle very far beyond the confused discomforts and uneasiness of today, and the changes and complications of human life will remain as they are now, very like the crumplings and separations and complications of an immense avalanche that is sliding down a hill. And in this tremendous work of human reconciliation and elucidation, it seems to me it is the novel that must attempt most and achieve most.

There is much in that which Forster would applaud. It is the spirit of his conclusion to the lectures, when he speculates about whether the novel will fade away or develop into an efficient criticism of our lives today. He is hopeful and speaks of the possible development of the human brain and suggests that in this the novel may have a part to play.

Between the invocation and the conclusion, the lectures deal with the usual aspects, the story and the plot and the characters. These offer the emotional pleasures of the novel. Then come the intellectual pleasures, which interest him more; fantasy, prophecy, pattern and rhythm. He is a little arbitrary about his definition of these words and right at the beginning he gives arbitrary definition to the novel: 'Any fictitious prose work over 50,000 words will be a novel for the purpose of these lectures.' This looks like taking us away back beyond the two hundred year lifetime of the novel deep into antiquity, but he is confined by the terms of the lectureship to discuss what has been written in the English language. Confined in time, he is more sadly confined in space and cannot discuss the greatest novels, the Russian and the French. 'English fiction is less triumphant: it does not contain the best stuff written yet.' Then comes the first inspired idea to illuminate the subject. He asks us 'to visualize the English novelists...as seated together in a room—all writing their novels simultaneously...They are half-mesmerized, their sorrows and joys are pouring out through the ink, they are approximated by the act of creation'. An interesting Canadian critic, Mr Johnstone in his *Bloomsbury Group,* has told us that Forster sees all of them together in that great room because, since 'writers draw their inspiration from the subconscious they have all through history felt more or less the same while writing'. It is a little difficult to be sure what authors felt any time these two hundred years but we do know that this is the way we read novels when we are young and before we have any historical perspective. It is also an expression of the mystery of the classics, the books that stay alive, the mystery of the ink of two hundred years ago being some-times more fresh and refreshing than the ball-point of today.

Then comes another kind of refreshment, which we should have lost if the lectures had been edited, the little break in the tension of argument, the digression which gives the audience time to catch its mental second wind. He denounces pseudo-scholarship which is usually the craft of passing examinations, and quietly puts his finger on a very present trouble, putting our national affairs so much in the hands of clever examinees. 'Learning is connected with earning' he says, and we wonder how many in his audience understood what he had said when he added on that first afternoon of his Clark

Lectures: 'If another ladder to employment was contrived, much
so-called education would disappear, and no one would be a penny
the stupider.'

Lectures will always be enriched by asides like these. They help
the speaker in the preliminary test which Aristotle first laid down,
that he must persuade the audience to give him their attention. After
that, it is the test of the lecturer on literature to persuade his
audience to read the texts and enjoy them with more lively intelligence. A favourite way of doing this is to read to them, and Forster
all through these lectures explores his great gift for reading aloud.
He does so here, to illustrate his fantasy that all these novelists are
writing at one time together and at the end he offers two more
illuminating comments: 'The final test of a novel will be our affection for it, as it is the test of our friends, and of anything else we
cannot define.' The other comment is a major one, expressing the
essence of the novel's contribution in literature: 'The intensely
stiflingly human quality of the novel is not to be avoided; the novel
is sogged with humanity; there is no escaping the uplift or the down-
pour, nor can they be kept out of criticism. We may hate humanity,
but if it is exorcised, or even purified the novel wilts, little is left but
a bunch of words.'

It is the natural comment of the intellectual novelist. Two kinds
of writing are full of people, the play and the novel. But the dramatist detaches from his characters and the audience watches a
spectacle. In the novel, writer and reader are involved, critically and
emotionally, and neither of them can escape from the people in the
tale. The heart-felt cry is related to the famous little cry in the next
lecture, about the story. 'Yes—oh dear yes—the novel tells a story.
That is the fundamental aspect without which it could not exist...
and I wish it was not so, that it could be something different—
melody, or perception of the truth...' Are we hearing now why he
gave up the novel? He probed truth for his own country and his own
people in *The Longest Journey* and in *Howards End*, and then he
sought to make it a note in music in writing about India. We cannot
say he failed. It was neither failure nor success that stopped him,
but he wrestled no more with what he called this 'low atavistic
form'. On the last day of the year before these lectures he was

sitting with Sassoon and Arnold Bennett who tells us in his diary that Forster said 'he had not begun a new novel, and hadn't got any ideas for one. So I cursed him and urged him to get on with a novel: but of course I knew it would be no good.' What we are hearing in these lectures is his farewell to the novel.

A mere story, he says, is like 'a tape-worm, for its beginning and end are arbitrary', and he returns to his repellent simile: 'wriggling and interminable, the naked worm of time—it presents an appearance both unlovely and dull', and later: 'it is never possible for a novelist to deny time inside the fabric of his novel: he must cling however lightly to the thread of his story, he must touch the interminable tape-worm.' He wants something more than that: 'there seems something else in life besides time, which may conveniently be called "value".' What that means in this context is immediately seen in a sustained attack upon the Waverley Novels. It may not seem very fair, and it ignores the passionate historical judgements on civil war in *Waverley* and *Redgauntlet,* which most would rank high in the achievements of the English novel. It ignores the connection of prose and passion in the vibrating Lowland Scots spoken by the peasant characters. But it leads him to stating his real quarrel with the story: 'Intolerance is the atmosphere stories generate.' There, there is a significant secret of the silence.

There is a useful comment on *War and Peace* just before that which leads us back to Forster's own work. He begins by distinguishing place and space. 'Many novelists have the feeling for place... Very few have the sense of space...Space is the lord of *War and Peace* not time.' As we should say, time-space, and suggest Thackeray as an English novelist who had all western Europe for space and, from *Barry Lyndon* onwards, lived in time like an historian or like Hardy in *The Dynasts.* Whereas Forster is very local, even when he places the scene in the vast plains of India, just occasionally giving us a hint of that feeling of the air about us resting on endless land space. It would have been interesting if he had returned to the questions of time and space—'as soon as fiction is completely delivered from time it cannot express anything at all' —with our modern conception of time-space. It might have affected his clear distinction between story and plot which he appropriately discusses after his two lectures on 'People', but which we may look at now.

In a plot, he says, the emphasis falls on causality. ' "The king died and then the queen died" is a story. "The king died and then the queen died of grief" is a plot. The time-sequence is preserved, but the sense of causality overshadows it.' He is naturally for plots and we are not surprised to hear that the story arouses only curiosity but 'a plot demands intelligence and memory also'. Intelligence and memory in the reader are as closely connected as time and space and are an essential combination for the reader of Forster's novels. 'Memory and intelligence are closely connected for unless we remember we cannot understand.' Then comes a fine description of a plot: 'Every word or action in a plot ought to count: it ought to be economical and spare...organic and free from dead matter... and the final sense will be...of something aesthetically compact, something which might have been shown by the novelist straight away, only if he had shown it straight away it would never have become beautiful'. Like the power for tranquillity in the house called Howards End.

And there are other moments in this chapter on plot which illuminate Forster's novels. When he speaks of human beings in novels being 'enormous, shadowy, and intractable, and three-quarters hidden like an iceberg' we think of Stephen Wonham, who was so much too big for his companions in *The Longest Journey*. And Helen Schlegel who, if never unwieldy, was always 'three-quarters hidden'. In a rare personal moment he says 'the work of Hardy is my home and that of Meredith cannot be', yet when he is describing the plots of the renounced Meredith, we think of *Howards End*, which moves through time-space from one scene to another: 'A Meredithian plot is not a temple to the tragic or even to the comic Muse, but rather a series of kiosks most artfully placed among wooded slopes, which his people reach by their own impetus, and from which they emerge with altered aspect.'

And once again there are the joys the lecturer loves to offer, the malicious fun at the end about Gide and the old lady who cried out contemptuously: 'How can I tell what I think till I see what I say?'

When we consider what he says about People, those characters made up of words who are the stuff of prose fiction, we see how intellectual is Forster's approach and the pleasure his work gives. The characters are exercises for intellectual analysis and the most interesting of them are those who are remote enough from the author and his readers to make the idea of personal relationships a challenge, Gino, a kind of Italian we shall never meet, Stephen Wonham, the natural inhabitant of the Rings, the erratic Helen Schlegel, Dr Aziz, that never-to-be-met amalgam of various Mohammedan types.

It is here that Forster introduces the discussion about the nature of history and the nature of prose fiction, a comparison which brings us nearer to the name and nature of the art of creating characters and displaying them in interesting situations. He opens the chapter by suggesting a new emphasis: as soon as we turn from the story, the concern about what happens next, and look at the characters, there is 'emphasis upon value'. Almost at once we have the first suggestions of a comparison with people in history, 'real people', as we call them, though we remember that the historian also relies entirely on word-masses. It seems likely that there are no heroes in the human story but the word-masses go on building them up and tearing them down. The word-masses of the novelist survive because they have created a person in whom we can believe and in whom we can be interested. 'The novelist...makes up a number of word-masses roughly describing himself...gives them names and sex, assigns them plausible gestures, and causes them to speak by the use of inverted commas, and perhaps to behave consistently. These word-masses are his characters.'

The historian, he goes on to say, is a man who records 'whereas the novelist must create'. Fortunate novelist who begins with a clean page while the historian begins with many word-masses often apparently contradictory. So the historian finds out and interprets, whereas the novelist creates and in doing so interprets. History, he says, is based on evidence while a novel is based on evidence plus or minus an unknown quantity which is the temperament of the novelist. He goes no further than this, presumably taking for granted the obvious reflection that the chief character in every novel is the author of it. A novel is a brain child and we recognize the parent of it. The novelist is the god of his novel, and everything depends on how his God made him. Nothing could possibly give a man away more than writing a novel. A prose fiction is as individual as a fingerprint, and if the author is a shallow man it will at once appear. The novelist, unlike the dramatist, never escapes from his novel.

There are kinds of writing which reach perfection when the author becomes detached, and this is notably so in the lyric. Of the achieved lyric Forster says: 'The poet wrote the poem no doubt, but he forgot himself while he wrote it, and we forget him while we read.' That is in his essay on 'Anonymity', written in 1925, not long before the lectures were composed, and it is in this essay that he deals more fully with the writer as creator. He says there is the upper personality, the one with the name, the one we can see 'dining out, answering letters etc' and there is the lower one: 'The lower personality is a very queer affair...unless a man dips a bucket down into it occasionally he cannot produce first-class work...It has something in common with all other deeper personalities, and the mystic will assert that the common quality is God, and that here, in the obscure recesses of our being, we near the gates of the Divine.' This is a fine expression of the human heritage, the condition that makes man the glory and the riddle of the world. It is a creative condition in which (so far as literature is concerned) readers as well as writers participate: 'What is so wonderful about great literature is that it transforms the man who reads it towards the condition of the man who wrote, and brings to birth in us also the creative impulse. Lost in the beauty where he was lost, we find more than we ever threw away, we reach what seems to be our spiritual home, and remember that it was not the speaker who was in the beginning but the Word.' So the world of man's own creation is one in which we all have equal rights and we enjoy them according to our abilities. Those of us who have read the *Alexandria* will feel that we are breathing the atmosphere of the ancient library again.

We can return to our lecture room now to hear the lecturer say that the worlds of our creating have a fulness that our 'real' world does not offer. 'In daily life we never understand each other, neither complete clairvoyance nor complete confessional exists...But people in a novel can be understood completely by the reader, if the novelist wishes; their inner as well as their outer life can be exposed.' Then comes an early statement about doublethink. Forster says that characters in novels 'even if they are imperfect or unreal... do not contain any secrets, whereas our friends do and must, mutual secrecy being one of the conditions of life upon this globe.' If only Orwell had had time and space enough to discuss this compassionate side of doublethink.

Our lecturer by this time is discussing 'the main facts in our own lives' as they appear in the novel, birth, food, sleep, love and death. Birth usually happens off, food is social, it brings characters together, sleep is used in a perfunctory way, love comes in far too much and death is very useful to the novelist. He does not dwell on his own dependence on death in his novels and as for love, he does not tell us why he preferred to be independent of it.

We are much more with him when he returns to his books and picks on *Moll Flanders* and with the skill of the born lecturer makes us run to take it up again. Here is one of the most delightful analyses in the lectures. Moll has a delightful sponsor and she repays him by providing him with material on the main theme of his lecture: people in novels 'are people whose secret lives are visible or might be visible: we are people whose secret lives are invisible.' The last words complete his conception of the novelist as creator: 'And that is why novels...can solace us; they suggest a more comprehensible and thus a more manageable human race, they give us the illusion of perspicacity and power.' The desire of the preacher to manage the race.

The second lecture on 'People' has the famous things on flat characters and about the novelist 'bouncing' us into accepting what he says. Of flat characters many of us may think that we know them in life as well as in fiction. Flat characters, 'humours' in the seventeenth century, 'are sometimes called types and sometimes caricatures'. They are sometimes normal and sometimes are given a twist or bias to express exaggeration. They are useful in novels because 'they are easily recognized whenever they come in...they never need reintroducing, never run away, have not to be watched for development, and provide their own atmosphere.' Round characters, on the other hand, are 'full of the spirit of mutiny...they try to live their own lives and are consequently often engaged in treasons against the main scheme of the book. They "run away", they "get out of hand": if they are given complete freedom they kick the book to pieces.' So the novelist employs flat characters. Anything more like real life it is difficult to imagine. Social life and public life and most of the business of government depends on treating us all as flat characters. He quotes Norman Douglas saying to D. H. Lawrence: 'That is the novelist's touch. It falsifies life.' Generally, the aspects of a character in a novel are developed which cause the required reactions in other characters. That is all there is time for, that is all that is appropriate. But what is true of fiction is to some extent true of life. We live on a series of generalizations similar to those seventeenth-century characters. In our domestic life we meet plumbers and lawyers, postmen and doctors and we behave towards them in relation to their work and may have little time or chance to know them in any other way. Most of their personalities remain submerged and life, like the novel, would not get on if we attempted more.

It all comes back to personality in real life as in the novelist, as Forster implies when he talks about 'the power of the writer to bounce the reader into accepting what he says'. That is the gift of the novelist, to create so that we believe absolutely and, as we shall never analyse the gift, Forster's easy word for it is as accurate as any other. Percy Lubbock, he has just been saying, holds that method in the craft of fiction depends on the point of view the novelist adopts, whether he stays outside his characters or gets inside or becomes one of them, or adopts one of the possible intermediate attitudes. Forster pays tribute to the talent and insight of Lubbock's discussion, but says what we should all say, that the novelist can adopt any method he likes but, if he has not the power to make us believe, the method will not help him. We know that novelists have found that they can bounce us more easily by one method than another. Forster adds to that by reminding us that a great novelist can mix his methods—'it came off with Dickens and Tolstoi'. Then comes the old warning about the Thackeray method: 'may the writer take the reader into his confidence about his characters? Answer has already been indicated: better not...it generally leads to a drop in the temperature, to intellectual and emotional laxity, and worse still to facetiousness.' Some of us may think that once again it all depends and we enjoy ourselves as much when Fielding or Thackeray are talking as when their characters are talking. But Forster has gone on to another valuable suggestion: 'To take your reader into your confidence about the universe is a different thing. It is not dangerous for a novelist to draw back from his characters, as Hardy and Conrad do, and to generalize about the conditions under which he thinks life is carried on.'

What have we gleaned from two lectures on the characters in a novel? Some flashes of insight which are invaluable as they come from the personal experience of writing. But the discussion has always been on a cool level, an intellectual determination not to be carried away and not to be bounced into extravagance or undue warmth about the God's plenty of splendid characters in the range of English fiction. He never asks where, outside God's world, you will find so many amusing characters, often with more roundness than the plot requires. No hint of this from the apostle of personal relations and we wonder, perhaps, whether the gospel of personal relationships gets us any farther than intense communication with a few chosen spirits. Nothing more wonderful, nothing more admirable, and nothing more confining to the spirit of man.

We come to major truth when we come to the lecture on Fantasy and Prophecy. The series is mounting to its climax as he discusses what is in effect comedy and tragedy in the novel. He had begun himself as an almost purely comic or fantasy novelist and proceeded to the other kind before falling silent and in all of them we feel a reaching towards the perfection of which the novel form is capable. Now the simplest and most obvious thing about a novelist is that he has observed humanity. He may have turned fantasist as a result and avoided it as in *Zuleika Dobson,* or created 'the army of unutterable muddle' as in *Tristram Shandy,* or made 'a dogged attempt to cover the universe with mud' as in *Ulysses.* But in every case the novelist has been reacting to the human scene and as Forster says at the end of these two lectures 'the human mind is not a dignified organ' and not always strong and it is the sensitive spirits who escape into fantasy. Stronger ones, he names them—'I can only think of four writers to illustrate it—Dostoievsky, Melville, D. H. Lawrence and Emily Brontë'—are able to prophesy.

But to separate fantasy and prophecy is as false as to separate time and space. The stuff of novels is human beings and their surroundings and that is the stuff of the world. But in the novel there is something more, for the novel is the product of mind and mind contemplating human beings and their surroundings can translate what it sees prophetically or fantastically and these powers are connected so there is a 'fantastic-prophetical axis'. A novelist can get on with his characters and his plot and the background against which they move and be satisfied. But there are novelists in whom the fantastic-prophetical axis is essential: 'Deprive Sterne or Virginia Woolf or Walter de la Mare or William Beckford or James Joyce or D. H. Lawrence or Swift, and nothing is left at all.'

So we must find a new formula. In a delightfully satisfying simile he opens his lecture by reminding us how easy it is for theory to soar away from fact. 'Perhaps our subject, namely the books we have read, has stolen away from us while we theorize, like a shadow from an ascending bird. The bird is all right—it climbs...The shadow is all right...But the two things resemble one another less and less.' He applies it to criticism, there in Cambridge in which our most forceful academic critics were then young: 'lecturer and audience may awake with a start to find that they are carrying on in a distinguished and intelligent manner, but in regions which have nothing to do with anything they have read.'

We continue to look for our formula and our lecturer reminds us that: 'Our easiest approach to a definition of any aspect of fiction is always by considering the sort of demand it makes on the reader.' The fantasist says: 'Here is something that could not occur' and he asks us to believe it. It is our old friend, willing suspension of disbelief, and eventually he defines fantasy thus: 'It implies the supernatural but need not express it.' A working formula for one part and if we are literalists we had better leave *Tristram* and *Zuleika* alone. Their mythology is not for us. Perhaps we shall enjoy the mythology of the prophetic novelists, 'the deities of India, Greece, Scandinavia and Judaea'. If we are to do so, we must make the necessary sacrifices: 'the prophetic aspect demands two qualities: humility and the suspension of the sense of humour.' Our lecturer does not like the sacrifices: 'Humility is a quality for which I have only a limited admiration', and to him the sense of humour is the 'estimable adjunct of the educated man', but the sacrifice must be made if we are to catch the prophetic 'accent in the novelist's voice' for prophecy 'in our sense is a tone of voice' and so in our discussion of it 'we may come nearer than elsewhere to the minutiae of style'. It is an instinctive reaction of the lecturer to a subject which 'promises to be so vague and grandiose'.

So prophecy here has nothing to do with the narrow sense of foretelling the future and it is quickly distinguished from preaching — George Eliot preaches, Dostoievsky prophesies. The novelist-prophet is not just an inspired teacher, as we see from the judgement on *Moby Dick*: 'There has been...no explicable solution, certainly no reaching back into universal pity and love.' We sense his difficulty in defining prophecy when he speaks in terms of music: 'The essential in *Moby Dick*, its prophetic song, flows athwart the action' and again, on D. H. Lawrence: 'he is the only living novelist in whom song predominates, who has the rapt bardic quality.' It sounds like Dylan Thomas, who did not have much to say but who provided meaning enough in the sound of his saying.

In the end he equates the prophetic gift with what we call 'genius' to get us out of farther analysis. The greatness of D. H. Lawrence, he says, rests 'upon something aesthetic' and concludes his appreciation thus: 'What is valuable about him cannot be put into words; it is colour, gesture and outline in people and things, the usual stock-in-trade of the novelist, but evolved by such a different process that they belong to a new world.' Many of us now would go back to Forster's phrase about 'minutiae of style' to explain Lawrence's special quality, his power of giving illumination to a word in its context which we usually find in great verse. Re-creating and evoking with words, such as prophets use. He returns to the musical comparison when he speaks of Emily Brontë: '*Wuthering Heights* is filled with sound—storm and rushing wind—a sound more important than words or thoughts.' (The quiddity of the lectures lies in the phrases dropped about individual novels. What could be better than describing Heathcliffe and Catherine as externalizing their passion 'till it streamed through the house and over the moors'?) Emily Bronte connects the prose and the passion, and once again it comes back to words and she who uses them. The paradox would seem to be that in the intensely individual characters which the great novelists create there is also an abstraction or essence of human character generally, and in this sense, prophecy is the ontological content of a novel. The sense in which Forster himself excelled.

To clinch the argument we must go back to the beginning of the lecture on Fantasy, where he says: 'There is more in the novel than time or people or logic or any of their derivatives, more even than Fate. And by "more" I do not mean something that excludes these aspects nor something that includes them, embraces them. I mean something that cuts across them like a bar of light, that is intimately connected with them at one place and patiently illumines all their problems, and at another place shoots over or through them as if they did not exist.' There are moments in Forster's novels when this bar of light shoots across the mind of the reader: the moment in *Howards End* when Margaret realizes that Helen is with child, the moment in the court scene in *A Passage* when Adela sees the beauty in the figure of the punkah wallah.

The other power Forster attributes to prophecy, to provide a mythology, brings us even more closely to his own work and, if we think of it, to D. H. Lawrence. When Forster turned from comedy, it was to give expression to his sense of our need of an island mythology, a faint adumbration of what it would be. (It would be interesting to study why these novelists felt a special need for prophecy). In his World's Classics Introduction to *The Longest Journey* he says: 'I caught fire up on the Rings' and compares the experience with the one he had when his first short story came to him. The short stories often celebrate Greek mythology, the two English novels one that might be native to our island. He was serious about it: 'Once I even tested the magic by staying with Lytton Strachey not very far from the Rings' and we can be serious about the suggestion today when there is urgent need for vital belief. The mythology of *Howards End* is the one we have inherited from Rome, the teeming city, from which men looked longingly at the country, where was solitude and silence and the poise that comes from contact with our native earth. *Howards End* was in a companionable county and brought peace to both kinds of Forster's Londoners, the philistine and the intellectuals.

As we finish the lecture we may feel that we have not found any very precise formulae, but we have a new sense of the novel form. We have a new sense also of how the ideal form of the novel pursued our lecturer in his own work. We recall how the early novels left the impression of exercises, trials, and how each of the three which followed was obviously an essay or attempt. He was trying to discover how far he could expand his form. He ceased abruptly and the likeliest explanation is the nature of the times in which he was living, a time of the breaking of nations, not expansion.

We come to the last lecture, which will help us to look back on the series and find new value in every part. At the end, as in the novel, it will be like Beethoven's Fifth Symphony: 'when the orchestra stops, we hear something that has never been actually played.' He calls his final subject Pattern and Rhythm and tells us it is the search for beauty in the novel. Once again there is a close relationship, pattern being the shape, which makes it 'an aesthetic aspect of the novel' and because it is beauty the lecturer's voice quickens and gathers emphasis: 'Here, here is the point where the aspect called pattern is most clearly in touch with its material, here is our starting point...Beauty is sometimes the shape of the book, the book as a whole, the unity' and he proceeds for half his lecture to offer one of these perceptive analyses of a work of imagination which are a model for us all, an analysis of *The Ambassadors* by Henry James.

That is beauty appearing in unity and when unity is lacking the beauty that is present he calls 'rhythm'. Rhythm is of two kinds, the one you can tap to and the one you can't but which 'some can hear'. The simpler kind is like Forster's famous echo: 'The little phrase crosses the book again and again, but as an echo, a memory' and a little later he adds: 'this seems to me the function of rhythm in fiction, not to be there all the time like a pattern, but by its lovely waxing and waning to fill us with surprise and freshness and hope', and again 'the effect can be exquisite...it lessens our need of an external form.' The simple kind of rhythm is thus related to pattern.

The deeper rhythm is described by that parallel to the Fifth Symphony, when the orchestra stops we hear it, and every part of the symphony is heard as a unity: 'all enter the mind at once, and extend one another into a common entity.' He admits that he cannot find any analogy: 'Yet there may be one; in music fiction is likely to find its nearest parallel.' The reader need not seek far for a likeness, for the distinguishing property of Forster's serious novels is this sense that the novelist's mind is a glowing bundle of atoms which race about hitting one another, raising echoes which become a harmony.

And certainly we enjoy in his three serious novels the final effect he suggests that the novel can offer. Again the analogy is with music: 'Music...does offer in its final expression a type of beauty which fiction might achieve in its own way. Expansion. That is the idea the novelist must cling to. Not completion. Not rounding off but opening out.' And he asks: 'Cannot the novel be like that?' and the audience must have remembered how the ending of *Howards End* was the opening up of opportunity to the old house and the ending of *A Passage* was a prophecy of greater opportunities for personal relationships between the inheritors of the ancient civilizations and the Western ones which must learn to grow old gracefully.

He sums up his argument for the other kind of rhythm by referring to the greatest novel of them all, *War and Peace*. 'As we read it do not great chords begin to sound behind us, and when we have finished it does not every item...lead a larger existence than was possible at the time?' The conclusion has an echo, back from the lecture on Prophecy when he said that the human mind is not a dignified organ. That is the kind of bleak scientific fact we often hear from Cambridge. Here, at the end of his course, the lecturer speaks like one of the great Cambridge scientists and the two cultures, as so often in Cambridge, speak as one: 'We may harness the atom, we may land on the moon [yes, it is 1927] we may abolish or intensify warfare, the mental processes of animals may be understood; but all these are trifles, they belong to history not to art.

History develops, art stands still. The novelist of the future will have to pass all the new facts through the old if variable mechanism of the creative mind.' Expansion, not completion! And as the prophecies are adumbrated the audience knows that all along it has been taken for granted that it all depends on who is writing the novel.

The actual ending of the series is a note in music, expressing the hope so many scientists have offered since Forster spoke, the hope that the human brain, 'not a dignified organ', is the one living organism capable of notable evolution. He turns back to what he has said about the two movements of the human mind 'the great tedious onrush known as history, and a shy crablike sideways movement'. He recalls that he laid it down that 'human nature is unchangeable' and that was the condition in which it went on producing prose fictions. And he ends: 'If we had the power or licence to take a wider view, and survey all human and pre-human activity, we might not conclude like this; the crablike movement, the shiftings of the passengers, might be visible, and the phrase "the development of the novel" might cease to be a pseudo-scholarly tag or a technical triviality, and become important, because it implied the development of humanity.'

Where Angels Fear to Tread

IT IS A fair presumption that when a young man of unusual intelligence sets out to be a novelist he will think first of the plot. He will decide against tragedy. That will come later. The atmosphere will be comic, which does not preclude seriousness or violence, but will give sufficient opportunity for his intelligence and wit. His experience will be limited and he must write of what he knows. In choosing his theme, he will be careful to hit on something that will amuse the novel-reading public. For the Edwardian novelist, that was the middle classes, the people who used the subscription libraries. They obviously enjoyed seeing themselves, especially when the novelist was critical of their lives. They were critical of their lives themselves, and enjoyed skilled help in being so. They thronged the theatres when Galsworthy and Shaw and Somerset Maugham were making fun of them. And they liked the continent. Especially Italy, for it was important to visit Italian churches and art galleries and museums.

So Forster in his first novel made fun of suburbia, not for the last time, and he took his characters to Italy. He had spent some time there himself after coming down from Cambridge and was well soaked in Baedeker and the Museums. In making fun of suburbia he was questioning values as he was to do with increasing seriousness in later books. He wrote with his Bloomsbury robes about him. In a sense, all his novels are attacks on social values, but here the attack is nothing more than gay fun. Suburbia is Sawston and Monteriano. There is no old man or woman in this novel to dishevel the hypocrisies.

We meet most of the characters in a well-managed scene on the departure platform at Charing Cross, the first of the group scenes Forster managed so well. Lilia enters, the story is about her; Irma, her fatherless daughter; and her mother, Mrs Theobald. Mrs Theobald has come down from Yorkshire with a Mr Kingcroft to see them off and they will return to Yorkshire and we shall hear very little more of them. We shall stay in Sawston with Lilia's mother-in-law, Mrs Herriton and her children, Philip and Harriet. Finally, there is Miss Abbott, who is going to Italy with Lilia and the development of this young woman's character will be the most interesting thing in the book. Mr Kingcroft is dispatched for foot-warmers—no one has to make sure about passports as we are in Edwardia—and Philip, her brother-in-law, gives advice. 'Love and understand the Italians, for the people are more marvellous than the land.' Here is our first Forsterian echo, for Lilia is to take this advice with both hands and all her heart. Two more glimpses on that platform; of Miss Abbott 'tall, grave, rather nice-looking' and then, as the train moved 'they all moved with it a couple of steps, and waved their handkerchiefs, and uttered cheerful little cries. At that moment Mr Kingcroft reappeared, carrying a foot-warmer by both ends.'

We return to Sawston and are immediately engaged in speculating about Lilia's future. She is thirty-three, vulgar and a widow and she is after another husband. Philip has sized her up: 'I believe she would take anyone. Right up to the last, when her boxes were packed, she was "playing" the chinless curate.' His mother feels sure that Lilia is safe in Italy, and Philip agrees for 'Italy really purifies and ennobles all who visit her'. Italy, we shall find, does not manage that with Lilia and does strange things to Caroline. It is the second reading of a Forster novel which provides the more delicious entertainment, the echoes are heard, and that is as true of this first novel as of the others.

There is a lull in the brilliance while we go back in time to Lilia's affair with Charles Herriton and their marriage and his death and the tussle for the child between the grandmothers, which Mrs Herriton won. Mrs Herriton's interest in Lilia is because of the child of her dead son; if Lilia remarried she might take the child away. We return to the present and skim through time as letters come from Italy. Then one day everything happens together, a letter from Lilia, now in Monteriano (good Italianates will recognize San Gimignano), a little gardening, trouble with the servants and a letter by the afternoon post from Yorkshire. Lilia is engaged to be married. All is flurry and speed again, with Mrs Herriton, the true English matron, in charge. Wire Italy, get money from the bank in case Philip must go out at once, look up Baedeker about Monteriano, a delicious skit that Baedeker entry, this energetic young novelist has time for everything, an equivocal telegram from Miss Abbott and Mrs Herriton directs at once that Philip must go out. We go back to the source of the quotation which is the title and we find:

> For fools rush in where angels fear to tread,
> Distrustful sense with modest caution speaks,
> It still looks home, and short excursions makes;
> But rattling nonsense in full volleys breaks,
> And never shock'd, and never turned aside,
> Bursts out, resistless, with a thundering tide.

How very true, as we shall see. Meantime, as always, in the comic novel, we are referred back to the ordinary and the trivial. The gardening had been forgotten and the row of peas she had just sown had all been eaten by the sparrows.

Lilia defeats Mrs Herriton by marrying Gino before Philip arrives to interfere. There is a good deal of comedy about Gino's status. From being of noble family he comes down to being the out-of-work son of a small-town dentist. He is equally deceived about Lilia's wealth and wishes he had not married her so that he could take the bribe Philip offers him to go away, just like the concierge in 'The Eternal Moment'. Gino makes the best of it and gradually imposes his will on Lilia until the woman who made passes at curates is the docile, lonely Italian wife, who spends most of her time at home and never dreams of going out alone. A child is born and Lilia dies. Gino becomes a character in the round so great is his affection for the child, so touching his care for it. When Philip comes again with another bribe, this time to be allowed to take the child back to Sawston, it is such a ridiculous idea that Gino does not understand. Then comes the violence. Harriet Herriton, an obtuse young woman, attempts to kidnap the baby, which is killed when the carriages of Harriet and Miss Abbott collide. There is more violence when Gino tortures Philip in the agony of losing his child. Miss Abbott intervenes, 'This thing stops here', stops the fight and makes the men control themselves. From that moment to the end, the story is about Miss Abbott. They are in the train and Philip is very near to proposing marriage. Neither he nor she can hope to settle back in suburbia after the excitement they have lived through in Italy. For back of all this Gino business was the beauty and intensity of living in Italy. She confesses that she is in love with Gino and would have given herself to him body and soul. She knows exactly what has happened to her and she despises herself for being at the mercy of physical love—and with the son of a dentist with a pretty face. She must live with that in suburbia: 'All the wonderful things are over.' And for Miss Abbott the future is: 'I love him, and I'm going to Sawston, and if I mayn't speak about him to you sometimes, I shall die.'

The young novelist is indeed exercising himself. He has set himself to arouse his readers' sympathy for the incurable pain of hopeless love. Gino is marrying again and for so many other reasons Caroline Abbott can never have him. 'Here was the cruel antique malice of the gods, such as they once sent forth against Pasiphae. Centuries of aspiration and culture—and the world could not escape it.' Then the final bitter irony that she knew she 'could have pulled through' and escaped the bondage of the hopeless passion if she had never seen Gino again. But she had to go back to stop the fight and save Philip. She had held Gino in her arms then, and now she was in bondage to him. 'For the thing was even greater than she imagined.' The novel that began on Charing Cross Station ends in a train returning towards England but in a very different mood, heightened out of suburban triviality and farce. We are, in fact, encountering the emotion that teases us so much in *Howards End,* when we cannot believe that Helen Schlegel would have given herself to Leonard Bast. 'Get over supposing I'm refined', Caroline says to Philip. 'That's what puzzles you. Get over that.' And his reaction is this, which raises it from being pathologically morbid into the acceptance of the coarse nature of life: 'As she spoke she seemed to be transfigured, and to have indeed no part in refinement or un-refinement any longer. Out of this wreck there was revealed to him something indestructible—something which she, who had given it, could never take away.'

Then Caroline speaks again and we learn that Gino worshipped her as a goddess and that saved her. He could not ask and she could not give. And Philip's response to that was to see 'the fair myth of Endymion. This woman was a goddess to the end. For her no love could be degrading: she stood outside all degradation. This episode, which she thought so sordid, and which was so tragic for him, remained supremely beautiful.' Tragic for Philip because he was an Edwardian gentleman and could not make love to a woman who was or had been in love with an Italian peasant. If that is difficult to believe it may help to remember the case of Colonel Leyland in 'The Eternal Moment', the short story published in the same year, who found himself in precisely the same predicament and reacted in the same way. So *Where Angels Fear to Tread* is a love story, inspired by the classics where every kind of love is found, the love for a beautiful boy which can never be consum-mated. It is stated quietly and sympathetically and the young novelist is able to end without a false note or any embarrassment. A remark and an incident are echoed. The remark is sympathetic. Philip would have liked to tell her that he worshipped her too but, as she had said: 'all the wonderful things have happened.' The incident was the smut in Harriet's eye on a previous train journey and now, as the train enters the tunnel: 'They hurried back to the carriage to close the windows lest the smuts should get into Harriet's eye.'

Emotion has been contained. It has also been very well expressed and the young novelist could look forward confidently to richer themes and fuller expression of them. And now we can return to chapter two, with all the special advantages of knowing the end of a Forster novel. Almost the first thing we read is that Philip thinks Caroline is 'young only because she is twenty-three: there was nothing in her appearance or manner to suggest the fire of youth.' Then we hear her saying to the Sawston curate: 'Oh, but you must let me have my fling. I promise to have it once and once only. It will give me things to think about for the rest of my life.' Every sentence is a start of pain to the reader who has become involved with her at the end.

We return at once to comedy, the innocent questions Philip puts about the unknown Italian and the embarrassed replies she offers. At the hotel everything is comically embarrassing, Lilia's brazen attitude, Gino and his clothes, the dinner, and Philip's interview with Lilia. Only when she calls in Gino does embarrassment evaporate and permit us the purely comic mood for hearing the startling news that Lilia has already married Gino. To make sure of her escape from suburbia, she married him the moment she heard an envoy from Sawston was coming. We have an undertone of uncomical realization that she has chosen a more stifling suburbia. After this boisterous scene in which Philip is accidentally knocked over by Gino (which explains the way the fight goes later), the quiet description of the house where Lilia will gradually become confined, compelled into obedience by this youngster of twenty-one who becomes her husband and lives on her money. 'It was in this house that the brief and inevitable tragedy of Lilia's life took place.' Stark enough. This young novelist has all the stops at his command. Gino's first victory is to make sure his family do not occupy his house. To make quite sure, he helps them with Lilia's money to leave the town. Forster's comment is typical of his attitude to charity: 'she liked nothing better than finding out some obscure and distant connection—there were several of them—and acting the lady bountiful, leaving behind her bewilderment, and too often discontent.' The comic spirit enjoys these observations. We very soon have another example, a description of Italian manners for English readers, a custom that was to afflict Lilia. 'In the democracy of the café or the street the great question of our life has been solved, and the brotherhood of man is a reality. But it is accomplished at the expense of the sisterhood of woman.' Some sentences fall like knells. 'And all the time the boy was watching her and growing up.' Later, when he had compelled her to adopt the conventions of Italian women: 'she never took a solitary walk again, with one exception, till the day of her death.' Then the comic spirit takes charge again and we have Gino and his Customs friend talking together. Only one echo amidst that fun, Gino declaring that he will never, of course, see Philip again but he was sorry he was boisterous and toppled him on the bed. It was Isherwood who first pointed out Forster's way of imitating life by making the trivial everyday occasions the norm and the heightened moments always measured against the norm and brought back, as always in life, to the ordinary things. So a bitter moment is set in this scene. Gino persuades his friend to go home with him, for Lilia so badly needs company, and she becomes animated and they all have a gay time. Outside again, Gino decides he will never take another friend to meet his wife and the friend agrees that it is not a safe thing to do. It is a stage in Lilia's isolation.

Comedy would be an unsatisfying and distorting medium if it did not admit pathos and the story of the relationship between Lilia and Gino is almost purely pathetic. 'No one realized that more than personalities were engaged; that the struggle was national; that generations of ancestors, good, bad, or indifferent, forbade the Latin man to be chivalrous to the northern woman, the northern woman to forgive the Latin man.' We watch her ineffectual struggles as she is spiritually suffocated, her one unpremeditated attempt to run away, her one intercepted cry to England for help: 'Lilia had achieved pathos despite herself, for there are some situations in which vulgarity counts no longer. Not Cordelia nor Imogen more deserve our tears.' The narrative, like the comment, is managed with proficient economy. It ends when the child is born: 'As for Lilia, some one said to her, "It's a beautiful boy." But she had died in giving birth to him.' She had escaped at last. She has left the stage and made room for Philip Herriton and Caroline Abbott. Gino remains to frustrate their happiness also.

We have a portrait of Philip: 'He had a fine forehead and a good large nose, and both observation and sympathy were in his eyes. But below the nose and eyes all was confusion.' We had better go on to the self-portrait of thought and experience: 'he had got a sense of beauty and a sense of humour, two most desirable gifts. The sense of beauty developed first...At twenty-two he went to Italy with some cousins...He came back with the air of a prophet who would either remodel Sawston or reject it...In a short time it was all over.' Nothing had happened and then come the phrases which have such a familiar ring to Forsterians: 'He concluded that nothing could happen, not knowing that human love and love of truth sometimes conquer where love of beauty fails.' So, we are told, he came to rely more and more on the second gift, the sense of humour.

In a few days, Philip finds himself with Caroline in the London train. They seemed to be very much children of the railway age, these two. Caroline knows by this time that Lilia is dead but, by decree of Mrs Herriton, no one is to know that a child has been born. Caroline longs to confess; she has that love of open talk that the young Edwardian novelist so much liked in his women. Caroline herself says: 'Women—I heard you say the other day—are never at their ease till they tell their faults out loud.' This time the echo comes from Pope, a few lines below the title line: 'Who to a friend his faults can freely show?' When Caroline has done, Philip suggests she has described her conduct rather than explained it and Caroline responds with an outburst against Sawston: 'I hate the idleness, the respectability, the petty unselfishness' and she means exactly what she says for 'everyone here spent their lives in making little sacrifices for objects they didn't care for, to please people they didn't love'. Then Caroline praises Lilia, who 'somehow kept the power of enjoying herself with sincerity'. In such phrases and in the character of Gino we find the unacknowledged sources of much of D. H. Lawrence's work. Then we learn that Italy has had the same effect upon Caroline as on Philip. They are twin spirits, for she declares: 'I wanted to fight against the things I hated—mediocrity, dullness and spitefulness and society.' The journey ends and Caroline goes 'to buy petticoats for the corpulent poor'.

The rest of the chapter builds up to the second 'excursion' to Monteriano, this time to save the child. Lilia's daughter Irma learns she has a little brother from postcards sent by Gino. Irma talks

4

at school and Miss Abbott gets to know. It is all very tiresome. Harriet has a conscience and that becomes a nuisance and she is packed off to the Tyrol. That conscience of hers is going to be an even greater nuisance later. The effect of Caroline Abbott's concern is to make Mrs Herriton think of taking over the baby. Philip knows perfectly well that the baby is nothing to do with them but he is up against a sin of suburbia, insincerity: 'Philip started and shuddered. He saw that his mother was not sincere.' But he is dominated by her stronger character: 'Her ability frightened him.' But he can be critical and her meaningless existence is compared with the better ways of Harriet, who has her religion, and Lilia 'with her clutches after pleasure'. The Edwardians were as concerned with the empty meaninglessness of life as we are, as all materially prosperous peoples must be. Caroline at this stage sees Gino as a thoroughly wicked man and will do anything to rescue the child from sin. The 'excursion' is undertaken because Caroline declares she will go and rescue the child herself and bring it up. Intolerable, under the social laws of suburbia and Philip is packed off to collect first his sister and next, if he can, the child.

When they arrive in Monteriano, Caroline is already there. The Edwardian young lady rushes in 'resistless, with a thundering tide', and Harriet and Caroline meet after a thundering row on the stair-case of the hotel. They end the day in the opera and everything is gay. Eleven years later, D. H. Lawrence is to describe a similar evening, following again in Forster's footsteps, but tonight Philip and Caroline are gay and 'convinced each other that Romance was here'. As it happened, Gino also was there and hilariously throws a bouquet to Harriet. She is outraged, the two ladies leave the theatre and Philip joins Gino and his friends in their box. He is 'Fra Filippo' who has 'come all the way from England and never written', he is a friend, nay more, a relative. Only connect. Clearly, but for the ladies, there would be no difficulty. But Caroline is there 'to champion morality and purity, and the holy life of an English home'. And Harriet is there, with her conscience. Meantime, Caroline goes to see Gino an hour before Philip is due to go. She knows how strong the man is, she understands him, and she is more likely to be successful than Philip. It is a stormy interview, the most exciting passage in the book, the meeting of a man and a woman in sincerity and truth. It can be judged by the phrases set into it. He senses that she has been watching him for some time: 'it is a serious thing to have been watched. We all radiate something curiously intimate when we believe ourselves to be alone.' Then we learn the quality of the love Gino had for the baby. He would have no relations with him: 'They would separate our thoughts.' But he will take another wife, to look after the baby. He is the exceptional man 'who comprehends that physical and spiritual life may stream out of him for ever', that the generations from his son will keep him immortal. These esoteric Edwardian beliefs are appealing and we do not have to wait for the ruined greatness of D. H. Lawrence to enjoy them. The scene culminates in a sacramental washing of the child. 'The Virgin and Child, with Donor' Philip thinks, when he comes in. Poor Caroline Abbott. She had fallen in love, crudely, passionately, and she runs away, ashamed.

She has quite come round to Gino's side. He will not part with the baby, and she faces Philip with the truth when he muddles himself with hypocritical words. 'Do you want the child to stop with his father, who loves him and will bring him up badly, or do you want him to come to Sawston, where no one loves him, but where he will be brought up well?' Philip still lives in the aura of his new friendship with Gino. 'The access of joy that had come to him yesterday in the theatre promised to be permanent. He was more anxious than heretofore to be charitable towards the world.' But he is weak. Both women see how weak he is. He will achieve nothing. They also know that Gino will never be persuaded to part with the child. No one is surprised that Philip's interview is a failure but he continues in his agreeable state of euphoria and: 'the two young men parted with a good deal of genuine affection. For the barrier of language is a blessed barrier, which only lets pass what is good... we may be better in clean new words, which have never been tainted by our pettiness and vice.' Somehow the tower of Babel has turned upside down.

So the carriages are ordered and all three visitors will go away that evening. Harriet has been hovering on the other side of the square as Philip and Gino talk. We know what happened. Harriet, the zealot who could never understand, stole the baby, allowed Philip to suppose she had traded for it with Gino, and then the accident. Philip honourably returns, to tell Gino. Caroline generously returns, knowing what it will cost her, to save Philip.

Italy had written his first novel for him very well. Italian feeling had helped him to temper the comedy with tenderness and with flashes of real insight into the heart and mind. In this novel England is Sawston, and little more than a suburban set of opinions. The joy and the sorrow, the foolish excursions and the stupid violence are all in Italy, and the English characters become sentient in contact with Italians. Gino brings out the best in Philip, makes him for a moment a complete man, and he touches Caroline with the spirit of Pan. She is outraged, but it develops in her generosity and compassion that are more sympathetic to us than her gift for seeing things without confusion and expressing things truthfully. Gino and Philip become simpatico, and Philip and Caroline just fail, for their feet are in Sawston, to achieve that most agreeable personal relationship described by Gino's friend: 'The person who understands us at first sight, who never irritates us, who never bores, to whom we can pour forth every thought and wish, not only in speech but in silence—that is what I mean by simpatico.' The definition gathers resonance in the great scenes of this novel and will gather more as we study the others.

The next novel he published was *The Longest Journey*. But *A Room with a View* had been planned and the Italian part written earlier. In conception and mood it goes with *Where Angels Fear to Tread* and will be considered now.

A Room with a View

WE BEGIN IN a Florentine pensione. A girl and her chaperon are offered more suitable rooms by an old man and his son, rooms with a view over the Arno. It is quite impossible to accept the offer because we are Edwardians. But the vicar intervenes. He thinks that we should all try to help one another to be happy, and his intervention makes the offer acceptable. The offer becomes a symbol. The old man who made it will help the girl to see things she might never have seen in her stuffy Edwardian suburban life.

Very soon we are in Santa Croce and Lucy, the girl, is deserted by the lady novelist who is her chaperon for the morning. There is a chance encounter with the old man, Mr Emerson, and his son George. Lucy knows that this is very embarrassing but the old man will not have it so and behaves as if they were all natural people. 'You are pretending to be touchy; but you are not really. Stop being so tiresome, and tell me instead what part of the church you want to see.' The next voice we hear is a familiar echo in Santa Croce. The English clergyman is telling his party that the church 'was built by faith' and Giotto was 'untroubled by the snares of anatomy and perspective'. Old Mr Emerson exclaims 'in much too loud a voice for church' and we see at once that Miss Bartlett, the chaperon, was right. The old man must be a socialist. 'Built by faith indeed! That simply means that workmen weren't properly paid...and as for the frescoes, I see no truth in them.' The humanist has disposed of his first clergyman, and at the end he will dispose of the other.

We are still in church when the old man makes his 'extraordinary speech' to Lucy on behalf of his son: 'But let yourself go. You are inclined to get muddled, if I may judge from last night. Let yourself go. Pull out from the depths those thoughts that you do not understand, and spread them out in the sunlight and know the meaning of them.' An early attack on muddle and the suburban mind. Then comes the appeal for the son which will be repeated so effectively at the end of the story: 'By understanding George you may learn to understand yourself. It will be good for both of you.'

We go through a volume of snobbery and suburban pretences before we hear the appeal again. We are in the trivial world which Forster pictured with such delicate venom in his first two novels— *The Longest Journey* was written later. In each there is a real character, Gino and Mr Emerson, completely out of tune with the others, a real person among Edwardian marionettes. Mr Emerson is the socialist humanist, not of the calibre of Cox and Salt and Carpenter, whom Goldie knew and Forster admired, but one of their disciples, a simple, not formally educated man of good sense and natural feeling, who is able to quote his friend Samuel Butler effectively: 'Life is a public performance on the violin, in which you must learn the instrument as you go along.' Strange how these Edwardian novels still have connexion with us, although their world was so completely destroyed in the European upheavals. We cross the gap most easily with Wells and Shaw, with science and socialism, for their world seems to us real and serious, opposed to the Edwardian emptiness and triviality. There were too many people in these novels with too little to do. We enjoy the trivial puppetry best in Saki and Max and in those Edwardian hangovers, Ronald Firbank and P. G. Wodehouse, for they fill the emptiness with hilarity and make it graceful.

Forster makes us uneasy, even in these Edwardian sketches of suburbia. The wit is nimble and flashes. The characters behave appropriately and their actions and interactions are suitably comic. But their creator is critical. He does not like muddle. He is for the intelligence, which requires order. He is for sympathy and tolerance and the spirit of suburbia would collapse under these virtues. In his world of ladies unbruised by toil, with a sprinkling of parsons and men with enough money to support them in genteel cultural idleness, he is aware of the poor. He has inherited a Claphamite conscience. Later, it will be Leonard Bast. Here, much less unpleasantly, it is an old man with rheumatism and his son who has a situation on the railways.

There are other little breaks in the film of pretence which gave such security to suburbia. There is a flash of anger, which, as so often in Forster and real life, gives a moment of truth. There is a very momentary one when Lucy Honeychurch is quarrelling with her mother and warns that she may break away from home and even share a flat in London with another girl:

> 'And mess with typewriters and latch-keys', exploded Mrs Honeychurch. 'And agitate and scream, and be carried off kicking by the police. And call it a Mission—when no one wants you! And call it Duty—when it means that you can't stand your own home! And call it Work—when thousands of men are starving with the competition as it is.'

Memory recalls how true that rings; every girl who tried to break suburban bonds being labelled 'Suffragette' and told she had no right to work while men were unemployed. Later, there is a recognizably Forsterian scene in the woods, for Pan is there, when the men throw off their clothes and plunge into the pool:

> for some reason or other a change came over them, and they forgot Italy and Botany and Fate. They began to play. Mr Beebe and Freddie splashed each other. A little deferentially they splashed George. He was quiet: they feared they had offended him. Then all the forces of youth burst out. He smiled, flung himself at them, splashed them, ducked them, kicked them, muddied them, and drove them out of the pool.

Then there is a great fuss when a choice assembly of the other characters come that way, but all is well and there is a chapter ending which approves it, with that faint air of Edwardian nostalgia which we are beginning to enjoy again.

On the morrow the pool had shrunk to its old size and lost its
glory. It had been a call to the blood and to the relaxed will, a
passing benediction whose influence did not pass, a holiness, a
spell, a momentary chalice for youth.

Pan in very decent mood.

In a curious sense the novel is a love story and we have Lord
David Cecil's word for it that Forster 'tells a story as well as anyone
who ever lived'. Though Somerset Maugham, on the other hand,
thought Forster could hardly be bothered with getting on with a
story at all. In this novel, it is the wrong love story that is told,
simply, perhaps, because the true lover is almost completely
inarticulate. True, he rescues Lucy when a man is stabbed in front
of her in the Piazza, that sudden violence familiar in Forster's
novels, introduced here to give George the status of her protector.
She faints in his arms, the only way she can get there in this Edwardian novel, for clearly he is of an unsuitable class to make love to her.
His father will have to make the running for him, putting truth and
passion before the suburban niceties. Meanwhile George, when she
recovers, saves her from the sight of truth by throwing her Medici
reproductions into the Arno. They were smeared with the blood of
the stabbed Italian. A little later George does behave truthfully in an
instinctive reaction when she falls among the violets suddenly from
nowhere. He kisses her. Pan was near by, the young cabbie and his
amorata have shown us that.

When Forster was planning and writing the first part of this
novel, probably as early as 1903, he seems to have thought of a
heroine rather like Caroline Abbott, only this time she was to be
allowed to realize herself. Caroline and Philip failed to achieve
passion, Lucy and George were to do so. With a great deal of help
from the people around them. So Lucy had to be provided with all
that becomes a heroine, and Forster gives her one gift precious to
him, the ability to play Beethoven on the piano. In order to establish
her as a performer, we are taken to Tonbridge Wells and Mr Beebe,
the vicar, is made use of to show us how good she is. Instead of a
simple piece, to his surprise she is attempting the first movement of
Opus 111:

He was in suspense all through the introduction, for not until the pace quickens does one know what the performer intends. With the roaring of the opening theme he knew that things were going extraordinarily; in the chords that herald the conclusion he heard the hammer strokes of victory.

In the story as it unfolds the gift is honorary, for nothing is made of it. There is no great scene in which she plays to the hero and he can no longer be silent. There are, in fact, very few scenes between them because of that job on the railways which absorbed so much of his time.

The false suitor, on the other hand, has plenty of time. Cecil Vyse is a languid youth: 'I have no profession...It is another example of my decadence. My attitude—quite an indefensible one—is that so long as I am no trouble to anyone I have a right to do as I like.' He does however intend to exert himself when he becomes engaged to Lucy. He is a Meredithian character who will mould the woman to his design. He is going to make something of his suburban choice. He serves his purpose of being a foil to the real man and he is even used to bring the real man to live near Lucy, for until he did so it was very unlikely that hero and heroine would ever meet again.

Cecil is sketched without enthusiasm, without the comic zest which goes to making these preposterous spinsters Miss Bartlett and the novelist Miss Lavish. Without the trace of sympathy which goes to making the kindly clergyman, Mr Beebe, the suburban vicar, attractive to spinsters. But his creator decides against him in the end and gives him a little scene in which he shows himself to be the prim celibate who instinctively shrinks when he hears from Cecil that he is going to marry Lucy: 'The clergyman was conscious of some bitter disappointment which he could not keep out of his voice.' It explains the scene at the end when he learns that George and Lucy are in love. It is a glimpse of celibate feeling extra to the necessities of the story. 'He was very quiet, and his white face, with its ruddy whiskers, seemed suddenly inhuman. A long black column, he stood and awaited his reply.' And later: 'I am more grieved than I can possibly express. It is lamentable, lamentable—incredible.' He is lost to grace, as clergymen are apt to be in these humanist novels, and it is the old socialist who helps her towards beauty and

truth: 'But remember the mountains over Florence and the view.'
The priest, the man of births and marriages and deaths, is unable to
help her but the old man 'had made her see the whole of everything
at once'. He was not only a socialist, he was a humanist: 'He had
robbed the body of its taint, the world's taunts of their sting; he had
shown her the holiness of direct desire.'

We learn afterwards that there had been an endearing collusion
to give old Mr Emerson his opportunity to bring Lucy and George
together. The spinster chaperon, Miss Bartlett, most Edwardian of
mocked characters, who has always been so tender in protecting
Lucy's sensibilities, knows perfectly well that Lucy will find the old
man in the study and she decides against all the rules to give him his
chance and says nothing. It is like a sudden flood of warm feeling on
an aridly satirical scene. It is prelude to the natural warmth that the
old man is able to release. The wheel of novel fortune turns and as
the clergyman goes down the spinster comes up. The scene in
which the old man succeeds is a typical Edwardian expression of
intellectual and emotional conflict. It is Beebe versus Emerson for
Lucy's soul, the medieval against the classical, the obscurantist
against the classicist who bids her see the view: The old man is
speaking:

> Now it is all dark. Now Beauty and Passion seem never to have
> existed. I know. But remember the mountains over Florence
> and the view. You have to go cold into a battle that needs
> warmth, out into the muddle that you have made yourself...
> Am I justified?...Yes, for we fight for more than Love or
> Pleasure: there is Truth. Truth counts, Truth does count.

Never has father stood in for a son with better effect. She asks him
to kiss her, to give her strength, so that she can try. We can feel the
old man's sincerity still in this highly wrought page, one of those
intense pages that come in all three later novels. The young novelist
brings it off, this violence which changes the course of the story.
Then, as chapter ending, there comes a paragraph precious to the
Edwardian connoisseur. How very good they were at these quiet
paragraphs of recollection in tranquillity of a violent scene:

> He gave her a sense of deities reconciled, a feeling that, in

gaining the man she loved, she would gain something for the whole world. Throughout the squalor of her homeward drive – she spoke at once – his salutation remained. He had robbed the body of its talent, the world's taunts of their sting; he had shown her the holiness of direct desire. She 'never exactly understood', she would say in after years, 'how he managed to strengthen her. It was as if he had made her see the whole of everything at once.'

Without more ado, we have the benign concluding Edwardian chapter, when everything is warm and cosy again. George and Lucy are happily married, the only ones, though they will never know it, in their creator's world, to enjoy the full innocence 'of direct desire'. We are back in the Florentine pensione where we began and we are in the same rooms and the romantic spirit of Florence is about them. There is a refrain from a cabbie below: 'Signorino, domani faremo uno giro' to which eventually her response: 'Lascia, prego, lascia. Siama sposati', and the cabman drives away singing, as merry as the one who drove them up into the hills in the beginning. Romantic echoes. George has become articulate and sympathetically interprets the spinster chaperon: 'I do believe that, far down in her heart, far below all speech and behaviour, she is glad.' A touch of gentle pathos mingles with romance.

How do such slight novels live? Not merely because they are the first pieces by a novelist who was to turn to higher themes with increasing success. But because in themselves so much wit and intelligence shines through, because there is so much salt in the satire, and because in each there is a character who is in the round and can impart life and roundness to the flatly comic characters when he comes in contact with them. These two novels would have been very slight little sketches without Gino and Mr Emerson, and these vivid characters foretold the books to come. There was to be no return to this light comic manner. Events made that impossible. After the next two novels, with their serious treatment of island themes, the first war and the consequent disintegration of European society. So the fifth novel undertook a problem in a society untouched by the European earthquake but foretelling its own. After that, could there have been a return to the comic manner? Not for anyone so concerned about society and mankind as Forster. In the face of approaching calamity there was much to say, but in the defence of values and in appeals for sanity. It had to be preaching, not prophesying. It did not need a prophet to foresee farther calamity and no one could prophesy how things would be straightened out after another holocaust in Europe.

There was another reason why he could not return to comedy. His enemy had disappeared, a war casualty. His comedy depended on opposition to Edwardian suburban life, which was stuffy with strictly enforced behaviour patterns. Gino and Italy gave freedom from them. Mr Emerson defied them and we shall see that Stephen Wonham was unaware of them. They were the opponents of suburbia, but when war opened the windows of suburbia to the free air of the world, Forster's comic stock-in-trade had gone. He had to go to India to find little English communities which still lived by the old rigid suburban rules, and when he opposed them there it was no longer with a comic sensibility.

The Longest Journey

ONCE AGAIN the young novelist is experimenting with his form and this time he attempts a more serious theme. He tells us in his Introduction to the World's Classics edition when the idea came to him. It was entered in his diary on 18 July, 1904: 'An idea for another novel—that of a man who discovered that he has an illegitimate brother.' He tells us that gradually 'other ideas intervened to confuse or enrich the original theme'. He lists them: 'the metaphysical idea of Reality'; 'the ethical idea that reality must be faced'; 'the idea, or ideal, of the British Public School'; 'there was the title, exhorting us in the words of Shelley not to love one person only; there was Cambridge, there was Wiltshire'. No mention of a story, no mention of characters, only places and ideas, so we find that the most interesting things are the descriptions, the animated descriptions of Cambridge, the Hardyesque descriptions of Wiltshire, with the suggestion of search for some native spirit in the English earth to take the place of Pan; and the ideas, the ideas that come flooding in on the undergraduate mind, expressed sometimes so succintly that we could contrive a calendar of Thoughts from this text, sometimes as questions asked of life and sometimes as the comment that comes naturally from the action. It was the Cambridge of G. E. Moore, his ideas were in the air and Forster would hear them all around him. They 'sought for reality and cared for truth', as others have done.

The Spirit of Place is consciously developed; Cambridge, where truth is pursued intellectually, Wiltshire, where truth appears in nature and in the nature of things, and Sawston, English suburbia, last, worst abiding place of English hypocrisy and pretence. It is undergraduate Cambridge, a recent, warm memory for the writer. On the Wiltshire Downs there is a house, as in *Howards End,* with character and influence consonant with prehistory in the Downs. It is not made much of here, but the most intriguing and sympathetical insinuation in the novel is the hint of ancient religious power rising from the haunts of the dark little men who flourished there so long before the Romans came.

The story is simple and begins in the middle, in Rickie's happiest days, in Cambridge, as an undergraduate. This is the preferred novel because of this recall of his own first really happy days, in Cambridge, as an undergraduate. Forster confesses in the World's Classics Introduction that he is 'always puzzled when elderly men reminisce over their respective public schools so excitedly' and that it 'sounds as if they must have had a dullish time since'. But he has no difficulty in celebrating undergraduate life and he does it very well. He gets the story going also, for Agnes, whom Rickie will eventually marry, bursts in on an undergraduate tea-party and her brother, the schoolmaster who will help his sister so much in destroying Rickie, is suitably introduced. His school is in Sawston, where civilization is 'a row of semi-detached villas, and society a state in which men do not know the men who live next door', but seem to be on edge all the time about what they may be thinking.

The opposition to the hypocrisy and pretence comes in this story from the truthfulness of Ansell, the undergraduate friend, a truthfulness which was the result of academic discipline, and of the half-brother, Stephen, the truthfulness of the primitive. From this middle state the story must probe backwards and reach forwards, backwards to Rickie's childhood and the story of his father and mother, backwards again to the begetting of the bastard (that was in Stockholm and one of the earliest echoes in the book is sounded when we are shown a photograph of Stockholm on the wall of

Rickie's room). Forwards from Cambridge to marriage and school-mastering, from youthful freedom to being dominated by the brother and sister and again towards freedom with Stephen, who eventually provides him with the escape of death.

The action of the novel is not so much story as conflict, shown in the little scenes Forster managed so well; scenes in different times and places, knit together in a way more familiar now than to the Edwardians. Conflict between the spiritual death of suburbia and the spirit that struggles for life, seen in Rickie, who dies; seen in his mother who runs away and dies, seen in Stephen, who avoids and lives. Seen in Rickie's father, who, to avoid a suburban scandal, takes back the wife who has run away and then runs away from her and his lame son. Seen in Agnes, the wife of Rickie, who seeks suburban fulfilment in marriage and money and pursues what she needs with feminine dedication. Seen in her brother, who fights for his housemastership and takes holy orders to secure his position and relentlessly struggles against Rickie whose actions and connections may bring discredit on the House and the School. Seen in Aunt Emily, who devotes her energies to securing fame for her dead husband, editing his old-world socialist essays, full of sweetness and light, while her agent oppresses the peasantry and she is malicious to Stephen whom she has fostered. She moves the action forward when, in a moment of pique, a cause too trivial for any but a malicious nature, she unnecessarily opens up the past and tells Rickie and Stephen they are brothers. Rickie, who hears it first, supposes they are their father's sons, and it is Ansell, the ideal undergraduate, the philosophical Jew for ever seeking reality, who explodes the truth over him, that he and Stephen are related through their mother.

Agnes has given all her energies to suppressing the scandal and Ansell, who hates her for ruining Rickie, observes that and foils her. Action becomes tumult. The brothers meet, part and are thrown together again and the release of Rickie by death is contrived. The tragic convention is continued into a final chapter in tranquillity now, all passion spent, the old fashioned review of the characters who are left alive. There are not many; the death roll has been formidable.

These bare bones are given life and significance by many details, many ideas and observations, many of the echoes so familiar in Forster's novels. The pages are rich not only with the sharp little scenes but with the thoughts and comments that Forster pours into them. In the other two early novels it is the comic spirit which carries us along. Here, the mood and the intention are different, Penseroso to their Allegro, and we shall be thoughtful throughout. Never dull, but prepared to exist on a diet which includes classical references—'Those elms were Dryads—so Rickie pretended and the line between the two is subtler than we admit'; thoughts— 'For drudgery is not art and cannot lead to it'; sallies—'not a curl crooked. I should say he will get into the Foreign Office.' There are some comments which carry the accent of the mature writer, as this note on the sprawl of houses from Salisbury into the Downs: 'They neglect the poise of the earth and the continents she has decreed. They are the modern spirit.' Always the fastidious pessimist when not the gay companion. And this plea for the country life: 'It is easier to know men well. The country is not paradise, and can show the vices that grieve a good man everywhere. But there is room in it, and leisure.'

These are mature reflections but the outlook of the observer is refreshingly undergraduate and young. 'It's a story of youth, written by a young man', as Forster said of an early Tolstoi. He has the outlook of a young man gazing from his college window into the world, meeting the tumultuous excitements of the world, seeing people with the seriousness of youth, as this comment on Rickie's father: 'he never did or said or thought one single thing that has the slightest beauty or value.' Or this glimpse of a covey of dons, watching road repairs: 'throwing up their hands with humorous gestures of despair. These men would lecture next week on Catiline ...Luther...Evolution...Catullus. They dealt with so much and they had experienced so little.' Or this recurring, desolating statement, another comment like the first, on the emptiness of normal human life in such contrast to the undergraduate sense of importance in living: 'It is simply a question of beating time till I die.' That was Rickie's mother. In another place the novelist reflects that people 'must be convinced that our life is a state of some importance, and our earth not a place to beat time on'.

These brief quotations only hint at the atmosphere he creates, which is nearer poetry than the novel usually supports. It is the atmosphere he will create more easily and more definitely in the next novels. Here, he is learning how to do it, by creating scenes, each with its own temperature and emotion, without a regular narrative connexion and noticeably without the narrative quality which makes us go on to find out what happens. We watch people developing within themselves, reacting on one another in doing so. The people are related to ideas and that is how he holds our attention. It is the modern spirit and he foresaw it at the beginning of the century. The humanist intelligence is in charge, observing life in order to comment on it, to discover its quality and its dimensions.

Does the young novelist find an answer to this emptiness which is to be one of the main themes of later novels? We may think for a moment that we find it at the beginning of the seventh chapter, where he confesses the youth of the non-hero from the majestic height of a man six or seven years older: 'he is, of course, absurdly young...He has no knowledge of the world...He believes in humanity because he knows a dozen different people. He believes in woman because he has loved his mother.' Then, says the young novelist, experience comes. We must accept experience or we shall die. We go on absorbing it 'till we are quite sane, quite efficient, quite experienced, and quite useless to God or man.' It is the comment of youth on age. And how will this youth avoid the secular difficulty? He tells us: 'There comes a moment—God knows when—at which we can say, "I will experience no longer. I will create. I will be an experience." ' It may be a sufficient answer to the threat of panic and emptiness. It was a test the writer brilliantly passed in his later work, but Rickie, his non-hero, failed. It is here, at the opening of chapter seven, that Rickie's failure is described as tragedy. He could not outface suburbia or understand the nature of his half-brother and these failures made the tragic release of death the fitting denouement. Many readers will find the solution to the problem of emptiness at the end of the book where it is symbolized by Stephen in an Adoration scene: 'He bent down reverently and saluted the child.' It was a gesture which said: 'He was alive and had created life...he believed that he guided the future of our race, and that, century after century, his thoughts and his passions would triumph in England.' That secular belief had not half a century in which to survive, but how surprising to find this in our humanist novelist, quite as surprising as the end of *A Passage*, where Mrs Moore is accepted into the One.

The tragic note is never sustained in the narrative, and only in a few moments is it sounded. First, when we see through the eyes of Agnes that Rickie has the possibility of greatness in him. It comes at the moment when Agnes has lost the man she was going to marry, Gerald, the subaltern, the 'young man who had the figure of a Greek athlete', who 'died that afternoon. He was broken up in a football match.' As soon as he heard, Rickie sought her out and pleaded with her to realize what had happened to her: 'It's the worst thing that can ever happen to you in all your life and you've got to mind it—you've got to mind it. They'll come saying, "Bear up—trust to time". No, no, they're wrong. Mind it.'

Her reaction is immediate. Rickie had only been a boy and a weakling to her. Now she sees 'that this boy was greater than they supposed' and she 'acknowledged that life's meaning had vanished'. At that moment, more than any other in the story, the mood reaches towards tragic intensity. Towards the end, when Rickie has run away and Stephen has escaped and she cannot get at Ansell, her actions are summarized in her own reflections:

> To her, life never showed itself as a classic drama, in which, by trying to advance our fortunes, we shatter them. She had turned Stephen out of Wiltshire, and he fell like a thunderbolt on Sawston and on herself. In trying to gain Mrs Failing's money she had probably lost money which would have been her own. But irony is a subtle teacher, and she was not the woman to learn from such lessons as these. Her suffering was more direct. Three men had wronged her; therefore she hated them and, if she could, she would do them harm.

At that moment she is the avenging woman and acquires tragic proportions. Normally, she is the suburban acquisitive, a big, strong, healthy, handsome girl who goes out to get what she wants. Her original entrance is dramatic. She stands in the door of Rickie's room and speaks of horsewhipping him. She is engaged to the young army officer who appears only to die. Two years later, Rickie is in love with her, describes her as an empress, and is seduced by her. She marries him when it suits her brother to have a married woman to run his school house. Her instinct was to shrink from Rickie's club foot, from anything abnormal. But she bears him a child which has a worse club foot than its father, and the novelist kills off the child in a few days, simply by exposing it to that deadly Edwardian complaint, a draught. Probably no novelist has killed his characters so casually.

In marriage one partner usually dominates and in England it is usually the woman. We are shown how Agnes gradually dominates Rickie, for she is 'the emissary of Nature' while 'man does not care a damn for Nature' and demands 'friends, and work, and spiritual freedom' all of which Agnes seeks to deny him as she grows menacingly possessive. But she will guide and guard him as she can, for he is her chief possession. She wants to help him when he takes his short stories to the editor and she weighs up his report of what is said, which confirms her view that she has not married a born writer. So she will have to defend him as a schoolmaster and that led her to her fatal blunder. She will defend Rickie and her brother and the House against the scandal of Stephen's existence. Ironically, she is put into this situation by her own acquisitiveness. She hoped to secure Aunt Emily's money for Rickie by ousting Stephen but when Stephen is ousted he learns he has a brother—one of Aunt Emily's betrayals, for she had promised Agnes that Stephen would never know—and Stephen, sweet child of nature, supposes that it would be pleasant for Rickie to know he has a brother. Agnes tries to buy him off. It is at a moment when she is flustered by continuous attacks from another enemy, Ansell, who has always seen Agnes as a catastrophe for Rickie. We see to what lengths Ansell will go to save Rickie, the fierce celibate friend interfering in the wrecked marriage. Agnes, unsettled by this enemy, misjudges the other, and when she tries to buy Stephen off, her defeat is total. She loses Rickie and then is freed of him by his death. With that calculated casualness of Forster's which keeps the reader alert, we learn in the coda that she has married again and has succeeded in bearing healthy children.

When we turn to the other women characters, we search in vain for someone agreeable. There is little to be said for Rickie's mother, who is resurrected for brief episodes. She is colourless and lacks taste. She returns to her husband as readily as she runs away from him. She begins to love her elder son only when she has given birth to a bastard and let him be taken away from her. Aunt Emily, on the other hand, has character but it is disagreeable. She has something of the senile irritability which we see developed in Ruth Wilcox and Mrs Moore. She brings up Stephen but is unable to cope with him at a difficult age and, when her mind is so easily poisoned against him by Agnes, she turns him out, cuts him off with an allowance and gets the parson to tell him to go to the colonies. She ought to have been able to see through Agnes' legacy hunting tricks but she is quickly vindictive and, when she dies, she has done nothing for her ward.

Her cruelty to Rickie is equally great and that is described for us by Agnes, herself an expert. Aunt Emily knew Rickie's nature, the points at which he was especially sensitive and in a fit of Sunday pique she tells him that Stephen is his bastard brother. Making every allowance for the Edwardian Sunday, it was unforgivably malicious. 'You told him to hurt him', says Agnes. 'I cannot think what you did it for. I suppose because he was rude to you in church. It is a mean, cowardly revenge.' Aunt Emily deteriorates. When Rickie visits her after leaving Agnes he finds: 'she has forgotten what people are like. Finding life dull, she had dropped lies into it...She loved to mislead others...But her own error had been greater, as it was spiritual entirely.' She had betrayed the true reality.

Is the non-hero any better in the tale? He is in obvious contrast to his wife. He is physically weak, deformed and, despite pitiless flashes of truth, is the average untruthful man. In literature, he is the predecessor of Maugham's Philip Carey and the Stephen Daedalus of James Joyce, which is a reminder that we must take a long leap over many books that we regard as the early classics of the century to get back to Forster's early novels. Like these characters, Rickie is partly autobiographical, especially in his love of Cambridge and in being a writer of short stories. 'I've got quite a pile of little stories, all hanging on this ridiculous idea of getting in touch with Nature.' Just the sort of stories Forster was writing.

Rickie had the same concern for reality which his creator was able to enjoy. The undergraduate search for reality is the simple theme which opens the novel: ' "The cow is there"...it was philosophy. They were discussing the existence of objects.' Later, the theme is developed into that favourite Bloomsbury question about the value of existence, and its answer 'useless to God or man'. At another point, in one of these rhetorically elaborated passages which were required to end chapters in Edwardian novels, Rickie struggles again to get nearer reality: 'He prayed to be delivered from the shadow of unreality that had begun to darken the world.' Then he faces the old moral dilemma of the artist: 'To do good! For what other reason are we here? Let us give up our refined sensations, and our comforts, and our art, if thereby we can make other people happier and better', and this popular utilitarian view, so attractive to Edwardians, is heard again, twenty pages later, in a note on Tony Failing: 'He loved poetry and music and pictures, and everything tempted him to live in a kind of cultured paradise, with the door shut upon squalor. But to have more decent people in the world—he sacrificed everything to that.' It is Rickie speaking and he is not prepared to go as far as that. But comments like this recur, the eternal questions raised, the eternal dilemmas stated and considered, and it is this which makes it the preferred novel and always attractive to us. Youth asks the questions and every reader responds in sympathy.

The satisfying thing in Rickie's outlook, again obviously a mirror of his maker, is that he believed in the intelligence, and we best see the quality of this belief when he is thinking about Herbert Pembroke, his brother-in-law, who was 'stupid in the important sense: his whole life was coloured by a contempt for the intellect'. Rickie's intellect 'was not remarkable'—a modest mirror—but he had the right attitude to it: 'it is in what we value, not what we have, that the test of us resides.' The effort which Cambridge had taught Rickie to make was 'not so much to acquire knowledge as to dispel a little of the darkness by which we and all our acquisitions are surrounded'. In a long life, Rickie's creator has never deserted that ideal.

Rickie came up against reality most awkwardly when he discovered that he had a bastard brother, for the Sawston suburban spirit surrounded him. His personal reaction was natural and was acutely sharpened when he learned that the relationship was through his mother. When he first heard that Stephen was his brother, he fainted and as soon as he recovered his training took charge and he felt he must tell Stephen. 'Because he must be told such a real thing.' But the women persuaded him against it and the lie won. We hear an echo from an earlier word from Tony Failing: 'we are punished if we lie.' As so often in Forster novels, the woman for the moment is the stronger. Agnes is all for concealment, as Mrs Herriton was for concealing from Irma that she had a brother, and Agnes wins and Rickie has a breakdown.

They are married soon afterwards and Rickie is imprisoned in Sawston and a classroom. The mind adjusts or we should not survive and Rickie's mind adjusted. 'No man works for nothing, and Rickie trusted that to him also benefits might accrue; that his wound might be healed as he laboured, and his eyes recapture the Holy Grail.' It is a tribute to the liveliness of the book that the eye runs easily over these occasional highly wrought Edwardian utterances. The prison closes in on Rickie. We hear it in an echo of a quotation heard in Rickie's days of undergraduate freedom. 'Pan ovium custos' appears in the text Rickie is teaching and we feel with him that his classroom is a prison.

Once again he urges Agnes to let him tell Stephen. She will not have it. 'It was the last time he attempted intimacy...they had destroyed the habit of reverence and would quarrel again.' The tragedy of personal relationships develops, 'the relations between them were fixed' and they echo again of that summary of human life: 'To the end of life they would go on beating time.' It is the turning point: 'Henceforwards he deteriorates...He remained conscientious and decent, but the spiritual part of him proceeded towards ruin.' For a bitter moment Rickie himself sees this, the high undergraduate hopes all gone: 'He was an outcast and a failure. But he was not again forced to contemplate these facts so clearly.' The bleak phrases have a tragic air.

Then we come to the storyteller's problem of letting out the truth about Stephen. Pembroke must know, Ansell must know and Stephen himself must know. The story, in order to go on, requires that they know. The devices by which they learn are perhaps a little too contrived, as if the artist thought such things unimportant, his eye being on the mental relationships between the characters and not enough on the mechanics of bringing them together.

It is at this point that Ansell fulfils his purpose in the story. He is to bring Rickie back to reality and resurrect his spirit. In the beginning he was the philosophical commentary on the characters and their actions. Here he discerns first the relationship between Agnes and Rickie. He is clearsighted intelligence, touched with sympathetic imagination. He is the only hero-type in the story in the sense that he has his creator's full approval. 'He had a great many facts to learn, and before he died he learned a suitable quantity. But he never forgot that the holiness of the heart's imagination can alone classify these facts.' (An echo there of a favourite quotation which appears thirty years later in 'What I Believe.') In that spirit Ansell looked on what Agnes and Rickie were making of life together: 'They live without love. They work without conviction. They seek money without requiring it. They die, and nothing will have happened, either for themselves or for others.' A young couple, in fact, in a contemporary idiom and a reminder that Edwardian problems were very like our own.

Ansell's function in the story is to try to rescue Rickie from Agnes and all the suburban life she represents. He has the Cambridge sense of comradeship and will go to any lengths to help his friend. So a meeting with Stephen is contrived and the violent discovery scene follows. That is the dramatic conclusion of the suburban theme and it ends with a brief three paragraphed chapter of moralizing: 'The soul has her own currency...But the soul can also have her bankruptcies.' This is the stuff of Edwardian bestsellers and in the last sentence we find the humanist paradox: 'Will it really profit us so much if we save our souls and lose the whole world.'

So we come to the third part, which is Wiltshire, the remaining fifth of the book, and its management is a technical triumph. It begins with the flashback which tells us how Stephen was begotten.

That is relaxation after high drama. There is some comedy in the treatment of free love with a quotation as climax from Walt Whitman, who was the poet for Edwardians in that area of human relationships. We have the comic touch that Tony Failing, the Shavian kind of socialist, conservatively recognizes the power of social opinion in such matters: 'they are not guiltless in the sight of man and therefore will inevitably pay.' While his wife, whom we have met as the peevish old woman, cries out when she hears of the seventeen day love story: 'Why, they're divine! They're forces of Nature! They're as ordinary as volcanoes...they are guiltless in the sight of God.'

And so we come to Stephen, the natural man. On the one hand Rickie, who arrived at truth through Cambridge and denied it through Sawston. On the other, his brother Stephen, who arrived at truth by natural living on the Downs, and we are given the sense of their strange influence from the earliest known human life on the island, the people of the Rings of thirty thousand years ago. Forster had fallen under their influence. Which of us has not who has passed that way? 'I was then twenty-five years old, and had begun to warm to the Wiltshire downlands which I had hitherto condemned as bare and dull, and I caught fire upon the Rings.' This was in 1904, when the story was shaping, and it 'gave Stephen Wonham, the bastard, his home'. Stephen is a late example of that *lusus naturae,* the Natural Man, the idea which goes so far back and for example, which Cook sought in his voyages in the South Seas and which his editor, Hawkesworth, knew well for he had translated Fenelon's *Telemachus,* which comes so much earlier than Rousseau. If we want a comparison in literature for the brothers, we can go to Tom Jones and Blifil, who are neither of them concerned with truth and reality, as they lived in the eighteenth century and knew what was real and true without thinking about it. Tom and Blifil are in the usual comic opposition. Rickie and Stephen are each seeking truth and right action and come into opposition and that is of the nature of tragedy.

Stephen, begotten in that mad romantic affaire between his mother and the Wiltshire farmer, was brought up in Wiltshire by the Failings. Failing, whose conservative view about paying for illicit love turned out to be right, was the kind of back-to-the-land intellectual socialist familiar to Forster through Lowes Dickinson. We meet them in the Dickinson biography. They wrote and they farmed or played at farming. They were very keen on the small-holding which produced independent citizens in contrast to factory workers. It is a recurrent idea which appears much later in Huxley's *After Many a Summer*. In Failing's case the actual management of the farm was left to the agent, Mr Wilbraham, who 'knew his place, and kept others to theirs. Everything with him was graduated— carefully graduated civility towards his superiors, towards his inferiors carefully graduated incivility.' Such men have always been the backbone of English society, carrying things on while their masters behaved like civilized people, much too civilized to notice what was going on in their name.

Stephen had to be withdrawn from his first school after 'a violent spasm of dishonesty—such as often heralds the approach of man-hood' and expelled from his second for 'rowdiness and indiscipline'. After that, he lived with the widowed Mrs Failing, who left him to his own devices among the shepherds. 'It is one of the shepherds', she whispers to Agnes when Stephen comes in at teatime. He is represented as gawky and quarrelsome, rawly natural. Later, he develops the peaceful touch of the countryman. At that first meeting an echo is contrived and amplified when there is talk of accidents at a place on the railway line. The hint of doom is heard again next day when Rickie says to Agnes: 'I always have in this house the most awful feeling of insecurity' and then 'Dear—dear—let's beware of I don't know what...'

The crisis is mounted skilfully. Rickie and Stephen go off riding to Salisbury and Stephen is shown in the worst light, drunken and coarse, and Rickie leaves him with the soldier who is invented to separate them. Things at Cadover continue to go wrong. There is a trivial quarrel with Aunt Emily which happens because church upset them all, as it sometimes does, and lunch was late and they were tired and hungry and snappish. Then there is a clamour of echoes, Rickie saying to Agnes, who is going to ruin him: ' "You're changing me", he said gently. "God bless you for it." ' He looks at the railway lines where the child was killed as they travelled down and where he is going to be killed. 'The line curved suddenly: certainly it was dangerous.' Then the Shelley quotation which gives the novel its title, followed by an echo of Madingley and the peevish revelation 'your brother'. He faints, as he faints when Ansell hurt him with the further revelation. Stephen does not know and is not to be told, so Agnes cries: 'Dear, we're saved.' And Rickie is overborne. Stephen disappears from the story while the corruption of Rickie proceeds in Sawston.

Stephen's return is artificially contrived. Agnes' plan to get Mrs Failing to turn him out has succeeded only too well, for he is turned out with the papers that tell him that Rickie is his half-brother. So he naturally comes to share this good news with Rickie. We see him through Ansell's eyes as they wait together for Rickie in the garden. 'He gave the idea of an animal with just enough soul to contemplate its own bliss.' Obviously 'he was simple and frank...He had not the suburban reticence.' He then receives through Ansell's eyes full benefit of the Natural Man idea: 'He was not romantic, for Romance is a figure with outstretched hands, yearning for the unattainable. Certain figures of the Greeks, to whom we continually return, suggested him a little...he had been back somewhere—back to some table of the gods, spread in a field where there is no noise...' The very accent of the little stories Forster was writing then. Stephen continues his story, telling Ansell how he was kicked out, and why he now seeks his brother.

Agnes hopes she can cope with the emergency and tries to bribe Stephen, and gets for response: 'Here's a very bad mistake' and he goes off. We are left with the melodramatic scene in which Ansell tells Rickie that Stephen is his mother's son. Another measure of artificial contrivance is needed to bring the brothers together again. Stephen gets a job with a London firm of hauliers and we are given views on Londoners. It hardly seems necessary to the tale, but a young writer likes to have his say on anything he feels strongly about and we note this particular interest because we shall hear so much about it in the next novel. 'The London intellect, so pert and shallow, like a stream that never reaches the ocean, disgusted him almost as much as the London physique, which for all its dexterity is not permanent, and seldom continues into the third generation.'

We hear a strong echo there from Jack London's *The People of the Abyss* (1903): 'Year by year, and decade after decade, rural England pours in a flood of vigorous strong life, that not only does not renew itself, but perishes by the third generation.' Stephen comes to Sawston where by mistake a man tips him a sovereign: 'On the action of this man much depends.' For Stephen promptly gets drunk and turns up at Rickie's place again.

It is the saving of Rickie for the moment. He takes the insensible Stephen in and puts him to bed. Something has happened to Rickie. Ansell has taken him 'behind right and wrong to a place where only one thing matters—that the Beloved should rise from the dead'. He and Agnes and Pembroke are all in a state of exhaustion and accept good sense and right action as the exhausted must. But for Rickie there is regeneration. He cries out to Pembroke the Shelley quotation: 'I never did belong to that great sect whose doctrine is that each one should select' and 'the quiet of months and the remorse of the last ten days had alike departed'. Once again we are told that: 'He had journeyed—as on rare occasions a man must—till he stood behind right and wrong.' To understand this we must recall something earlier: 'the Primal Curse, which is not...the knowledge of good and evil, but the knowledge of good-and-evil.' We are familiar with good-and-evil, though not as a curse. Meister Eckhart had preached about the function of evil in exercising good. Milton in the *Areopagitica* spoke of good-and-evil, and in eastern thought the two are related with the suggestion of a state of being behind it in which these twin conditions no longer exist. The Primal Curse would seem to be the conflict that is in the nature of all existence. What is still more interesting is the repetition of the idea of continued existence: 'On the banks of the grey torrent of life, love is the only flower. A little way up the stream and a little way down had Rickie glanced, and he knew that she whom he had loved had risen from the dead, and might rise again.' This is the resurrection also of the spirit, influencing those now alive, and it is to become a main theme in the novels which follow. Rickie's reaction to this recovery of belief is typical of his condition: 'Let me die out. She will continue' and we know later that his wish is fulfilled.

But his wish that Stephen will stay with him cannot be fulfilled.

Stephen sees that Rickie does not care for him at all and is merely using him to recover a sense of his mother's presence. Stephen is transformed. He was 'a man who probably armed the world...In a few hours he had recaptured motion and passion and the imprint of the sunlight and the wind...his hair was beautiful against the grey sky, and his eyes, recalling the sky unclouded, shot past the intruder as if to some worthier vision.' This leads us back, gasping, to Meredith, to the Pre-Raphaelites, to Wagner. Seeing Stephen thus put Agnes completely off balance and for a moment she thought she saw her one love, Gerald, again.

Stephen has to go. But he asks Rickie to go with him. We hear his simple philosophy again: 'We're alive together and the rest is cant.' His voice continues in the thick morning mist through which: 'Only the simplest sounds, the simplest desires emerged.' 'Come', the voice said, 'I will take care of you, I can manage you.' And Rickie went, for 'a voice...lies nearer the racial essence and perhaps to the divine; it can, at all events, overleap one grave.' It is the first time that we hear this note in Forster's novels. The pitch is higher than narrative prose can normally offer. It is nearer drama, more like the veiled utterance of verse. The young novelist was experimenting, seeing how far he could go, how much he could make the novel form contain. He will have to handle these higher temperatured prose techniques confidently if he is to present the themes of the next two novels successfully.

Forster tells us that the book designed itself: 'it is the only one of my books that has come upon me without my knowledge.' We may sum it up with the help of a phrase in Helen's first letter in the next novel. This novel 'is sometimes like life and sometimes only a drama'. For it is not a complete success. There is only one round character and that is the author, who is seeking a technique for serious expression in novel form. He has the spirit of place, admirably in Cambridge and Sawston, not so strongly in the countryside of England as in the next novel. He has conflict and passion and something of romance, but he does not yet have the power to fill out his characters and give them to us in the round. The novel is an idea and not yet an achievement; that will come with the next novels.

If we think of it again as a young man's experiment in the difficult art of writing a novel, we can be sure that one part of the experiment would encourage him. His prose already had hints of having the magic in it. He does not attempt many heightened scenes and even so there are occasional echoes of the Edwardian failing for highly wrought pulsating prose. Very occasional, for usually the prose is clear, fresh, lively. It is these qualities which keep the three first novels alive today and the interest of *The Longest Journey* to the student of the novel is that Forster, in his first essay into serious comment in fictional form, wrote persuasively. His characters are not very amiable or their antagonisms very absorbing, but we find ourselves engaged and we read on to the end. For the real character, the author, never loses our attention.

The carnage among the characters is tremendous. Forster tells us that 'Will Beveridge...pleasantly calculated that the percentage of sudden deaths (infants excluded) amounted to over 44% of the adult population'. To which we may pleasantly add that a bare 34% of the adult characters survived the tale. Was it an attack of the college spleen which exterminated so many and tarnished all the ladies in the tale? If so, there is compensation in the next novel.

Howards End

Look into your hearts and look into the past, and remember that all this beauty is a gift which you can never replace...You can make a town...but you can never make the country, because it was made by Time.

Abinger Pageant.

HOWARDS END is a house and we meet it in the opening words: 'It is old and little and altogether delightful—red brick.' It is a Hertfordshire farmhouse: 'From hall you go right or left into dining-room or drawing-room. Hall itself is practically a room.' There are three bedrooms above and three attics above that, which gives you 'nine windows as you look up from the front garden'. The house is typical of its county: 'Hertfordshire is England at its quietest, with little emphasis of river and hill; it is England meditative.' The words are being quoted in a Hertfordshire house and they are still as true as, this later note on the county: 'Having no urgent destiny, it strolled downhill or up as it wished, taking no trouble about the gradients, nor about the view, which nevertheless expanded... Though its contours were slight, there was a touch of freedom in their sweep to which Surrey will never attain...The comradeship, not passionate, that is our highest gift as a nation, was promised by it.'

All through the novel, as occasion offers, England is celebrated in these quiet word-patterns. By contrast, there are many of those London descriptions in which the Edwardian novelists excelled. London won them all and their prose quickens as they embark on a description. But here, for contrast to the country life, we have the London always in a state of flux, building and rebuilding, a city of nomads. Rush and hurry in an anonymous flurry of living. In the country, sane living in houses like Howards End. In the city, life in luggage, lived without proportion, a prey to panic and emptiness. It is the modern theme, urgent now as our planners frighten us with a nightmare future of life in enormously swollen cities and it was foreseen by the Edwardians while they celebrated the lively bustle of London.

These are the themes of the novel, prophetic about the future of England, preaching remedies—which now seem impossible to apply. In 1910 we are still in the classical tradition and the answer to life in the city is the answer Cicero found in Rome—leave it and live in the country. So the characters in this novel begin in Howards End in Hertfordshire, where the younger Schlegel girl and the younger Wilcox boy believe one night they are in love and pledge themselves and next morning correct the romantic mistake. After the turmoils which make the story, the three main characters gratefully settle there, where it is possible to connect the prose and the passion.

The owner of Howards End is Ruth Wilcox. She recognizes its quality and she knows that her husband and family do not. They are business men and philistines, city nomads. So when she is dying she pencils a note that she wishes Margaret Schlegel to have Howards End. Margaret and Helen are Edwardian intellectual spinsters, who met the Wilcoxes in Germany. The Schlegel girls, with their much younger brother, Tibby, live in their house in Wickham Place, where they receive not only the Wilcoxes but a character from a different world, Leonard Bast. He is a clerk, at the very bottom of the infinite gradations of the Edwardian middle classes and always near what they called the 'abyss', homelessness and starvation. He becomes a casual acquaintance of the Schlegels and, as they are advanced Edwardian women and could not let well alone, they take him up.

When Mrs Wilcox dies, her wish that Howards End should go to Margaret Schlegel is ignored and must be fulfilled another way. The tenuous acquaintance between the families develops and in a couple of years Henry Wilcox sees in Margaret a successor to his late wife. She has grown to respect him as one of the practical men who through the generations had civilized England and made intellectual life possible, and eventually she accepts him. She has something of Ruth Wilcox's quality, placidity and understanding. Unlike her clever, mercurial sister, who sometimes acts so impulsively; as when she brought the Basts across England by train to Henry Wilcox's country house. Henry had told the Schlegels—not knowing their interest—that the insurance company in which Bast worked was unsound. The girls persuade Bast to leave it and work elsewhere for an even smaller salary. The insurance company proves perfectly sound and Bast's new job disappears from under him. Helen is furious and trails the Basts in her wake across England to face the man whose advice ruined them.

The fat is in the fire, for Bast's wife Jacky was Henry's mistress long ago. Helen's pleas for them are rejected and Margaret turns on her sister for being so foolishly impetuous. That night, while Bast's wife lies in a drunken stupor, Helen seeks to console Bast by lying with him. This has all to be straightened out, so the novelist takes Helen to her brother Tibby, now an Oxford undergraduate, and together they evolve a plan for saving the Basts from the abyss. She cannot confess her casual affaire, and disappears for a long while from the tale. Her long absence in Europe worries Margaret, who has married Henry Wilcox but not yet succeeded to Howards End. That requires more contrivance. Henry, with his practical good sense, suggests a plan to trick Helen into meeting Margaret.

The plan works and she meets Helen at Howards End and sees at a glance why her sister has been so evasive. She is with child. There is a great welling of affection between the sisters and Helen asks if Margaret will spend one night with her in this house. Henry refuses, for what to him is good practical reason, but Margaret acts by the rule of the affections and stays with her sister in Howards End. The house is quite ready for them, as an old countrywoman who was a friend of Ruth's has been looking after the house, and by some instinct, possibly some communication from Ruth, has prepared it for immediate use.

The story remains at Howards End. Leonard Bast is impelled down there in a febrile state of remorse. Henry's son Charles has been trying to find out who had seduced Helen so that the miscreant can be brought to book. Tibby unwittingly tells him and Charles pursues Bast to Howards End, begins to give him a beating and Bast collapses with a heart attack and dies. There is a charge of manslaughter and Charles goes to prison and his father is a broken man. The sweet influence of the house is used by Margaret to shelter both Helen and Henry. They recover and find happiness there and Howards End is at last given to Margaret.

The stories of which novels are made do not seem much when they are told bare. The characters have to come alive in them and give the story their quality and the characters in this novel are the best Forster has made. He knew them all well, except Leonard Bast and his wife, and he knew their backgrounds. He gives us frightening glimpses of their inner lives and the panic and emptiness there. But he also indicates that the prose and the passion can sometimes connect and peace and proportion be attained.

One character dominates them all, Ruth Wilcox. She belongs to neither party. She is not intellectual and she is different from her practical husband and these equally competent businessmen, her sons Charles and Paul. She enjoys the Forsterian virtues, tolerance and sympathy, and the source of her strength is Howards End and the countryside. We catch a Post-Impressionist glimpse of her in the letter from Helen which opens the book: 'Trail, trail, went her long dress over the sopping grass, and she came back with her hands full of the hay that was cut yesterday...Mrs Wilcox reappears, trail, trail, trail, still smelling hay and looking at the flowers.' The hay is an echo and a symbol throughout the story right to the end, when the closing words are Helen's again: 'The field's cut!...the big meadow! We've seen to the very end, and it'll be such a crop of hay as never!'

Ruth Wilcox is the most sympathetic character, as she must be in her divine role of shaping the lives of the others. She knows she is dying but keeps it secret, and seeks a spiritual heir for her beloved

Howards End where she was born and where she receives the strength necessary to help her husband and family. She must find someone equal to these responsibilities and arrange that they are undertaken. We meet her when she prevents a vulgar brawl between the families, when it is discovered that Helen and Paul have foolishly thought they were in love and should engage to marry:

> She seemed to belong not to the young people and their motor, but to the house, and to the tree that overshadowed it. One knew that she worshipped the past, and that the instinctive wisdom the past can alone bestow had descended upon her — that wisdom to which we give the clumsy name of aristocracy. High born she might not be. But assuredly she cared about her ancestors, and let them help her. When she saw Charles angry, Paul frightened, and Mrs Munt in tears, she heard her ancestors say, 'Separate those human beings who will hurt each other most. The rest can wait.'

She has the wisdom which gives her early knowledge of what goes on and the wisdom to be silent until speech is needed. 'It's all right dear. They have broken off the engagement', she assures Charles.

We see very little of her, even through the eyes of the other characters and this is for clear purpose. There are references to Margaret's appreciation of her good sense just before we learn that the old lady is seeking her friendship, and may have arranged meetings:

> Perhaps the elder lady…may have detected in the other and less charming of the sisters a deeper sympathy, a sounder judgement. She was capable of detecting such things. Perhaps it was she who had desired the Miss Schlegels to be invited to Howards End, and Margaret whose presence she had particularly desired. All this is speculation: Mrs Wilcox left few clear indications behind her.

Vague, because she is to be a greater influence as a spirit. The blurring is given a reason in the next reference, when once again we see her through Margaret's eyes:

> She was not intellectual, nor even alert, and it was odd that, all the same, she should give the idea of greatness. Margaret, zig-

zagging with her friends over Thought and Art, was conscious
of a personality that transcended their own and dwarfed their
activities. There was no bitterness in Mrs Wilcox; there was
not even criticism; she was lovable, and no ungracious or
uncharitable word had passed her lips. Yet she and daily life
were out of focus: one or the other must show blurred.

And again, just at the end of the same scene: ' "I am used to young
people", said Mrs Wilcox, and with each word she spoke the outlines
of known things grew dim.' The friendship between the two ladies
which is to be the sweet presiding influence in the story is cemented
in that scene and the chapter ends with a typical gently ironic twist.
The conversation ceased suddenly when Margaret went back to the
room: 'Her friends had been talking over her new friend and had
dismissed her as uninteresting.'

Certainly she was simple and may have seemed colourless but
her simplicity was of the order which is achieved beyond compli-
cation and is the voice of truth, as we learn only a few pages later
when her husband is speaking about her after the funeral:

> Ruth knew no more of worldly wickedness and wisdom than did
> the flowers in her garden, or the grass in her field. Her idea of
> business — 'Henry, why do people who have enough money
> try to get more money?' Her idea of politics — 'I am sure that
> if the mothers of various nations could meet, there would be no
> more wars.'

To pursue the tale 'the commentator should step forward' and
the novelist himself tells us Ruth Wilcox's reasons for asking that
Howards End be given to Margaret and not remain with her family:
'To them Howards End was a house: they could not know that to
her it had been a spirit, for which she sought a spiritual heir.' The
house did not come to Margaret for a long time, but it came at need.
Meanwhile, Ruth Wilcox's influence was at work on her at once,
for Ruth required a successor, not only to Howards End. So the
'Wilcoxes continued to play a considerable part' in her thoughts.
'She desired to protect them, and often felt that they could protect
her where she was deficient.' Their kind of life 'was to remain a real
force' to her. 'She could not despise it, as Helen and Tibby had

affected to do. It fostered such virtues as neatness, decision, and obedience, virtues of the second rank, no doubt, but they had formed our civilization.' At the end, when Margaret and Helen are at last in Howards End together, Margaret acknowledges the influence of Ruth Wilcox in their lives:

> I feel that you and I and Henry are only fragments of that woman's mind. She knows everything. She is everything. She is the house, and the tree that leans over it. People have their own deaths as well as their own lives, and even if there is nothing beyond death, we shall differ in our nothingness. I cannot believe that knowledge such as hers will perish with knowledge such as mine. She knew about realities.

A little later, her speculations go further. She wakes in the morning and looks out into the garden. Helen is still asleep, a moment of forgetfulness achieved. Margaret reflects: 'How incomprehensible that Leonard Bast should have won her this night of peace. Was he also part of Mrs Wilcox's mind?' In a final chapter of pastoral warmth, when Helen is questioning Margaret, we see in her replies the unrealized influence of Ruth Wilcox. Helen asks how Margaret managed so well. 'I did the obvious thing. I had two invalids to nurse. Here was a house, ready furnished and empty. It was obvious. I didn't know myself it would turn into a permanent home...There are moments when I feel Howards End peculiarly our own.' The spiritual successor has come into her inheritance. Then she speaks the benediction of Howards End and Hertford-shire: 'This craze for motion has only set in during the last hundred years. It may be followed by a civilization that won't be in move-ment, because it will rest on the earth. All the signs are against it now, but I can't help hoping, and very early in the morning in the garden I feel that our house is the future as well as the past.' The prayer will be echoed by the fortunate ones who are settled in Hertfordshire now.

The realities which Margaret cherished were those cherished by Edwardian women generally, as well as the Bloomsbury group, the sweetening of personal relations so that society could remain sane and wholesome. They were especial ideals for women before they could fulfil themselves in the professions and they are celebrated in Margaret and Helen in that decade when the breaking of Europe was imminent and women as well as men sought almost unconsciously the power to prevent catastrophe.

The relationship between the sisters gives us the greatest scenes in the book. Their feeling for one another reveals the most sensitive possibilities in personal relations. Between sisters there can be an unconscious sympathy which travels over space and time and offers a depth of understanding rarely achieved between human beings. In Margaret and Helen this transcended their contrasting qualities, for Margaret was the more ordinary and steady person, Helen the swift, brilliant brain who behaved erratically. Margaret lived to strengthen the bonds of affection between her friends. Helen lived to achieve herself as unconsciously as any other beautiful thing in nature.

Margaret's character matures. At the beginning she is inexperienced, though she has brought up her younger sister and still younger brother. She is apt to change her mind quickly. She has natural sympathy for the practical people, the Wilcoxes, and realizes their contribution towards achieving civilization and that without them civilization could not continue. She has also an understanding of the poor and submerged which stays in proportion and here, as with the businessmen, she contrasts with Helen, who runs to intellectual and emotional extremes. There is no suggestion that Margaret ever feels the panic and emptiness which haunts Helen and which Helen quickly detects is felt by the Wilcoxes. Margaret acquires the same poise and repose as Ruth Wilcox because, like her, she gives her time and thought for others. Eventually the house, Howards End, is the background which gives her strength, and the plot can be looked on as the story of her waiting for it.

She has the instinct to make a nest and as soon as she is taken down to Henry's house at Oniton she begins. The vicar turns out to be a friend of her father's, local people promise introductions so that by the time they come away: 'She loved her future home. Standing up in the car...she gazed with deep emotion upon Oniton.' That chapter ends with a paragraph of doom. 'She never saw it again...the Wilcoxes have no part in the place, nor in any place. It is not their names that recur in the parish registers. It is not their ghosts that sigh among the alders at evening.' The Wilcoxes are the commercial nomads of great cities. Houses belong to country people and Howards End naturally descends to Margaret though she had to take the name of Wilcox to inherit it. It is as if Forster were saying that real people live on the earth and those who live in cities are shadows. After the first war, profiteers bought up a great part of the English countryside, and in time became absorbed. Perhaps they read the little essay which opens chapter seventeen: 'The feudal ownership of land did bring dignity, whereas the modern ownership of movables is reducing us again to a nomadic horde. We are reverting to the civilization of luggage, and historians of the future will note how the middle classes accreted possessions without taking root in the earth, and may find in this the secret of their imaginative poverty.' The mystique of the house, any house, then follows: 'The Schlegels were certainly the poorer for the loss of Wickham Place. It had helped to balance their lives, and almost to counsel them.'

It fits the allegory that Margaret and Helen are athwart one another at Oniton and that they are reconciled at Howards End. In the last scenes, at Howards End, it is more than reconciliation of the sisters, it is translation of a sordid story into tragedy in the death of Leonard Bast—'Let Squalor be turned into Tragedy'—and the reconciliation of Helen and Henry to life. Margaret has come to Howards End mellowed and experienced. The house is not given to her. She takes it. For she disobeys her husband in using it for the night so that Helen can have her wish and they sleep there. She expects to leave her husband as a result and go to Germany where her sister will have her baby. But almost immediately, she needs the house to nurse her husband back to health after the shock of Charles being sent to prison. The result is that Margaret achieves relationships with her sister and her husband which saves them both and even makes them friends. The scenes with Helen in which this happens are the fine flowers of Forster's novels and will remain among the most true and tender scenes between women in our fiction.

At the back of the cult of personal relations is the struggle to realize the self, so that life has form and colour and design. In the last chapter, when the chief characters are together in a glow of friendly happiness which is the spirit of Howards End in Hertfordshire, Helen confesses to Margaret that she feels something wanting in herself, and Margaret from the sure background of the house is able to comfort and reassure her:

> All over the world men and women are worrying because they cannot develop as they are supposed to develop. Here and there they have the matter out, and it comforts them. Don't fret yourself, Helen. Develop what you have; love your child. I do not love children. I am thankful to have none. I can play with their beauty and charm, but that is all—nothing real, not one scrap of what there ought to be. And others—others go farther still, and move outside humanity altogether. A place, as well as a person, may catch the glow. Don't you see that all this leads to comfort in the end? It is part of the battle against sameness. Differences—eternal differences, planted by God in a single family, so that there may always be colour; sorrow perhaps, but colour in the daily grey.

The differences between Margaret and Helen were great. Margaret is rather like the Goodness in the Max Beerbohm cartoon, who sat placidly while Evil hurried about and explained to Goodness that she had won the world just by being so active. It is Helen who is so impetuous. She writes as soon as she believes that she and Paul Wilcox are in love. If she had waited to sleep on it she would have discovered she was wrong. That would have denied us the easy comedy opening with Aunt Juley being driven by Charles in his car and confusing Charles and Paul with embarrassing results. It is Helen who snatches up the wrong umbrella when she hurries from the Queen's Hall concert, and that begins the acquaintance with Leonard Bast. It is Helen who sweeps the Basts back into their flat and out again and down to Oniton, where she seduces Leonard and the story of his wife's illicit relationship with Henry Wilcox tumbles out. It is Helen who goes off to Germany and is so vague about herself and stays away so long that our curiosity is aroused. In short, it is Helen who provides the story element which is such a help to the lesser sort of novelist whose readers stay with him because they must find out what happens. It is Helen who provides the big scenes in the novel in the sense of the big rows. She is quite infuriating in Wickham Place when she simply will not let young Bast go but will persist in her clever questions. She is so much more infuriating at Oniton that even Margaret turns on her: 'You have been most self-indulgent. I can't get over it. You have less restraint than more as you grow older.'

It is a flaw which is corrected by her sufferings, when she has the social shame of carrying a bastard and finally by the healing steadying influence of Howards End. But there is another flaw for which there is no help. She behaves improbably. Again and again in the five novels Forster asks us to believe things of his characters we cannot believe and sometimes the improbable act is a hinge on which the story turns. They are things which could happen, but not to the characters as Forster has made them. They are calculated, like the sudden deaths which Forster uses more than most authors, but the sudden deaths must be accepted as the actions out of character cannot be. For a novel is an organism made up of characters and the things that happen to them, and the organism comes alive and remains alive when the characters behave according to their nature. As soon as a character behaves out of character the illusion cracks and the little world becomes a shadow of a shade.

The author can do what he likes with his characters. He can kill them abruptly as Forster does and that is acceptable; it is what the Author of the fiction in which we all exist does to us all. But when the characters themselves act or induce action it must be probable that they do what they do. To most readers the whole of the Helen-Bast story at Oniton is false except for the reactions of Margaret and Henry Wilcox and the unfortunate Jacky. The most improbable thing of all is the seduction. Perhaps it is unfair to call it so. Call it a casual affaire, as Helen in retrospect sees it. 'I pressed him to tell me.' That is certainly in character. Helen had no notion of the blessedness of not knowing. 'Right up to the end we were Mr Bast and Miss Schlegel...I saw his eyes, and guessed that Mr Wilcox had ruined him in two ways, not one. I drew him to me. I made him tell me. I felt very lonely myself. He is not to blame. He would have gone on worshipping me.' The staccato accents have the air of truth and her speculation that her action was a growth from her brief and innocent affaire with Paul is acceptable: 'Both times it was loneliness, and the night, and the panic afterwards. Did Leonard grow out of Paul?' But it remains too difficult to accept. What *is* stark and believable is that Helen while the child grew in her should forget her lover. 'I ought to remember Leonard as my lover... It is no good pretending. I am forgetting him.'

The reader who has no difficulty with these things is fortunate, for he can enjoy altogether one of the most exquisite relationships in English fiction, the complementary creation, Margaret and Helen. Probably every reader is able to forget his difficulties from that point in Chapter 37 when the sisters are completely reconciled: 'Helen still smiling, came up to her sister. She said "It is always Meg". They looked into each other's eyes. The inner life had paid.' From that moment, the pastoral comedy takes charge: ' "Little boy, what do you want?" "Please, I am the milk." ' It is sad to be querulous about this central thing. Clearly the wonderful relationship between the sisters had to be tested and the testing had to be severe to be of any value at all and it could not be severe without violence, even violence to the character of one of them. But the relationship between author and reader requires truth also.

The contrast to the Schlegel view of life is provided by the Wilcox men: 'they avoided the personal note in life. All Wilcoxes did. It did not seem to them of supreme importance. Or it may have been as Helen supposed: they realized its importance but were afraid of it. Panic and emptiness could one glance behind.' Father and son, Henry and Charles, are fine studies in the Butler manner, and after one or two casual meetings early in the novel, we see them discussing Ruth Wilcox's pencilled request that Howards End be given to Margaret Schlegel. Mrs Wilcox 'was quite a poor woman —the house had been all her dowry, and the house would come to Charles in time. After the funeral Mr Wilcox is sent the note: 'I should like Miss Schlegel (Margaret) to have Howards End.' The men react immediately. This is a question of property and everyone knows the intense excitement that can be generated over property when wills are read.

5*

But this is not a will. It is only a pencilled note. Charles suggests undue influence. The father 'whose nature was nobler than his son's' will not have that. Then the son falls back on the suggestion that it is not his mother's writing. His wife says that pencil doesn't count and is put down for saying anything at all. Then: 'the two men were gradually assuming the manner of the committee-room. They were both at their best when serving on committees. They did not make the mistake of handling human affairs in the bulk, but disposed of them item by item, sharply...They were the average human article, and had they considered the note as a whole it would have driven them miserable or mad. Considered item by item, the emotional content was minimized, and all went forward smoothly.'

At that point the commentator slips in to exonerate the Wilcoxes and reports that 'it is natural and fitting that after due debate they should tear the note up and throw it on their dining-room fire'. But the comedy continues with a sharper satirical edge. They thought of the mother who had written that note: 'and all they could say was "Treachery". Mrs Wilcox had been treacherous to the family, to the laws of property, to her own written word.' Later, Mr Wilcox defends Margaret against Charles. She did not know. But he blames his wife instead. She had tricked them all by not telling them she was ill and in terrible pain. If she had told them they would have been with her and the note would not have been written. The denouement is more easily amusing. Charles wrote Margaret to ask her whether his mother had wanted her to have anything. The Wilcoxes had to be sure that she did not know what Ruth Wilcox had wished: 'her husband wrote later on, and thanked me for being a little kind to her, and actually gave me her silver vinaigrette. Don't you think that is extraordinarily generous?' We are indeed in Samuel Butler's England!

The novelist has woven it into his plot that these two fall in love and marry. To do that they must obviously go on meeting and we get the impression that Forster never worried about such details. Between the will scene and the meeting of the sisters and Mr Wilcox on the Embankment we are told two years have passed, and the chapters have been concerned with other characters, principally with creating Leonard Bast and giving him a personal relationship with the Schlegel girls. Now Mr Wilcox is brought back to say that Bast's insurance office is unsound. That starts Bast off on the way to the abyss, which was the usual Edwardian word for being out of work and penniless and therefore homeless. Wilcox, as we meet him on Chelsea Embankment, is that familiar figure, the business-man buoyant with success. Full of bonhomie. 'With a good dinner inside him and an amiable but academic woman on either flank, he felt that his hands were on all the ropes of life, and that what he did not know could not be worth knowing.' We are still in Butlerian England.

The next meeting is during a collision between Bast and the girls at their house. He arrives with his daughter and when there is a scene he offers his services. Margaret, ironically in the event, sends Helen to deal with Bast and get rid of him gently, while Wilcox instructs her: 'You must keep that type at a distance. Otherwise they forget themselves. Sad, but true. They aren't our sort, and one must face the fact.' Is Forster telling us that there must be proportion in personal relations? Is he remembering his socialist friends who went to live with agricultural labourers, (Goldie and Cox and Salt in the Life of Goldie and Henry Carpenter in *Two Cheers*) and the young men he and his friends met when they went lecturing to the workers? We are on surer ground in accepting this as true narrative of the divisions and distances between the broad range of the middle class at that time and at any time until the social upheaval of the last war.

Meanwhile, Forster still has the task of bringing Margaret and Henry Wilcox together, and he uses this scene to do it: Margaret praises Bast to him: 'He's a real man. As she spoke their eyes met, and it was as if Mr Wilcox's defences fell. She saw back to the real man in him. Unwittingly she had touched his emotions. A woman and two men—they had formed the magic triangle of sex, and the male was thrilled to jealousy, in case the female was attracted by another male.' Crude, but it does the trick, and we are able to lunch at Simpson's in the Strand and Margaret notes: 'He and she were advancing out of their respective families towards a more intimate acquaintance.'

Time is not wasted any longer and the next scene is the proposal.

The mechanics which lead us to these scenes are often crude but the scenes themselves are excellent entertainment. This proposal scene not least among the scenes of human comedy. Everything about the proposal is appropriate. They are middle-aged. He has lost a wife and it is a great compliment to her memory that he wants to marry again, and to marry someone who was her friend. We sense in him, because he is a businessman and twenty years older than Margaret, the deference to a woman he has decided he wants badly and we see nothing of his habitual arrogant sureness. He is pleading. Margaret, when her intuition tells her he is going to propose, acknowledges to herself that she is an old maid and lonely. At first she imagines that her intuition must be the wishful thinking of an old maid. Then sympathy, compassion and understanding grow in her for this older man whom she has come to respect, of whose proposal she can be proud. His abrupt manner when they meet tells her again that something is on the way. The scene then builds up. The middle-aged do not rush into these things. He may have made up his mind but he still requires reassuring signs from her. She happens to express the right ideas that morning and his emotion grows. When at last he proposes she manages to give that little start he would expect. His reactions are natural: 'You aren't offended?...I wish I had written instead...Ought I to have written?'

Before they marry we have that scene of 'telegrams and anger' down at Oniton. The discovery that Jackie Bast has been his mistress is a test of personal relations. He behaves as he should, giving her back her freedom. She, grown mature, realizes it was no concern of hers but of Ruth's, that it can be forgotten and that she loves him and will not let him go. It is here that we have Margaret's Apology for all the Wilcoxes. If they hadn't 'worked and died in England for thousands of years, you and I couldn't sit here without having our throats cut. There would be no trains, no ships to carry us literary people about in, no fields even. Just savagery.' It is the descendent of the Claphamites confessing on behalf of Bloomsbury that it takes the other sort as well to make a world.

Later, we admire the energetic man of affairs when Margaret is trying to meet her elusive sister, trying with a growing sense that something very serious is wrong. Henry produces an effective plan.

There is a good deal of humour in the care with which the trap is set, and the denouement is that scene of sympathetic tenderness between the sisters. Henry's reaction is different, and it will be as well to summarize the sequence again. He will have Helen's seducer named and brought to book. He must marry her and if he cannot he 'must be thrashed within an inch of his life'. Henry will not agree to Helen and Margaret sleeping at Howards End. They do and Leonard Bast appears and young Charles arrives to thrash him according to the code he and his father hold. Leonard Bast collapses with heart failure, a caseful of books falling on him symbolically as he falls, and Charles goes to prison for manslaughter. It leaves Henry a broken man. He had made the storm and had not the strength to withstand its fury.

It is at the first stage in this sequence that Margaret turns on him in anger, and in the white heat of emotion tells him all that the Schlegels have against the Wilcoxes. He has refused her sister's request that she may sleep at Howards End and he remains unmoved after all her appeals:

> 'Not any more of this!' she cried. 'You shall see the connexion if it kills you, Henry! You have had a mistress — I forgave you. My sister has a lover — you drive her from the house. Do you see the connexion? Stupid, hypocritical, cruel — oh, contemptible! — a man who insults his wife, when she's alive and cants with her memory when she is dead. A man who ruins a woman for his pleasure, and casts her off to ruin other men. And gives bad financial advice, and then says he is not responsible. These men are you. You can't recognize them, because you cannot connect. I've had enough of your unweeded kindness. I've spoilt you long enough. All your life you have been spoiled. Mrs Wilcox spoiled you. No one has ever told you what you are — muddled, criminally muddled. Men like you use repentance as a blind, so don't repent. Only say to yourself, "What Helen has done, I've done."'

A classical example of the quality of the feminine mind when roused and a valuable comment on the theme of 'only connect', that it involves using the brains that have been given us. It is the cry of the intelligence against the stupid and lazy mind which mars

personal relations. 'It is a flaw inherent in the business mind'
Forster says much earlier, when he is giving a fair example of
doublethink fifty years before Orwell labelled this typical English
mental condition. It was when Margaret and Henry were discussing
where they should live when they marry and it comes out that the
flat in Ducie Street which he was trying to let to her 'has huge
drawbacks. There's a mews behind.'

> Margaret could not help laughing. It was the first she had heard
> of the mews behind Ducie Street. When she was a possible
> tenant it had suppressed itself, not consciously, but auto-
> matically. The breezy Wilcox manner, though genuine, lacked
> the clearness of vision that is imperative for truth. When Henry
> lived in Ducie Street he remembered the mews; when he tried
> to let he forgot it; and if anyone had remarked that the mews
> must be either there or not, he would have felt annoyed, and
> afterwards have found some opportunity of stigmatizing the
> speaker as academic. So does my grocer stigmatize me when I
> complain of the quality of his sultanas, and he answers in
> one breath that they are the best sultanas, and how can I
> expect the best sultanas at that price? It is a flaw inherent in
> the business mind, and Margaret may do well to be tender to it,
> considering all that the business mind has done for England.

Now, at the end, his son in prison, and his wife determined to go
to Germany with her sister, Henry Wilcox confesses he is broken
and ended. 'He could bear no one but his wife, and shambled up to
Margaret [after the trial] and asked her to do what she could for him.
She did what seemed easiest—she took him down to recruit at
Howards End.' He did not completely recover. Fourteen months
later he is 'Not ill', Margaret tells Helen, but: 'Eternally tired. He
has worked very hard all his life, and noticed nothing. Those are the
people who do collapse when they notice a thing.' He has one more
duty to perform. He must formally, in the presence of his family,
make over Howards End to his wife. Ruth Wilcox willed it so and
when he had done what was necessary his creator released him to
the peace of Howards End.

> From the garden came laughter. 'Here they are at last!'
> exclaimed Henry, disengaging himself with a smile. Helen

rushed into the gloom, holding Tom by one hand and carrying her baby on the other. There were shouts of infective joy.

If Henry was the businessman imperfectly equipped mentally for personal relations (though in leaving him we may note that he chose his wives remarkably well) Tibby Schlegel by contrast had all the brains necessary but all the intellectual selfishness to cancel them out, so his sister sent him to Oxford and suggested he had better go into the Foreign Office. Unless he was created as a contrast to the Wilcoxes in imperfect manhood, it is not easy to see his function in the story. Not that the reader will dwell on that thought, for Tibby is a charming Edwardian creation in the ambience of Max Beerbohm and Saki, for which we are grateful. He is insipid as a boy and, like his creator, only comes into his own at college. He has that sharpness about his own comforts and easy irresponsibility about anyone else which is a familiar intellectual type, often drawn by Ronald Firbank. So he was sent to Oxford:

> The august and mellow University, soaked with the richness of the western counties that it had served for a thousand years, appealed at once to the boy's taste: it was the kind of thing he could understand, and he understood it all the better because it was empty. Oxford is—Oxford; not a mere receptacle for youth, like Cambridge. Perhaps it wants its inmates to love it rather than to love one another: such at all events was to be its effect on Tibby. His sisters sent him there that he might make friends, for they knew that his education had been cranky, and had severed him from other boys and men. He made no friends.

In his second year Margaret sees she ought to have a serious talk with him, as he is showing no inclination to choose a profession. She exhorts him tactfully: 'I believe that in the last century men have developed the desire for work, and they must not starve it. It's a new desire.' Tibby does not challenge this Claphamite interpretation of the Industrial Revolution and this gross libel on our excellent eighteenth century, but contents himself with: 'I have no experience of this profound desire to which you allude.' The scene continues with its accompaniment of undergraduate sighs and groans to its comic climax, with Margaret declaring:

'I want activity without civilization. How paradoxical! Yet I expect that is what we shall find in heaven.' 'And I', said Tibby, 'want civilization without activity, which, I expect, is what we shall find in the other place.' 'You needn't go as far as the other place, Tibbikins, if you want that. You can find it at Oxford.'

Collapse of ancient university, and Tibby disappears until he is approaching his final year at Oxford and his creator rehabilitates him to use him in the plot. Men had noticed that he had a character and a brain and to this young adult Helen comes, the only person she can turn to after the Oniton catastrophe, and she tells him all that happened there except of her affaire with Leonard. It is the neatest way of letting the reader know of what happened and of Helen's reactions. Tibby does what is necessary and remains in character: 'He had never been interested in human beings...and at Oxford he had learned to say that the importance of human beings has been vastly overrated by specialists.' His creator is quite relentless with him. He appears again when Henry Wilcox offers Howards End as a store for the Schlegel furniture: 'Margaret demurred, but Tibby accepted the offer gladly; it saved him from coming to any decision about the future.' He is kept in the background until he is needed to contribute to the speculations about Helen which arouse our curiosity and by that time he is 'mellowing rapidly...But he had not grown more human. The years between eighteen and twenty-two, so magical for most, were leading him gently from boyhood to middle age.'

He is useful once again. Charles Wilcox goes to see Tibby not only to find out about Helen but to see if he is capable of defending his family's honour. 'Their interview was short and absurd. They had nothing in common but the English language and tried by its help to express what neither of them understood.' But Tibby unwittingly discloses the name of Helen's seducer. It is Tibby's final appearance and his creator sums him up in a paragraph of quite notable asperity:

Tibby, on the other hand, had no opinions. He stood above the conventions: his sister had a right to do what she thought right. It is not difficult to stand above the conventions when we leave no hostages among them; men can always be more unconventional than women, and a bachelor of independent means need encounter no difficulties at all. Unlike Charles, Tibby had money enough; his ancestors had earned it for him, and if he shocked people in one set of lodgings he had only to move to another. His was the Leisure without sympathy—an attitude as fatal as the strenuous: a little cold culture may be raised on it, but no art. His sisters had seen the family danger, and had never forgotten to discount the gold islets that raised them from the sea. Tibby gave all the praise to himself, and so despised the struggling and the submerged.

It is that interest in the struggling and the submerged which is so typical of Forster and his Cambridge friends. It is an interesting chapter in the story of the middle class sense of guilt about the poor which accumulated for a hundred years before it crystallized into the Welfare State. Among the great range of references in the Edwardian decade, Galsworthy's play, *The Silver Box*, is the most apposite for it parallels *Howards End* in ascribing the same weakness to a rich character and a poor one and shows how differently they are treated and how differently they feel inside themselves about their weakness. Henry Wilcox had dishonoured Leonard Bast in the same way as Leonard had dishonoured him but by doublethink Henry was not even conscious of his fault.

There was one subject on which they were all agreed. Money was good, but it was this strong belief which made the gulf between the classes, for there was no power to make those who had it share. One of the best brief Edwardian statements on that question is Richard Whiteing's 1902 Preface to his slum novel *No. 5 John Street*:

Why was the one side so reckless and so defiant, the other so futile? The question of classes, therefore, pushed the one of mere persons entirely out of the way, and the figures that came before me in place of my primal pair were the poor man and the rich, as representing the whole social state to which it has pleased God to call us.

It was impossible to avoid certain conclusions—call them a moral, if you will. One of them was that, as a regenerative scheme, the pursuit of wealth for its own sake is a dismal failure. It makes far more ills than it cures. The poor, who alas! believe in it as much as their betters, are relatively as spiritually dejected as ever they were.

He continues with that intense moral questioning which is so familiar to anyone who has lived through the earlier decades of the century:

> it seemed to be a pity that wealth had so effectually slipped from the yoke of morals. The accumulation of it is now a business into which no questions of right and wrong are suffered to enter, other than those of the purely elementary order that concern the magistrate and the policeman. You win your money as you can, you spend it as you like, and the questions of how you spend and how you win are kept outside the domain of public and even of private account. You underpay, and thus indirectly underclothe and underfeed for long years; and one glorious day, if you are a very good man, you endow a technical institute. So I thought, and think, that the great thing is to bring the proud wilfulness of the money-maker under the curb of higher laws. What he seems to need in his singular pastime is a new spirit—perhaps, though one does not like to use such far-reaching expressions, a sort of new religion. One is on safer ground in saying that the most ravenous appetite of our nature needs a more austere control.

The decade echoes with such statements. The sense of class guilt produces here in *Howards End* the most baffling character in the book, Leonard Bast. Where Forster could have found such a character we can only speculate. He is designed as a George Gissing character and his function is to disturb the social conscience of the other characters and the reader. His chief interest is that his creator should have created him, a clerk according to a King's man. Frank Swinnerton, who knows about Edwardian clerks, has some pungent things to say about Leonard Bast in his *Georgian Literary Scene* and we are usually aware until the final scene that he is a made character, outside his creator's direct experience, but also too much within his sense of social responsibility. He is placed at the centre of the story and powerfully affects all their middle class lives, wrecking their security and so emphasizing the function of Howards End in restoring a sense of peace. He is in contrast to the Schlegels in seeking a false and useless intellectualism and to the Wilcoxes in being poor and proudly honest in an area in which doublethink has led them to wealth. He is typically sensitive about his poverty and pretends to himself and others until the crisis in his affairs when at last he says to Helen that money matters more than anything else and yet proudly rejects the competence she later offers him.

He represents the town as against the country dweller, the type we hear about first in Forster through Stephen Wonham's eyes: 'The London intellect, so pert and shallow, like a stream that never reaches the ocean, disgusted him almost as much as the London physique, which for all its dexterity is not permanent, and seldom continues into the third generation.' He is a type as dead as the dodo, largely thanks to the preoccupation with it of all these good Edwardians who played their part in founding the Welfare State.

Set in *Howards End*, Leonard Bast, like Gino before him and Dr Aziz after him, is the singular character at the centre of the tale, different from the others, rather unknown to them and therefore unpredictable. It is a mystery that their creator should have fashioned them so convincingly for he could not have known any of them intimately. We can only say that it is the story-teller's business to convince and after all most readers know less about Edwardian clerks, provincial Italians and Muslim doctors than the writer who gave us them. That may sound ungrateful, so we must note that more energy went to the creating of these characters than to those whom we can easily recognize. And certainly his creator's feelings about the poor young man were sincere. 'He was not in the abyss, but he could see it, and at times people whom he knew had dropped in, and counted no more.' He is regarded with great sympathy: 'The boy, Leonard Bast, stood at the extreme verge of gentility...He knew that he was poor, and would admit it: he would have died sooner than confess any inferiority to the rich... But he was inferior to most rich people...He was not as courteous as the average rich man, nor as intelligent, nor as healthy, nor as lovable. His mind and his body had alike been underfed, because he was poor, and because he was modern they were always craving better food.'

A good deal of time is given to showing us this craving for mental food and expectable digs are made at popular names, Stevenson, Jefferies. One interesting passage reminds us of the progress of the English social conscience. We learn that Leonard 'was trying to form his style on Ruskin: he understood him to be the greatest Master of English Prose.' Then the Edwardian tells us how much further Edwardians had got than Victorians in this social work:

And the voice in the gondola rolled on, piping melodiously of Effort and Self-Sacrifice, full of high purpose, full of beauty, full even of sympathy and the love of men, yet somehow eluding all that was actual and insistent in Leonard's life. For it was the voice of one who had never been dirty or hungry, and had not guessed successfully what dirt and hunger are.

Ruskin gave Leonard the feeling 'that he was being done good to' and that 'he would one day push his head out of the waters and see the universe'. The creative effort put into Leonard Bast ranges widely. We are taken into his flat, where this conversation hints at the sub-cultural level of their daily lives:

'I met Mr Cunningham outside, and we passed a few remarks.'
'What, not Mr Cunningham?'
'Yes.'
'Oh, you mean Mr Cunningham.'
'Yes, Mr Cunningham.'

P. G. Wodehouse himself, that great Edwardian, could hardly have used the same words more often to say the same thing and he certainly would not have blighted them with the sickening emptiness that Forster contrives to throw over them. Later, with the Schlegel girls, Leonard has a moment of sincerity which recalls the undergraduate sincerity of Forster himself with Goldie which began their friendship:

'But was the dawn wonderful?' asked Helen.
With unforgettable sincerity he replied 'No'. The word flew again like the pebble from the sling. Down toppled all that had

seemed noble or literary in his talk, down toppled tiresome Stevenson and the 'Love of the earth' and his silk top-hat. In the presence of these women Leonard had arrived.

He is given quite early a well-wrought Edwardian sentimental chapter ending:

> It remained...as a hint that all is not for the best in the best of all possible worlds, and that beneath these superstructures of wealth and art there wanders an ill-fed boy, who has recovered his umbrella indeed, but has left no address behind him, and no name.

Leonard was then nineteen and in a very few years and three hundred pages he is to get Helen with child and die of heart failure. It sounds like melodrama but it does not strike us so. Perhaps it should, for these actions, like so many in Forster's novels, are not very probable. The contrivances the author uses to bring the Schlegel girls and Bast together will not bear much scrutiny. But they do not worry the reader unduly. The possible errors are in detail and leave the general effect true and powerful, so that we know we should be much poorer in our understanding of our Edwardian origins without Leonard Bast. We have no better study of the thirst for cultivated ideas and the eagerness to copy accepted social conduct. It was without material acquisitiveness and the only snobbery in it was inverted. It is easy for us to forget that the only glimpses of comfortable and cultivated lives available to the Basts were books and the stage, where like as not they only heard the exaggerated language of melodrama. Margaret must have forgotten that when she was embarrassed at the Queen's Hall by his exaggerated courtesies. We are long before the cinema and radio and television. The struggle was obvious to these Cambridge men and we see here, as in some of the plays of Galsworthy, how painful it was to the intelligent upper middle classes to see it.

In the 41st chapter Leonard Bast is transformed. He is no longer a clerk, a specimen of a species, he is no longer manipulated by Helen or Jackie. He is a man tortured by Remorse and the picture of mental anguish is developed until we see him driven to action by what is going on in his own mind, action of which he is almost unaware, so concentrated is his mental suffering. In his last hours, his anguish is presented by wild nightmares and a vestigial stream of consciousness technique which we may note predates all the work of Dorothy Richardson and the others with whom the technique is associated. This is a new development in Forster's novels, much beyond anything in *The Longest Journey* and preparing us for the most intense moments in *A Passage*. This is elemental suffering, true and intense. It is the climax of the novel, as powerful as the panic and emptiness Helen hears so often. Leonard Bast is released from Remorse in the only possible way. He dies and he dies easily. It was a generous gesture by his creator, and it is a prim thought that his death was also a contrivance for the fulfilment of Ruth Wilcox's wishes for Howards End.

This complicated novel gives the impression, like *The Longest Journey* and *A Passage to India* of being composed at a white heat in which action and interaction echo and rebound. It will be interesting to look at the public themes it introduces, and first the England which Forster shows us in the first halcyon decade of the century. Howards End we have seen. It was Ruth Wilcox's only dowry and it was saved for her by her practical husband who paid off the mortgages and put the house and grounds in order: 'without fine feelings or deep insight, but he had saved it.' It might be the story of many a Hertfordshire house after neglect during the last war. He 'pulled down the outhouses; drained, thinned out I don't know how many guelder roses and elder-trees, and inside the house I turned the old kitchen into a hall, and made the kitchen behind where the dairy was. Garage and so on came later. But one could still see it's been an old farm.' Blackberries as well as guelder roses and elders are still the invaders as soon as a Hertfordshire garden is neglected. The wych-elm beside the house was an equal influence and we see it best through Margaret's eyes: 'No report had prepared her for its peculiar glory. It was neither warrior, nor lover, nor god; in none of these roles do the English excel. It was a comrade, bending over the house, strength and adventure in its roots, but in its utmost fingers, tenderness...It was a comrade.' There is a photograph of the house in 1885 but not the elm, in *Marianne Thornton*, with

Forster, a very young equestrian, in the foreground. The wych-elm has now gone.

Margaret sees with Forster's eyes, and through her eyes we can go on: 'She recaptured the sense of space, which is the basis of all earthly beauty and, starting from Howards End, she attempted to realize England...an unexpected love of the island awoke in her, connecting on this side with the joys of the flesh, on that with the inconceivable.' That is the story of so much English poetry and as we read the little background descriptions against which his characters move and think and feel, we see prose celebrating what verse had celebrated often before. In the story we get about by train and motor car and the car is sufficiently new to offer comic possibilities: ' "This is very good of you", said Mrs Munt, as she settled herself into a luxurious cavern of red leather, and suffered her person to be padded with rugs and shawls...Young Wilcox was pouring in petrol, starting his engine...The great car began to rock, and the form of Mrs Munt, trying to explain things, sprang agreeably up and down among the red cushions.' Later, we have a motor accident, when a car ran over a cat and Margaret, when her cries to stop and investigate were ignored, 'jumped straight out of the car. She fell on her knees, cut her gloves, shook her hat over her ear.' Cars go faster now. Her general reaction to motoring is no different from ours, for the great speed of motor travel made her feel that 'their whole journey from London had been unreal. They had no part of the earth and its emotions. They were dust, and a stink, and cosmopolitan chatter.' Which suggests that perhaps the best historical novels are those which were written of contemporary life and have remained vividly alive.

The most sustained celebration of England is offered as opening to chapter 19. The Edwardian novelist had no fear of rhetoric, it was expected of him and, when it comes off, the reward is great:

Seen from the west, the Wight is beautiful beyond all laws of beauty. It is as if a fragment of England floated forward to greet the foreigner—chalk of our chalk, turf of our turf, epitome of what will follow. And behind the fragment lies Southampton, hostess to the nations, and Portsmouth, a latent fire; and all around it, with double and treble collision of tides, swirls the sea. How many villages appear in this view? How many castles! How many churches, vanished or triumphant! How many ships, railways, and roads! What incredible variety of men working beneath that lucent sky to what final end! The reason fails, like a wave on the Swanage beach; the imagination swells, spreads, and deepens, until it becomes geographic and encircles England.

Even here, we do not escape thoughts of the city: 'Bournemouth's ignoble coast cowers to the right, heralding the pine-trees that mean, for all their beauty, red houses and the Stock Exchange, and extend to the gates of London itself.' Later, the essential country life. Margaret is standing in a room at Howards End which 'conveyed the peculiar sadness of a rural interior. Here had lived an elder race, to which we look back with disquietude. The country which we visit at weekends was really a home to it, and the graver sides of life, the deaths, the partings, the yearnings for love, have their deepest expression in the heart of the fields.' That still goes. The Englishman has never learned to build cities or to live in them. His heart remains in the country and he still feels as Margaret felt at Howards End: 'The peace of the country was entering into her. It has no commerce with memory, and little with hope. Least of all is it concerned with the hopes of the next five minutes. It is the peace of the present, which passes understanding.'

Howards End stands for understanding and peace. The contrast is London, with its 'sense of flux. London was but a foretaste of this nomadic civilization which is altering human nature so profoundly, and thrown upon personal relations a stress greater than they have ever borne before. Under cosmopolitanism, if it comes, we shall receive no help from the earth. Trees and meadows and mountains will only be a spectacle, and the binding force that they once exercised on character must be entrusted to Love alone.' It might have been a sermon for our aeroplane age. But it was part of that criticism of London we first heard in *The Longest Journey* from Stephen Wonham. We hear the same complaint in Howards End. We are looking through Schlegel eyes at Leonard Bast:

...a young man, colourless, toneless, who had already the

mournful eyes above a drooping moustache that are so common in London...One guessed him as the third generation, grandson to the shepherd or ploughboy whom civilization had sucked into the town; as one of the thousands who have lost the life of the body and failed to reach the life of the spirit... Margaret, noting the spine that might have been straight, and the chest that might have broadened, wondered whether it paid to give up the glory of the animal for a tail coat and a couple of ideas.

We are sometimes invited to enjoy London. We enjoy the concert in the Queen's Hall and are diverted by an early script for a Walt Disney fantasy film as commentary on Beethoven's Fifth. We lunch at Simpson's in the Strand, 'where saddles of mutton were being trundled up to expectant clergymen'. And once we drive through London, as George Moore did a little earlier in the opening of *Memoirs of my Dead Life*. Here, we are looking again through Margaret's eyes, fresh from the country, welcoming the familiar:

Hallo, Parliament's back!
Mr Wilcox glanced at Parliament contemptuously. The more important ropes of life lay elsewhere. 'Yes, they are talking again,' said he.

and we are reminded once again that things do not change and our criticisms were our grandfathers' criticisms.

But it is the countryman's view of London we are offered mostly: 'London thwarted her; in its atmosphere she could not concentrate. London only stimulates, it cannot sustain.' 'London came back with a rush...all whom he passed looked at him with hostility that was the more impressive because it was unconscious.' Impossible to greet them, as we do one another on a country road, there are so many, all wearing that glazed expression like a plastic mask over the face. 'Certainly London fascinates. One visualizes it as a tract of quivering grey, intelligent without purpose and excitable without love...It lies beyond everything: Nature with all her cruelty, comes nearer to us than do these crowds of men.' This is the London of Wells, and Bennett, of Shaw and Galsworthy, of Conrad and Somerset Maugham, but this young novelist sees it as 'the architecture of hurry...the language of hurry on the mouths of its inhabitants—clipped words, formless sentences, potted expressions of approval or disgust...The population still rose, but what was the quality of the men born?'

It is worth looking at one of Wells' notes on London, from *The New Machiavelli*, published in the year after *Howards End*:

> I realized that building was the enemy...The serene rhythms of the old-established agriculture...were everywhere being replaced by cultivation under notice...I suppose one might have persuaded oneself that all this was but the replacement of an ancient tranquillity...it was manifestly no order at all. It was a multitude of unco-ordinated fresh starts.'

The echo to that passage in *Howards End* will be:

> bricks and mortar rising and falling with the restlessness of the water in a fountain, as the city receives more and more men upon her soil...And again a few years, and all the flats in either road might be pulled down, and new buildings of a vast-ness at present unimaginable, might arise where they had fallen.

As indeed they are doing today as Wren's dream of London, a sea of rooftops with great spires rising among them in controlled formation, becomes truer than ever before. But for the novelist's purpose, London is flux, 'as humanity piled itself higher and higher on the precious soil'. 'I hate the continual flux of London', Margaret says. 'It is an epitome of us at our worst—eternal form-lessness; all the qualities, good, bad, and indifferent, streaming away—streaming, streaming for ever.' And much later, when she is married but has no permanent home, she feels acutely that: 'Marriage had not saved her from the sense of flux. London was but a foretaste of this nomadic civilization which is altering human nature so profoundly.'

The repeated solution in the novel to the recurring townee problem is proportion. Forster is Greek in that and Roman in his championship of the country life. Expectably, he cries out for a pure English mythology. 'Why has not England a great mythology? Our folklore has never advanced beyond daintiness, and the greater melodies about our country-side have all issued from the pipes of

Greece. Deep and true as the native imagination can be, it seems to have failed here. It has stopped with the witches and the fairies.' The clue to the eternal restlessness in the island may be here. Mythology and religion have been imported and a country which cannot produce its own may be in flux forever. Forster's admired Samuel Butler had indulged in a little wishful thinking along these lines in *Erewhon*, nearly forty years before: 'I cannot help thinking that the Erewhonians are on the eve of some great changes in their religious opinions.'

In a society in flux, personal relations are as difficult as they are necessary and the essence of them, Forster would seem to say, is proportion. The idea comes first in talk between Mrs Wilcox and Margaret, comes again when Mrs Wilcox's bearing in her last illness is described, and finally is used by Helen when Margaret tells her she is going to marry Mr Wilcox. We see proportion as a property of the intense activity of living. First, as Margaret offers her own apology for living to Mrs Wilcox: 'To be humble and kind, to go straight ahead, to love people rather than pity them, to remember the submerged—well, one can't do all these things at once, worse luck, because they are so contradictory. It's then that proportion comes in—to live by proportion.' And when Margaret has done, Mrs Wilcox gives her blessing to the younger woman's ideas: 'Indeed, you put the difficulties of life splendidly...it is just what I should have liked to say about them myself.' We learn later that Mrs Wilcox knew then that she was dying and her conduct of her last days is spoken of thus: 'Some leave our life with tears, others with an insane frigidity; Mrs Wilcox had taken the middle course, which only rarer natures can pursue. She had kept proportion.' Much later, it is a great blow to Helen to learn that her Margaret will marry Mr Wilcox. But she quickly recovers and, being Helen, sees it as a challenge which Margaret will meet successfully: 'You mean to keep proportion, and that's heroic, it's Greek, and I don't see why it shouldn't succeed with you. Go on and fight with him and help him.'

Helen perceives what Margaret had already determined. Henry Wilcox outwardly 'was cheerful, reliable, and brave; but within, all had reverted to chaos, ruled, as far as it was ruled at all, by an incomplete asceticism...he had always the sneaking belief that bodily passion is bad, a belief that is desirable only when held passionately...he could be a little ashamed of loving a wife.' Margaret read him clearly and she sees that to help him reach balance and proportion she must teach him to 'connect the prose and the passion...Live in fragments no longer. Only connect, and the beast and the monk, robbed of the isolation that is life in cities, will die.'

A little later, we are told about the conditions in which this connexion will most easily be made. It will be in the country, in a house like Howards End. It will be man in connexion with nature, an idea implicit in all Thackeray's descriptions of villages and great houses in the English countryside, implicit in the later letters in *Humphry Clinker,* when the exiled Smollett expresses what he felt when he went round the island for a last view of it, implicit in so much of European writing for two thousand years, as when Cicero, tired of Rome, speaks of the country life: 'nothing better, nothing more attractive, nothing more suitable for a free man.' It is the classical view of the human dilemma and it is contained within man's social condition. It may be useful to compare it for a moment with the greater dilemma in the natural world which the scientists have identified, which has been in the air in Cambridge all through Forster's working life and which he faces in his last novel. There, the panic and emptiness comes from the disintegration of all human values in those Jain caves, a confrontation with the natural world where there are no values but only a fight for life at the price, whenever necessary, of anything else there is.

Forster's Edwardian world was still the classical world and it is his reaction at that time to London life which Margaret expresses: 'The sense of flux which had haunted her all the year disappeared for a time. She forgot the luggage and the motor-cars, the hurrying men who know so much and connect so little. She recaptured the sense of space, which is the basis of all earthly beauty and, starting from Howards End, she attempted to realize England.' It has been quoted before but now we can go on: '...an unexpected love of the island awoke in her, connecting on this side with the joys of the flesh, on that with the inconceivable. Helen and her father had known this love, poor Leonard Bast was groping after it, but it had been hidden from Margaret until this afternoon. It had certainly come through the house.' The dilemma was within the compass of man and his works. Then, we are told, Margaret's mind 'dwelt on ruddy bricks, flowering plum-trees, and all the tangible joys of spring'.

Later, when she was down at Howards End, her thoughts are echoed. It is in the passage which begins by saying that the graver sides of life 'have their deepest expression in the heart of the fields'. Then she goes on to give a universal connotation to the theme 'only connect'.

> All was not sadness. The sun was shining without. The thrush sang his two syllables on the budding guelder-rose. Some children were playing uproariously in heaps of golden straw. It was the presence of sadness at all that surprised Margaret and ended by giving her a feeling of completeness. In these English farms, if anywhere, one might see life steadily and see it whole, group in one vision its transitoriness and its eternal youth, connect — connect without bitterness until all men are brothers.

This is the twentieth century echoing and answering the nineteenth. There are two subjects relevant to the main theme in which the Edwardian speaks more openly than his fathers usually dared. Right at the beginning we hear of 'panic and emptiness' as they listen to Beethoven's Fifth. The modern listener may find it difficult to detect these things in our contemporary interpretations of that robust work, but the important thing is that one of the characters can feel them to be there. Panic and emptiness must be felt at times by anyone who thinks at all and especially by anyone who is unable to absorb religious conviction of personal immortality. The music suggested at one point to Helen 'that there was no such thing as splendour or heroism in the world'. Once, at any rate, she 'had seen the reliable walls of youth collapse'. The passage is repeated: 'It was as if the splendour of life might boil over and waste to stream and froth...Panic and emptiness! Panic and emptiness! Even the flaming ramparts of the world might fall.' A creation without values, realized here (it is enough) in terms of the human condition. Helen had already noted panic and emptiness in the Wilcox men. It was on that difficult morning after she and Paul had absurdly plighted themselves: 'I felt for a moment that the whole Wilcox family was a fraud, just a wall of newspapers and motor-cars and golf clubs, and that if it fell I should find nothing behind but panic and emptiness.' Again the phrase is applied to the Wilcoxes, this time on the morning after their mother's funeral: 'they avoided the personal note in life. All Wilcoxes did. It did not seem to them of supreme importance. Or it may have been as Helen supposed: they realized its importance, but were afraid of it. Panic and emptiness, could one glance behind.' We hear the phrase once again, and from Helen, in the first extravagance of her reaction to the news that Margaret intends to marry Henry Wilcox. ' "Don't, don't do such a thing! I tell you not to— don't! I know—don't!" "What do you know?" "Panic and emptiness", sobbed Helen.'

It is obviously a disease of the mind to which the Wilcoxes of this life are prone. But they have a remedy. They avoid thinking and one of the things which helps them in the resolute pursuit of non-thinking is money. The Victorians were reticent about money. The Edwardians quite often openly extolled it, in contrast to the mood we noted in Richard Whiteing, when it worried them. A few years before *Howards End*, in 1905, Bernard Shaw wrote in a preface to *The Irrational Knot*:

> It is the secret of all our governing classes, which consist finally in people who, though perfectly prepared to be generous, humane, cultured, philanthropic, public spirited and personally charming in the second instance, are unalterably resolved, in the first, to have enough money for a handsome and delicate life, and will, in pursuit of that money, batter in the doors of their fellow-men, sell them up, sweat them in fetid dens, shoot, stab, hang, imprison, sink, burn and destroy them in the name of law and order. And this shows their fundamental sanity and rightmindedness; for a sufficient income is indispensable to the practice of virtue.

Forster, descendent of bankers, puts it thus:

> 'Money pads the edge of things', said Miss Schlegel. 'God help those who have none.'

'But this is something quite new!' said Mrs Munt, who collected new ideas as a squirrel collects nuts, and was especially attracted by those that are portable.

'New for me; sensible people have acknowledged it for years. You and I and the Wilcoxes stand upon money as upon islands. It is so firm beneath our feet that we forget its very existence. It's only when we see someone near us tottering that we realize all that an independent income means. Last night, when we were talking up here round the fire, I began to think that the very soul of the world is economic, and that the lowest abyss is not the absence of love, but the absence of coin.'

The great argument for money returns in the debating club to which the Schlegel girls belong, when they are discussing how best to give money to men like Leonard Bast:

'Money's educational. It's far more educational than the things it buys.' There was a protest. 'In a sense', added Margaret, but the protest continued. 'Well, isn't the most civilized thing going, the man who has learned to wear his income properly?'

The meeting protests, but Margaret goes on, quite naturally, considering her author, to suggest the economic policies we learned to associate, twenty years later, with Maynard Keynes. 'When your Socialism comes it may be different, and we may think in terms of commodities instead of cash. Till it comes, give the people cash, for it is the warp of civilization, whatever the woof may be. The imagination ought to play upon money and realize it, for it's the— the second most important thing in the world.'

Money is discussed once again, in the unbelievable context of the evening Helen and Leonard spent in the Shropshire hotel. Belief in money is now expressed by Leonard, the lowest of the middle classes. He renounces his precious books and the spirit of adventure which attracted Helen to him.

'My books are back, thanks to you, but they'll never be the same to me again, and I shan't ever again think night in the woods is wonderful.'

'Why not?' asked Helen, throwing up the window.

'Because I see one must have money.'

'Well, you're wrong.'

'I wish I was wrong, but—the clergyman—he has money of his own, or else he's paid; the poet or the musician—just the same; the tramp—he's no different. The tramp goes to the workhouse in the end, and is paid for with other people's money. Miss Schlegel, the real thing's money, and all the rest is a dream.'

Helen takes the other part and tells him he has forgotten death. He does not understand, so she explains:

'If we lived for ever, what you say would be true. But we have to die, we have to leave life presently. Injustice and greed would be the real thing if we lived for ever. As it is, we must hold to other things, because Death is coming. I love Death—not morbidly, but because He explains. He shows me the emptiness of money. Death and money are the eternal foes. Not Death and Life. Never mind what lies behind Death, Mr Bast, but be sure that the poet and the musician and the tramp will be happier in it than the man who has never learned to say "I am I".'

It is the argument of the Gospels but there is much to be said for England now on the other side. It is best to remember proportion, although, as Margaret says, to fortify us in exploring both sides: 'truth, being alive, is not halfway between anything. It was only to be found by continuous excursions into either realm, and though proportion is the final secret, to espouse it at the outset is to ensure sterility.'

The philosophical comments in the novel contrast with those in *The Longest Journey* where they come as undergraduate questioning, asking the right questions but not yet being sure of the answers. Here, the comment is mature, the natural observations of the creator on his world. And his world appears to be created to give him a chance of saying what he wants to say about the Edwardian world. It is true that the Edwardian reader expected it of his authors, just as he expected rhetoric and literary references. It is equally true that the novelist loved to provide them and it is an obvious argument that the novelist created the taste. The Victorians were not the only writers lost to the pulpit. Forster here, as in his earlier English novel, sufflaminates like any evangelist and this is natural, for we are all, writers among us, carefree in other people's countries but responsible and moral in our own.

So there is not only the cause and effect which make the plot but a dazzle of comment all along the way as opportunity for a paragraph sermon offers. The story is controlled by Howards End and its owner, Ruth Wilcox, and when she dies it is carried on through her spiritual heir, Margaret Schlegel and the old countrywoman, Miss Avery, who looks after the house. Miss Avery is apparently senile but she makes the house habitable and ready for when it will be suddenly needed and her comments, like flickers of insight, give us the feeling that some influence instructed her what was going to happen and what had to be done. The characters who are managed by Ruth Wilcox are her own family and the Schlegels and, at the end, Leonard Bast, when he comes to Howards End and under her influence, we may say, is released from the burden of living. It is a story of natural contrast to the point of opposition between a business family and an intellectual one, whose intellectual integrity the author assures in an Edwardian convention by giving them a German father. There is a reference to the other view on Germany, the economic rival with whom war was possible but surely unthinkable, but the accent, if any, is on the intellectual cultivated German, who was probably the kind Forster met when he lived with Elizabeth in her German garden.

Howards End has been called Forster's masterpiece and if he had not written *A Passage* it would have been. For in *Howards End* he is attempting more and achieving more than in the earlier novels. As in *The Longest Journey* we have the impression that he is testing himself, setting himself a standard which he must reach to satisfy himself, a standard of what a novel by him must achieve. He must have characters and they must be shown reacting to situations and for that there must be a plot. In *Howards End* the characters were seeking a working solution to the problems of personal relations in this island at the beginning of the century. In that context it is natural that the character and quality of a house should come into it, for stability and security were still possible and only city dwellers were social nomads. It was equally natural that the problem of class

6

and the economic ambience of poverty and wealth should come in, for the Edwardians sensed these things were to be revolutionized. But the light and grace of the novel is the relationship between the sisters and the sweet influence of a woman who had died. These are the essence of the pleasure.

Two years later he went to India with Goldie and Trevelyan and there he found a plan for a novel on the questions which had interested him most in *Howards End*, personal relationships and the dominating influence of someone dead. The war interrupted him and he was sent to Alexandria where he enjoyed the Mediterranean harmony and became absorbed in studying how Alexandrians had processed the Christian religion to make it palatable for Europeans. So when he came back to his Indian novel, with essential new material from a most fortunate second visit to India, he was able to develop another *Howards End* theme much more powerfully, the theme of panic and emptiness. So the theme of the Indian novel became the search for the Friend and the possibility of the rescue of the individual spirit from cosmic panic and emptiness.

If he had written another novel presumably it would have been about his own society. The war had revolutionized it. Bernard Shaw, in one of his tributes to the society in which he found himself, had pointed out that the war was at any rate partly about economics and for many of the victors victory meant being penniless and unemployed. The Edwardian sense of guilt and the Edwardian dream of social betterment had turned for a time into horror and chaos. Then in Europe chaos coagulated into totalitarian horror and Forster's energies were exerted to defend freedom of thought and speech. He had no thought but to be involved in the fight to preserve these things. In this flux the calm of mind for great creative-critical achievement was impossible. So *Howards End* remains as Forster's last creative comment on English society. Ruth and Margaret and Helen are still very much alive and in essence their problems are our problems and those of every generation. The novel is part of the evolving social conscience of the English people.

A Passage to India

THIRTY YEARS after he published *A Passage to India*, Forster spoke about it to India. He says it came into being because he had the great good luck to make a Muslim and a Hindu friend. The Muslim was Sir Syed Ross Masood, known all over India in later days as Chancellor of the Muslim University of Aligarth. The Hindu was the Maharajah of Dewas Senior, the subject of *The Hill of Devi*. The Muslim could trace his ancestry to the Prophet, the Hindu less certainly to the sun. For each of them Forster had the rich affection which is common between English and Indians, and because these friendships seemed under threat and because they were so rich that he wanted them to continue, he wrote the novel.

The novel has its prophetic theme, the modern theme, of friendship between people of different races, more urgent now that nations can destroy one another more resolutely. It is a secular theme in India, the Hindu preoccupation with friendship and the Muslim search for the Friend, for they are both male societies. The novel has an even deeper theme, a probing for truth which continues the Alexandrian studies a few years earlier. 'I can assure you that my book was trying to be creative', he says in that talk, 'that it was aiming at something even deeper than India' and he reminds his hearers that after the book was finished he found the title in a poem by Walt Whitman. He quotes it:

Passage to more than India!
Are thy winds plumed indeed for such far flights?
O soul, voyagest thou indeed on voyages like those?
Disportest thou on waters such as those?
Soundest below the Sanscrit and the Vedas?
Then have thy bent unleashed.

The end of the quotation comes aptly as we remember the stormy
spiritual voyaging of Mrs Moore:

O my brave soul!
O farther, farther sail!
O darling joy but safe! are they not all the seas of God,
O farther, farther, farther sail...

Not like one of Professor Godbole's songs, but effective in our
cruder western ears, and in Forster's words: 'India becomes what
indeed she has often been—a symbol of the universe.'

The plot, with its two great themes, friendship and truth,
requires the novelist to give himself an organism on the grand scale
to manage. He takes the vast Gangetic plain and all the generations
of men, Hindu and Muslim, who have lived there, for background.
We feel their presence throughout the book. And against that
impressive background he sets his little scenes and manipulates his
characters. He had discovered a gift for describing nature on the
grand scale in *Alexandria* and he uses it with magnificent effect
here. The actual opening is quiet, a description of the little town of
Chandrapore on the banks of the Ganges downstream from Patna.
At the end, the pitch rises in the description of the sky, and the tone
of this imaginative enterprise is set:

The sky settles everything—not only climates and seasons, but
when the earth shall be beautiful. By herself she can do little—
only feeble outbursts of flowers. But when the sky chooses,
glory can rain into the Chandrapore bazaars or a benediction
pass from horizon to horizon. The sky can do this because it is
so strong and so enormous. Strength comes from the sun,
infused in it daily, size from the prostrate earth.

Then the characters begin to come in and first the Muslims.
These enchanting young men, so familiar to anyone who has lived

anywhere near the great Moghul centres, Delhi and Agra and all their collaterals from Lucknow eastwards, are discussing the possibility of friendship with English people. Hamidullah (who must be very like Forster's friend Syed Ross Masood, very intelligent, compact of courtesy and understanding, poised and full of commonsense) contends that it is possible in England but not in India. In general they agree that it was only the exceptional English person who could be friendly and kind. ('We have not met an Englishman like you previously', said the Indore preacher to Forster, a phrase we often heard, for so few had met any Englishmen at all.) 'Aziz did not know, but said he did. He too generalized from his disappointments—it is difficult for members of a subject race to do otherwise.'

Aziz is central to the story, like Gino in the first novel. He is a poet and by profession a surgeon. We go with him to the Civil Surgeon's bungalow where he is snubbed by two Englishwomen. It is the first rude glimpse of the conflict which makes the story. He walks home and on the way he turns into a mosque to seek peace. We recall what Forster has written about mosques, the Great Mosque at Delhi and the Mosque of Amr in Cairo where the friends of the Prophet have left the impress of their spiritual quietness for ever. The mosque into which Aziz now turns is a little one, of the kind that can be seen at the end of any lane in the democracy of Islam. Mrs Moore is there and they meet and are immediately attracted to one another, the old English lady, who has fled from the English club to the peace of the mosque and the young Muslim. They are immediately in sympathy and he makes a gesture which we shall see again. Is there anything he can show this visitor to his country? He suggests the hospital but she has already seen over it. So all he can do is to escort her back to the club, where we meet the other visiting Englishwoman, Adela Quested.

Adela has come out to marry Mrs Moore's son, if she decides she can live in India. The novel is about the contact these two ladies make with the resident English, the Muslims and Hindus. The great themes, Friendship and Universal Love, are developed through what happens to these two women and the people whose lives are affected by meeting them. The two ladies are middle class Edwardians,

untouched by the suburbanism of Sawston, representing the grace
of age in Mrs Moore and intellectual emancipation in Adela
Quested. They resemble Ruth Wilcox and the Schlegel girls.
Sawston and suburbanism is found in the little English community,
friendship is found among the Muslims and Universal Love is
found in the one Hindu of any consequence in the book, the old
Brahmin teacher, Professor Godbole.

The theme of friendship, the Muslim theme, was introduced in
the mosque. The theme of universal love is introduced at the very
end of the next chapter. There is no apparent reason for recording
that Mrs Moore noticed a wasp asleep on the peg: 'Going to hang
up her cloak she found the tip of the peg was occupied by a small
wasp..."Pretty dear", said Mrs Moore to the wasp. He did not
wake, but her voice floated out, to swell the night's uneasiness.'
These two brief paragraphs and the long concluding paragraph of
the next chapter could well have been tacked on when Forster was
working on the Third Part of his novel and Professor Godbole by
the power of universal love projects the spirit of Mrs Moore into
the One. For the last paragraph of the next brief chapter is just as
apparently an extra as the wasp on the peg. A young Christian
missionary, Mr Sorley—who never appears again—is discussing
the divine hospitality: 'he saw no reason why monkeys should not
have their collateral share of bliss.' The writing is ironic: 'And the
jackals? Jackals were indeed less to Mr Sorley's mind, but he
admitted that the mercy of God, being infinite, may well embrace
all mammals.' Then we come to the echo: 'And the wasps? He
became uneasy during the descent to wasps, and was apt to change
the conversation.' Two years later in time and away across the great
Indian plain we shall see Professor Godbole in his annual religious
festival realizing universal love and the images that come to his
mind are the wasp and Mrs Moore and universal love embraces
them both. It is the climax of the meditations Forster began in
Alexandria on the great religions of the Middle East and India.

Mrs Moore's encounter with the wasp is the last of a series of
echoes in a chapter which is the counterpart of the previous chapter
in which Muslims discussed the possibility of friendship with
English people. The English view is put mostly by the young

magistrate, Ronny Heaslop, Mrs Moore's son by her first marriage. It was the case for magisterial aloofness, the argument that advantage was taken if friendly overtures were made. The other view, of natural friendship between professional people of different race, is hardly put at all. The normal condition was that they helped one another to bring India towards the modern world and were friends. Here, it is only a passing remark by the head of the local school: ' "Fielding! How's one to see the real India?" "Try seeing Indians".' It is because the visiting ladies do so that all the turmoil in the book begins and when it is over Fielding notes that the trouble with the young woman was that she wanted to see India but not Indians.

The collector, Mr Turton, goes to great lengths to help the ladies. He will arrange a Bridge Party, a party which will be a bridge between the peoples. The Indian community accepts, led by the Nawab Bahadur, but the party was not a success. Adela met Indian ladies but 'she strove in vain against the echoing walls of their civility'. Despite the difficulties, the two ladies do well and Fielding, the schoolmaster, applauds them. He, rather than the magistrates, is made the guardian of the little society. It is he who does most to make a bridge and after the party he invites the ladies to tea. It is another step in the plot.

Anyone who knew these little societies will recognize Forster's skill in bringing in all the old thoughts and phrases which marked the difficulties between the communities. He was not only the acute observer, he was the grave spectator of the imperial scene and there are two phrases in this chapter which mark him so. They are typical of many that follow and of his acceptance, like all Anglo-Indian novelists, of the duty to comment. One is about Indians adopting European clothes: 'the East, abandoning its secular magnificence, was descending into a valley whose farther side no man can see.' And the other is heard when the Indian men at this social occasion are watching their womenfolk overcoming their reticence at appearing in public: 'The sight was significant: an island bared by the turning tide, and bound to grow.' The phrases illustrate his great sympathy with the social evolution of India, and so speedy was the evolution that they were dated, almost historical, ten years later.

The novel is still at the social level and its criticism is most openly of the civil service which ruled India. He returns to it at the end of the chapter in a conversation between Mrs Moore and her son, the young magistrate. 'Your sentiments are those of a god', she tells him, 'And Englishmen like posing as gods.' He retorts that his service is there to hold India by force: 'We're not pleasant in India, and we don't intend to be pleasant. We've something more important to do.' It is a brutally plain statement of the magisterial view, which Forster expectably equates with the public school outlook. In fairness to a service which none of us really managed to love, it should be said that this view would never be heard by the late twenties. Ronny's mother looked at him: 'He reminded her of his public school days. The traces of young-man humanitarianism had sloughed off, and he talked like an intelligent and embittered boy.' Her reply to her son is the reply of age: 'God has put us on the earth in order to be pleasant to each other.' In the miserable condition of humanity, what else can we do?

These criticisms of Forster's have some validity, like his troubled prophecies of India's social evolution, and we already see another condition of poetry in these early chapters. The author's imagination is a burning coal which fuses the whole creation, and we hear echoes of what is to happen like sad presentiments. While Adela is talking to Fielding, she is half-consciously contemplating the distant hills. We shall come to see how strongly natural beauty affects her but she cannot know, as we know in a second reading, that an incident in these hills will free her from Ronny and India. All she can see is the bondage of India for an English girl and she, like Helen Schlegel, feels the panic and the emptiness:

> She and Ronny would look into the club like this every evening, then drive home to dress; they would see the Lesleys and the Callendars and the Turtons and the Burtons, and invite them and be invited by them, while the true India slipped by unnoticed. Colour would remain—the pageant of birds in the early morning, brown bodies, white turbans, idols whose flesh was scarlet or blue—and movement would remain as long as there were crowds in the bazaar and bathers in the tanks. Perched up on the seat of a dog-cart, she would see them. But the force that

lies behind colour and movement would escape her even more
effectually than it did now.

How true, and no wonder Forster did what he could to release this
pathetic society from the bondage of its existence.

The next chapter is given entirely to developing the character of
Aziz. We learn that the Civil Surgeon respects his surgical skill, and
that Aziz himself realizes his professional competence. We watch a
casual contact on the polo ground with a subaltern and after the
heat of the play there is 'the fire of good fellowship in their eyes'.
The next contact is with a Hindu colleague, the low-born ridiculous
Panna Lal and we sense the disdainful exasperation of the Muslim
as he makes fun of this quaint Hindu. At the end, he receives an
invitation from Fielding to a teaparty and the plot edges forward.
What have we learned of his character? That he has the Muslim
warmth and the Muslim mercurial nature. He has the Muslim
sentiment and the Muslim hauteur. He has the eagerness and
prickliness of Muslim youth and the next time we meet him he has
the poise of the professional man.

   The characters at the centre of the story will all come on stage
now at the lovely house which Fielding occupies, a remembrance,
Forster tells us, of a Garden House near Aurungabad. Here they
will meet and make arrangements that will change the lives of nearly
all of them. Fielding is developed for us a little before the meeting.
He is a 'hard-bitten, good tempered, intelligent fellow, on the verge
of middle age, with a belief in education'. By coming to India in
middle age he had a long lead over most professional Englishmen
who had come straight from school or college and had never worked
in their own civilization and learned the compromises which
make life tolerable. Youthful intolerance was one of our sins in
India. We did not know that life is much the same the whole world
over and that graft or any other social weakness in India is matched
in England. Fielding, we learn, had difficulty in getting on with his
countrymen in Chandrapore, partly because the womenfolk dis-
liked him. This seems natural, as he had no use for them. They
were insipid and it was a pity that they were there at all. His creed
was that the world 'is a globe of men who are trying to reach one

6*

another and can best do so by the help of goodwill plus culture and intelligence'. It is his creator's creed of personal relations and Fielding is in many ways made in his creator's ideal image of an Edwardian and had his approval until, much later in the tale, he gets married.

Aziz is first to arrive at the teaparty and there is the comedy of his supplying Fielding with a stud, with the eager generosity of the young Muslim, a little out of character perhaps in an older professional man. The ladies arrive and he found them easy to talk to as one was old, the other plain, and there was no beauty to disturb him. Forster is at pains to explain that 'Adela's angular body and the freckles on her face were terrible defects in his eyes'. But Aziz warms in talk and finds himself again issuing an invitation, this time to his home. At once: 'Aziz thought of his bungalow with horror. It was a detestable shanty near a low bazaar.' He turns the talk to the beauty of the old Muslim room in which they are sitting, calling it 'the architecture of Question and Answer'. An echo there, for soon he and Adela will be questioning Godbole. The old brahmin arrives and hardly interrupts the Muslim's excited flow of talk. Eventually Aziz finds himself inviting everyone there to a picnic to the Marabar Caves—anything to avoid having them at his bungalow. Adela questions him about these caves, she is as eager a questioner as Helen Schlegel and he is unable to answer. He knows nothing about these Hindu caves. Godbole undertakes to describe them: 'It will be a great honour.' Somehow he contrives to evade the honour and tells them nothing at all. Question and Answer went on:

> The dialogue remained light and friendly, and Adela had no conception of its underdrift. She did not know that the comparatively simple mind of the Mohammedan was encountering Ancient Night. Aziz played a thrilling game. He was handling a human toy that refused to work—he knew that much. If it worked neither he nor Professor Godbole would be in the least advantaged, but the attempt enthralled him and was akin to abstract thought. On he chattered, defeated at every move by an opponent who would not even admit that a move had been made, and farther than ever from discovering what, if anything, was extraordinary about the Marabar Caves.

And then Ronny appeared. He is awkward and breaks up the mood of the party. Fielding had taken Mrs Moore to look over the college, so he is not able to deal with the young magistrate. Adela remembers a Question and Answer of half an hour ago. Aziz had asked her why she did not settle altogether in India—inviting her, the story is shot with irony—and without thinking she answered: 'I'm afraid I can't do that.' Now she realizes that such a statement should have been made first to Ronny. The party is very soon breaking up in confusion and to cover her own confusion Adela says to Godbole that it is a shame they had not heard him sing. ' "I may sing now", he replied, and did.' It is a song of the milk-maiden to Shri Krishna, appealing to him to come but he will not come. 'The song is composed in a *raga* appropriate to the present hour, which is the evening.' It has always baffled Indians that we use the same musical scales all through the day.

> 'But he comes in some other song, I hope?' said Mrs Moore gently.
> 'Oh no, he refuses to come', repeated Godbole, perhaps not understanding her question. 'I say to him: Come, come, come, come, come, come. He neglects to come.'

Across the Indian plain and two years later in time Narayan Godbole, dancing himself into the trance of universal love, will recall the old lady and project her spirit into the One.

In the next chapter we remain with Ronny and Mrs Moore and Adela. Both the young people are irritable and wanted to fly out at one another and since 'they were both in India, an opportunity soon occurred'. They duly quarrelled and Adela realized that what she had said in the Garden House was true, she could not stay in India, which meant that she could not marry Ronny. It was her nature to tell him straight out and at once. He behaves well. Very soon they are engaged to be married and it is contrived simply, by using a memory from Forster's second visit to India. The young people meet the Nawab Bahadur who takes them for a drive. He tells his chauffeur which road to take and falls asleep. Ronny changes the route and there is an accident. The Nawab is extremely upset. He knows what had happened. The young people react in their own way. They have been in danger together and are drawn to one another and when they return they announce their engagement to Mrs Moore. They also tell her about the accident. 'Mrs Moore shivered: "A ghost!" But the idea of a ghost scarcely passed her lips.' It was indeed, as we hear later, but how did the old lady know? It builds up the feeling of things outside normal experience which are to become the stuff of the tale. At the end of the chapter, the weather is changing: 'blasts of wind, which seemed to fall perpendicularly out of the sky, and to bounce back into it, hard and compact, leaving no freshness behind them: the hot weather was approaching.' We have been living in the perfect season, the cold weather, and we who have lived in temperate climates cannot realize the power of weather over men. But in India, as Ronny said to his mother, the weather is 'the Alpha and Omega of the whole affair'.

The next chapter is Muslim, an overcast version of the first meeting with these attractive young men. Aziz has a fever and his friends come to see him and instead of gaiety there is crossness and muddle. Dr Panna Lal and another low caste Hindu are introduced and eventually Fielding, so that we can be given an embroidery of the racial differences under the Raj. Poor Dr Panna La speaks and behaves like an inferior babu and not at all like an Indian member of a hospital medical staff. Why did Forster caricature him? Why did he caricature so spitefully the only Eurasian among his characters, Mr Harris, the Nawab Bahadur's chauffeur? Why did he caricature the memsahibs? There were such people. They were all part of the Indian scene, but they were atypical. These mean characteristics are wrongly attributed. It would also seem that tolerance and generosity, the admired virtues, are not for the novelist.

The next brief chapter is prose embroidery, a pause before the key is changed and the theme continues on a new level. It corresponds to the first chapter, where: 'The sky settles everything... when the sky chooses, glory can rain into the Chandrapore bazaars.' Now these bazaars are paralysed and silent under the heat. When the friends of Aziz left his bungalow 'they were aware of a common burden, a vague threat which they called "the bad weather coming" ...The space between them and their carriages, instead of being empty, was clogged with a medium that pressed against their flesh, the carriage cushions scalded their trousers, their eyes pricked.' Direct experience there and Forster knew nothing of Indian hot weathers until his second visit. The embroidery goes on to include themes that recur in the book:

'The sun was returning to his kingdom with power, but without beauty—that was the sinister feature. If only there had been beauty!' and the sun 'was not the unattainable friend, either of men or birds or other suns, he was not the eternal promise'.

The next chapter concludes the first Part, and is of friendship. Aziz makes a gesture to Fielding and they exchange confidences and become friends. The gesture is to show him a photograph of his dead wife, as if admitting him as a brother within the purdah. They move on to the general question of friendship between Indians and English. 'Mr Fielding, no one can ever realize how much kindness we Indians need, we do not even realize it ourselves. But we know when it has to be given...Kindness, more kindness, and even after that more kindness.' Aziz is carried away on a wave of emotion. He has arranged this private talk by the simple device of telling his servant not to bring up Fielding's horse with the others. Fielding wishes he could respond to this emotion. 'Kindness, kindness, and more kindness—yes, that he might supply, but was that really all that the queer nation needed? Did it not also demand an occasional intoxication of the blood? What had he done to deserve this outburst of confidence, and what hostage could he give in exchange?' A touch of Edwardian condescension there, nothing of the democracy of nations which we very soon evolved, wherein all nations are equal and the men in them according to their attainments. Here, different social backgrounds were meeting. The one against which Fielding had developed left him an individual: 'he was content to help people, and like them as long as they didn't object, and if they objected pass on serenely.' The Muslim was firmly embedded in his society and had to play his part within it, which meant marriage and children. Aziz questioned Fielding and found that indeed he was not married and had no children. 'Then your name will entirely die out...This indifference is what the Oriental will never understand.'

Then the echoes begin to sound, for Miss Quested is introduced as a possible wife for Fielding, who confesses he finds her depressing as she 'goes on and on as if she's at a lecture—trying ever so hard to understand India and life'. He tells Aziz she is going to marry the City Magistrate and at once Aziz is relieved, 'for this exempted him from the Marabar expedition'. Once again, as the echoes of what is going to happen in the next part expire, Aziz says she is not beautiful.

The two men come back to each other, the contrast between them, the Englishman travelling light, the Muslim 'placed, placed', 'rooted in society and Islam' and the first Part ends with his dropping off to sleep, passing into a region where all his social joys 'bloomed harmoniously in an eternal garden, or ran down watershoots of ribbed marble, or rose into domes whereunder were inscribed, black against white, the ninety nine attributes of God'. He will go through much tribulation before he falls into that state again and 'the meadow disintegrated into butterflies' and he 'saw the thornbushes where pilgrims die before they have seen the Friend'.

The second part, The Caves, opens with another collector's piece for rhetoricians. The classical devices of highly-wrought English prose are exploited in this description of the Caves of Marabar. In actual fact, Forster tells us in a note, the Barabar Caves are 'known to be Buddhist, and their entrances are not unornamented'. Forster makes them absolutely unadorned, with bare polished granite walls, and Jain, like the Tower where Kipling had an experience similar to the one Adela Quested had in the Marabar, as we shall see. Once again, the prose changes key in a descriptive passage and we are prepared for drama. The Marabar Hills:

are older than anything in the world. No water has ever covered them, and the sun who has watched them for countless aeons may still discern in their outlines forms that were his before our globe was torn from his bosom. If flesh of the sun's flesh is to be touched anywhere, it is here, among the incredible antiquity of these hills.

The visit to the Marabar is bound to take place and is contrived

very simply. A servant overhears Adela saying that she would like
to have visited the Caves, that Dr Aziz had proposed it and Indians
seemed rather forgetful. The remark was repeated and grew, so that
when it reached Aziz he understood the ladies were deeply offended
and were daily expecting to hear from him. So the picnic was
arranged though no one was enthusiastic. There are improbabilities
in most stories and it is certainly improbable that two Englishwomen
would consent to go on a picnic in the hot weather or that the men-
folk would have encouraged them. Both Fielding and Ronny would
have had more sense. But the terrible silent heat was necessary, as
in Kipling's experience, for the mental states experienced by the
two ladies, so the picnic goes forward.

It begins in the comic spirit, retailing the hundred and one
oriental details that worried Aziz in the tremendous arrangements
he felt it necessary to organize. It is a touch of that splendid nonsense which Forster finds so pregnant with truth. In his excitement,
Aziz behaves like a boy and, like a boy, is nearly in tears when
Fielding and Godbole miss the train. (In actual life, he would have
stopped the train.) Mrs Moore steadies him and the spirit of
nonsense returns when Aziz asks his old cousin as the train trundles
along: 'what is in these caves, brother? Why are we all going to see
them?' Touched with the macabre.

In this chapter and still more in the next, the mind darts and
quivers, responding to emotion as the tension rises. The next
chapter begins with the two women, alone in the purdah compart-
ment. They plan a future which is never going to happen. We sense
a change in Mrs Moore. 'She was in rather low health', we are told,
and her thoughts reflect it: 'too much fuss has been made over
marriage; centuries of carnal embracement, yet man is no nearer to
understanding man.' Adela has all her life before her, and plans her
new household and her future. And in this sensitively managed
scene of preparation, stillness before violence, we are given this
background description:

India is the country, fields, fields, then hills, jungle, hills, and
more fields. The branch line stops, the road is only practicable
for cars to a point, the bullock-carts lumber down the side

tracks, paths fray out into the cultivation, and disappear in a splash of red paint. How can the mind take hold of such a country? Generations have tried, but they remain in exile. The important towns they build are only retreats, their quarrels the malaise of men who cannot find their way home. India knows of their trouble. She knows of the whole world's trouble, to its uttermost depth. She calls 'Come' through her hundred mouths, through objects ridiculous and august. But come to what? She has never defined. She is not a promise, only an appeal.

We can search all the writing in English about India and never find her spirit so poignantly expressed.

The little procession to the Caves, headed by the elephant for the ladies, soon moved off in the pallid morning air. 'As the elephant moved towards the hills...a new quality occurred, a spiritual silence which invaded more senses than the ear. Life went on as usual, but had no consequences, that is to say, sounds did not echo or thoughts develop.' It is the emptiness of chaos and old night. So many of these touches must have come after the second visit. He tells us he hoped to continue writing his novel during his second visit, but India was too much on top of him, which is the reason we have so little good writing from his stay in India. But during the second visit he was observing and sensing all the time, picking up the pregnant detail, as this quality of the hot weather which he only experienced during his second stay.

Now, just before the catastrophe, we are taken another step towards understanding the Muslim theme of friendship. Mrs Moore and Fielding, we learn, 'had strange and beautiful effects' on Aziz:

they were his friends, his for ever; he loved them so much that giving and receiving became one. He loved them even better than the Hamidullahs, because he had surmounted obstacles to meet them, and this stimulates a generous mind. Their images remained somewhere in his soul up to his dying day, permanent additions.

A little difficult, perhaps, to reconcile this completely with the feeling at the very end, but a great help to understanding what Forster was trying to do with his character. Aziz went on to talk of his beloved emperors and Adela questioned him about Babur's universal religion which she felt might help her to avoid becoming a typical Anglo-Indian memsahib. Aziz drew back from that: 'You keep your religion, I mine. That is the best. Nothing embraces the whole of India.'

Alas, they must do what they came to do. They must visit the caves and after the bitter irony of Aziz crying out to her, 'You will never be rude to my people' they climb up to the caves. The first accident is to Mrs Moore. Inside a cave, 'some vile naked thing struck her face and settled on her mouth like a pad...She hit her head. For an instant she went mad, hitting and gasping like a fanatic. For not only did the crush and stench alarm her; there was also a terrifying echo.' There is a natural explanation: 'the naked thing was a poor little baby, astride its mother's hip.'

But Mrs Moore has had enough and with polite reassurances to Aziz she urged him and Adela to visit the other caves without her. Left alone, she had a reaction, and the full horror of her experience came upon her. 'Pathos, piety, courage — they exist, but are identical, and so is filth. Everything exists, nothing has value.' (There is an echo in the festival in the final Part: 'the God could not issue from his temple until the unclean Sweepers played their tune, they were the spot of filth without which the spirit cannot cohere.') Mrs Moore was trying to write a letter to her children in England but her experience overcame her: 'suddenly, at the edge of her mind, religion appeared, poor little talkative christianity, and she knew that all its divine words from "Let there be Light" to "It is finished" only amounted to "boum". Then she was terrified over an area larger than usual.' The old lady is entering the valley of the shadow.

Meanwhile, Adela and Aziz are climbing in the heat with a guide. They visited caves, and the heat was exhausting. Adela, in a haze of fatigue, noticed nicks in the rock which reminded her of the pattern 'traced in the dust by the wheels of the Nawab Bahadur's car. She and Ronny — no, they did not love each other.' Aziz spoke to her and she shook herself out of her frightening discovery and made conversation. Her questioning habit did the damage. She asked Aziz if he had more than one wife. 'The question shocked the young man very much. It challenged a new conviction of his community, and new convictions are more sensitive than old.' In this palimpsest of 1913 and 1923 this must come from the earlier script. Aziz was so irritated that he broke away from her and went alone into a cave to recover.

When he came out Adela was nowhere to be seen. He questioned the guide but the man could not help and Aziz struck him. The man fled. Then Aziz noticed Adela, away down below, talking to another Englishwoman. He found Adela's field glasses, but that did not warn him and immediately afterwards he ran to greet Fielding, who had come in the car with the woman talking to Adela below. News comes that the two women have driven back to Chandrapore. Fielding senses trouble but Aziz, still feeling like one of his emperors, refuses to be concerned at this apparent rudeness. The picnic is packed up quickly, they return by train and the unbelievably horrible happens. Aziz is arrested. No explanation is offered. Aziz made a foolish move to run away but Fielding prevented him. Some silly mistake had been made and Fielding would go with him to the Police Captain, who would offer apologies for the error. But Fielding is called away by the 'authoritative tone' of the Collector and Aziz goes to prison alone.

Nothing in this is credible but the conduct of Fielding. Aziz would not have behaved like a foolish boy. The Collector and his police would not have made the arrest. If a foolish girl had had an accident on a foolish picnic she would have been taken to hospital and looked after by the Civil Surgeon with any necessary specialist help from the nearby medical school. Aziz would have been protected from infamy by the Civil Surgeon and Mrs Moore, and the guide would have been found if necessary. Even if they had been foolish enough to suspect Aziz, they would have remembered that Mohurram was coming along, the most difficult days in the year for communal disturbances, and the incident would have been played down.

Every aspect of the situation is absurd, but how many readers are to know? And have we any right to expect a novelist to be true to life? The novel falsifies life as Norman Douglas said, and Forster quoted him as saying so in *Aspects*, and if this novel had not falsified the English people, paper people all but Mrs Moore and Fielding, the novel would not have provided the medium for the novelist's thoughts on Friendship and Universal Love. The interesting thing is that these unbelievable antics, and the flaws in the Indian characterization as well, do not falsify these thoughts. The novelist's business is to 'bounce' us into believing his characters, he told us in *Aspects,* and we must be grateful to him for the word which so accurately describes many of the characters in this novel. The novelist's purpose now is to show that he found the English in India behaved like a herd and so could be carried away by emotion and the 'power of putting two and two together was annihilated'. All his training and his feeling was against that.

The experiences of Mrs Moore and Adela at the caves, on the other hand, are perfectly believable, and that is where the great value of the novel comes. The inner life is true. Adela had her heat stroke or whatever it was that brought her personal worries to a climax and a mental breakdown. Mrs Moore was on a spiritual pilgrimage and like all such pilgrims she had to pass through the dark valley. She embodies the second theme and this is part of its process.

In the social scene, Forster even drops the convention in Anglo-Indian novels that the administrators and magistrates should be free from criticism. Their work was done on prestige and even George Orwell respected the convention. He had worked in Burma and knew it was necessary. It was not difficult to do so, for these magistrates were intelligent men. Turton here behaves like a pompous ass, and that too was possible among the men in his service, but hardly likely in this situation.

Fielding quarrels with him and goes to see the policeman, McBryde, who was 'the most reflective and best educated of the Chandrapore officials'. Maybe, but the other officials had been to university and the excellent police service, which George Orwell adorned, was recruited straight from school. Forster spent in all a few weeks in British India and could hardly know all the ordinary things. It hardly matters, provided we treat *A Passage* purely as imaginative fiction and not as social history. Fielding's interview with McBryde shows how racial tension built up. Fielding is not allowed to see Adela. He felt sure that she had made a mistake and that he, and no one else in the English community, would be able to make her see it. He is not even allowed to see Aziz. The bridges were destroyed.

Fielding had to take sides and he took the side he knew to be right. He discussed the situation with Hamidullah and assured him of this. 'He regretted taking sides. To slink through India un-labelled was his aim...He foresaw that besides being a tragedy, there would be a muddle.' His day ended with a curious talk with Professor Godbole, who came to see him and actually hoped, although he knew what had happened, that the picnic had been a success. An extreme example of the Hindu conception of life as illusion. We are led along to the Hindu conception of right and wrong. 'Good and evil are different, as their names imply. But, in my humble opinion, they are both aspects of my Lord.' The old man babbles on, a little too naively for a brahmin of his education, we may think, and his discussion of good-and-evil does not carry us very far.

The next chapter, the twentieth, is managed with experienced virtuosity. A novel depends on the way the novelist manages his own thoughts and feelings. The opening of the chapter is satirical, an imaginary scene in the English Club, where the Collector calls a meeting. The Englishwomen are described contemptuously and vindictive sketches of Englishmen follow. The civil surgeon and the drunken subaltern are made to behave like boorish ignoramuses. The subaltern offers an arranged ironic echo: the Indian with whom he played polo on the maidan was all right. The caricature of the Civil Surgeon is particularly painful, for among all those who served India the doctors represented the professional virtues of skill, tolerance and generosity. They attack Fielding, who resigns from the Club. The novelist then passes from painting a picture of a society he did not know to the inner mind of a character he under-stood thoroughly. From the herd spirit at its worst to the private life of the compassionate mind of Fielding. The story has edged forward a little. Adela is a little better. Mrs Moore still has a temperature. Aziz has been refused bail, and then we leave that dubious melodrama to meet a sympathetic summary of our lives. Most of us must feel as we look back on life that we 'ought to have been working at something else the whole time'.

Fielding had gone out to his upper verandah to the cool night air at the moment of the quick tropical sunset. The beauty of it passed him by:

> he felt dubious and discontented suddenly, and wondered whether he was really and truly successful as a human being. After forty years' experience he had learnt to manage his life and make the best of it on advanced European lines, had developed his personality, explored his limitations, controlled his passions—and he had done it all without becoming either pedantic or worldly. A creditable achievement; but as the moment passed, he felt he ought to have been working at something else the whole time—he didn't know at what, never would know, never could know, and that was why he felt sad.

The next brief chapter records that Mohurram is beating up, but quite peacefully. It is a dangerous time, as the Muslims carry in procession their tazias, flimsy imitations of 'the tomb of the grandson of the Prophet, done to death at Kerbala', and communal violence often follows, for the Muslims have as many wrongs to avenge as the Irish. At the end of the little chapter, Professor Godbole slips away to his new appointment.

In the next chapter we meet Mrs Moore again at last. Adela returns home from the bungalow where she has been nursed. We learn a little more of what happened at the cave. She thought Aziz was there, about to touch her. Easy Freudian explanations for that: 'I hit at him with the glasses, he pulled me round the cave by the strap, it broke, I escaped.' But her present trouble was the echo: 'the echo flourished, raging up and down like a nerve in the faculty of her hearing, and the noise in the cave, so unimportant intellectually, was prolonged over the surface of her life.'

The description of the minds of these two women after their strange experience is the most difficult task the novelist sets himself and it is managed admirably. The novel is concerned throughout with these peripheral mental experiences and Mr Stewart remarks that Forster could not have done this if *Ulysses* had not been published. But we have noticed vestigial use of this technique in the death of Leonard Bast; Forster's technical precocity has been overlooked. Mind, in the Indian hot weather, can strip down to elemental feeling, as we have just seen in Fielding, but no other English novelist has attempted to explore this frightening region of the Indian scene. Kipling, as we shall see, merely indicates. Forster explores. Most of his characters are paper people but for compensation we have as clear an analysis of the horrors of the human mind as we find anywhere in the twenties, which specialized in these explorations.

The girl in her febrile state has a new reaction to her relationship with Ronny. How can she repay him for all he has suffered on her account? 'What is the use of personal relationships when everyone brings less and less to them? I feel we ought all to go back into the desert for centuries and get good. I want to begin at the beginning. All the things I thought I'd learnt are just a hindrance, they're not knowledge at all. I'm not fit for personal relationships.'

When she gets back, she finds Mrs Moore as absorbed in trivial things as Professor Godbole himself. She will neither sympathize with the girl nor help her: 'Her Christian tenderness had gone, or had developed into a hardness, a just irritation against the human race.' She tells Ronny roundly that she will not appear at the trial: 'I have nothing to do with your ludicrous law courts.' The old woman grumbles on and when at last she turns to her patience cards, Adela has a sudden realization and tells Ronny that Aziz is innocent. She has the illusion that Mrs Moore said so and when she asks her: 'Of course he is innocent', but she can give no other reason than Fielding's, that it was out of character.

We hear the echoes as the old woman grumbles on. She will be at the trial, a spirit called up, and she will be called up in spirit again at the festival of the birth of Krishna, and the echo of that is a Christian phrase: 'When shall I be free of your fuss? Was he in the cave and were you in the cave and on and on...and Unto us a Son is born, unto us a Child is given...and am I good and is he bad and are we saved?' Her mind falls out of time. She returns to them to say: 'I will not help you to torture him for what he never did.' But even that is not enough to convince Adela of her mistake, and Mrs Moore bleakly ends the talk: 'She has started the machinery; it will work to its end.' Ronny naturally feels that his mother should be encouraged in her plan to return to England and very soon she goes.

She is actually invited to share the cabin of the Governor's wife (Forster uses the 1913 title, Lieutenant-Governor): 'But she accepted her good luck without enthusiasm. She had come to that state where the horror of the universe and its smallness are both visible at the same time—the twilight of the double vision in which so many elderly people are involved...in the twilight of the double vision, a spiritual muddledom is set up for which no high-sounding words can be found.'

Her thoughts returned to the cave where all this mental trouble began: 'What dwelt in the first of the caves? Something very old and very small. Before time, it was before space also. Something snub-nosed, incapable of generosity—the undying worm itself. Since hearing its voice, she had not entertained one large thought.' Then, from the awfulness of this Ancient Night, the novelist addresses us directly: 'Visions are supposed to entail profundity but—Wait till you get one, dear reader! The abyss also may be petty, the serpent of eternity made of maggots.' It sounds very like heat-stroke.

We are rescued, but only into another strange dimension of echoes. She joins the mail train to Bombay, and the huts and houses and temples of the great Indian plain rush by the carriage window and among them she passes a place called Asirgarh. She knows nothing about it but because the line looped there in ten minutes she saw it again: 'it had looked at her twice and seemed to say: "I do not vanish." ' The reader goes on and forgets until the name echoes again at the end.

We have come to another of the great scenes, the trial scene, and it is introduced with befitting prose embroideries: 'existence had to be endured and crime punished with the thermometer at a hundred and twelve...Men yearn for poetry though they may not confess it; they desire that joy shall be graceful and sorrow august and infinity have a form, and India fails to accommodate them...men try to be harmonized all the year round, and the results are occasionally disastrous.' The girl at the centre of the stage is nervous and obviously still sick. Mr Turton has a glimpse of truth: 'it's our women who make everything more difficult out here'—an echo there back to young Richard Burton in Scinde who foresaw in 1850 that the memsahib would fracture our relations with the local peoples. But that was a secret thought of Mr Turton's, as was his forecast that this trial would be repeated in court after court as the appeal went up.

Any magistrate in his position would have seen that, as well as the potential Mohurram troubles, and the trial would never have taken place. If he had not, central authority would have stepped in. Why upset the town and expose the girl who had so foolishly gone on an ill-judged picnic? English people in India would not have behaved in the ridiculous way they are sketched at the trial[1] and yet out of it come more of these descriptions of the private mind which read so absolutely true. This time, it is the mind of Adela and it begins when she sees a beautiful object in the courtroom. She catches sight of the punkah-wallah, the meanest person in the scene, but beautiful:

> Almost naked, and splendidly formed, he sat on a raised platform near the back, in the middle of the central gangway, and he caught her attention as she came in, and he seemed to control the proceedings. He had the strength and beauty that sometimes come to flower in Indians of low birth. When that strange race nears the dust, and is condemned as untouchable, then nature remembers the physical perfection that she accomplishes elsewhere, and throws out a god—not many, but one here and there, to prove to society how little its categories impress her.

Then comes one of these touches which are a common indulgence with Forster, who is more concerned with the perfection of his design than with the reader, who cannot be expected to see them. A chant gathers volume outside the courtroom. It is the name of Mrs Moore, 'Esmiss Esmoor', repeated like an incantation. It rises in volume as her absence is discussed in the courtroom and after a crescendo: 'Suddenly it stopped. It was as if the prayer had been heard, and the relics exhibited.' No one present knew and the reader is not yet told that she is dead. But her memory has invaded the

[1] cf. George Orwell in his essay 'Rudyard Kipling' where he says that English people 'could not have maintained themselves in power for a single week, if the normal Anglo-Indian outlook had been that of, say, E. M. Forster.' Orwell had worked in Burma.

courtroom and steadied Adela. We are taken inside her mind again as she moves towards mental crisis and breakdown. She is back in the Marabar Hills and everything is very clear. The incidents recur with astonishing clearness and then all at once she falters and there is a pause. The stream of consciousness is interrupted and we find ourselves in the courtroom again and Fielding there, the only one to realize that this girl 'was going to have a nervous breakdown and that his friend was saved'. The charge is withdrawn, the court breaks up in clamour and confusion, and art asserts itself in another description of silent beauty. We see the punkah-wallah again, for:

> no one remained on the scene of the fantasy but the beautiful naked god. Unaware that anything unusual had occurred, he continued to pull the cord of his punkah, to gaze at the empty dais and the overturned special chairs, and rhythmically to agitate the clouds of descending dust.

There is once again what Professor Godbole would call an absence of truth in the next chapter. Adela renounces her own people. She would never have been allowed to do so. She would have been taken at once to hospital or to some hospitable bungalow. But the story requires conversation between the two Edwardian intellectuals, Adela and Fielding, so she is flung against Fielding outside the courtroom and he can do nothing but take her to his garden house. The victorious Muslims march on the hospital to rescue the Nawab's nephew, who, according to communal rumour, is having pepper shaken on his wounds. More absence of truth, or an exaggeration of what one community is prepared to believe of another. Dr Panna Lal saves the hospital by clowning. No community escapes the caricaturing spleen of this intolerant creator. All the stupidity he engraves with such skill could be seen in India but had to be ignored as much as possible by all the communities so that life could continue. It must also be recorded that Forster attaches his stupidities very often to people who could not have committed them, as here. Panna Lal behaves like some junior babu and not in the least like a Hindu member of a hospital medical staff. A little more experience of India would have saved him from these misfortunes.

The novelist has a good deal of clearing up to do after the trial and he performs his chores with what spirit he can muster. Fielding discusses with Adela what had really happened in the cave but she has lost interest. We learn now of Mrs Moore's death, which happened at sea before the trial. Aziz will demand twenty thousand rupees compensation from Adela and £1500 was a considerable sum then. In a long conversation and after an appeal to the memory of Mrs Moore, Fielding persuades Aziz to give up making any demand upon her. During that talk we learn of Aziz that: 'Imprisonment had made channels for his character, which would never fluctuate as widely now as in the past.' When we come to the Third Part we shall find a coherent Aziz.

There is an ungenerous record of Ronny's reactions. He is unkind to the memory of his mother and he decides he cannot marry Adela now as it would damage his career. He breaks off the engagement and is transferred to another district. An uneasy exit. Then Adela is led off the stage. It would seem that the novel is ending. The two lady visitors who were responsible for the story have gone. Adela has completely gone but Mrs Moore remains as a strangely living memory among all whom she has met.

There is a quarrel between Fielding and Aziz, as revealing as quarrels can be in life and in novels. Aziz carries to Fielding the rumour that Adela had become his mistress and in a rage Fielding calls him a little rotter. It was the word that was more deadly than a blow. Fielding, like his creator, treats Aziz more like a schoolboy than a friend in another profession. Dejected by the quarrel and by a compulsory attendance at the Club to which he had been re-elected, Fielding walks home past the little mosque where Aziz and Mrs Moore first met. There had been new faces at the Club. After the trial, officials had been moved for obvious reason, and the new ones looked to Fielding exactly the same: 'the more the club changed the more it promised to be the same thing.' India moulded the European in its own fashion. Fielding is the commentator within the tale. He foresees the dissolution of empire, but naturally he can only see it as a crash and not as escape for the English professional people.

Then comes a quiet intimation of the second great theme, the religious theme. As the theme of friendship fails, the other theme is indicated. Fielding reflects that every incident echoes now in India and the echoes are always evil:

'The original sound may be harmless, but the echo is always evil.' This reflection about an echo lay at the verge of Fielding's mind. He could never develop it. It belonged to the universe that he had missed or rejected. And the mosque missed it too. Like himself, those shallow arcades provided but a limited asylum. 'There is no God but God' doesn't carry us far through the complexities of matter and spirit; it is only a game with words, really, a religious pun, not a religious truth.

Mrs Moore had dismissed 'poor little talkative Christianity'. Now Islam is rejected. Hinduism is left. After dinner that evening, when Fielding and Aziz are wretchedly trying to mend their friendship, they turn to an innocuous subject, poetry. The exchange begins with a remark from Aziz which shows once again that Forster was consciously developing his character. Youth is giving way to experienced maturity:

'I was a child when you knew me first. Everyone was my friend then. The Friend: a Persian expression for God. But I do not want to be a religious poet either.'
'I hoped you would be.'
'Why, when you yourself are an atheist?'
'There is something in religion that may not be true, but has not yet been sung.'
'Explain in detail.'
'Something that the Hindus have perhaps found.'
'Let them sing it.'
'Hindus are unable to sing.'
'Cyril, you sometimes make a sensible remark. That will do for poetry for the present.'

What the Hindus have found will be shown in the final part and so, while the story seems to be petering out and the characters appear to be making their final exits, in fact the stage is being cleared for the greatest scene of all. Aziz leaves it bitterly. He goes off to the hills with his children and he persuades himself that Fielding is going to marry Miss Quested and that is why he was so keen that she should not pay Aziz compensation. Fielding wanted the money himself. It is unbelievable. Compassion is one of the attributes of Allah, and our Muslim friends are not only loyal in their thoughts but compassionate. The theme of friendship need not have been a theme that failed.

But Aziz had to be projected into a totally Indian State where he would find no English people and it required some powerful emotion to uproot him. Great care is given to preparing his mind in other ways too for the move. He is asked to write a poem for a new magazine which will cultivate the idea of India in which all Asians are friends. As soon as he tries to compose he thinks inevitably of bulbuls, the decay of Islam and the brevity of love. He struggled, and managed to form 'the vague and bulky figure of a motherland' and 'he longed to compose a new song which would be acclaimed by multitudes and even sung in the fields'. He realized that India must become a nation like Japan, so he hardened and prepared to make his gesture. He would work among Hindus. As he leaves the stage, his next entrance is prepared.

Last to go is Fielding. He too will leave Chandrapore and meantime he will go home on leave and the second part ends on an exquisite little prose embroidery on Egypt and the Mediterranean:

> The Mediterranean is the human norm. When men leave that exquisite lake, whether through the Bosphorous or the Pillars of Hercules, they approach the monstrous and extraordinary; and the southern exit leads to the strangest experience of all. Turning his back on it yet again, he took the train northward, and tender romantic fancies that he thought were dead for ever, flowered when he saw the buttercups and daisies of June.

The last sentence, as usual when a chapter ends, indicates a new theme, a suggestion of romance. Nothing is made of it. It had nothing to do with the chosen theme. In the next part, Fielding is already married and has given hostages to fortune and loses his creator's approval. Fortunately, his creator is concerned with more important matters than romance. The Third Part is Hindu, and shows what the Hindu has found. It could never have been written if Forster had not had the good fortune to go to India and stay in an

Indian State where that particular festival of the birth of Krishna was celebrated. It is not one of the great Hindu festivals, or in the main stream of Hinduism, but it is nearer to the Christian festival of the birth of Christ, and when we compare the highly wrought (and wholly successful) descriptions in *A Passage* with his original record in *Devi* we see how the likenesses to the Christian festival are stressed. The novel had refused to finish and had been laid aside. The manuscript was taken with him to India on this second visit but 'as soon as they were confronted with the country they purported to describe, they seemed to wilt and go dead and I could do nothing with them. I used to look at them of an evening in my room at Dewas, and felt only distaste and despair. The gap between India remembered and India experienced was too wide.'

Instead, he found his ending just by watching the festival. He had only to describe what he saw with the adaptations that art required and with the weaving in as naturally as possible of Fielding and Aziz to carry the friendship theme again.

The part opens in mid-festival with a crash of chords:

Some hundreds of miles westward of the Marabar Hills, and two years later in time, Professor Narayan Godbole stands in the presence of God. God is not born yet—that will occur at midnight—but He has also been born centuries ago, nor can He ever be born, because He is the Lord of the Universe, who transcends human processes. He is, was not, is not, was.

The background is sketched in: 'Hindus, Hindus only, mild-featured men, mostly villagers, for whom anything outside their villages passed in a dream' and when the villagers caught a glimpse of the image of the god 'a most beautiful and radiant expression came on their faces, a beauty in which there was nothing personal'.

Enter Professor Godbole: 'he pressed forward from the back, already in full voice, that the chain of sacred sounds might be uninterrupted.' The rhythm is eventually broken and the drummer introduces a new one:

This was more exciting, the inner images it evoked more definite, and the singers' expressions became fatuous and languid. They loved all men, the whole universe, and scraps of their past, tiny splinters of detail, emerged for a moment to melt into the universal warmth. Thus Godbole, though she was not important to him, remembered an old woman he had met in Chandrapore days. Chance brought her into his mind while it was in this heated state, he did not select her, she happened to occur among the throng of soliciting images, a tiny splinter, and he impelled her by his spiritual force to that place where completeness was to be found. Completeness, not reconstruction.

In that creative passage we see how much the artist can transform his material. This is universal love and it is the turn of our wasp to be included: 'he remembered a wasp seen he forgot where, perhaps on a stone. He loved the wasp equally, he impelled it likewise, he was imitating God.'

The noise and the jangle increases, 'they did not one thing which the non-Hindu would feel dramatically correct; this approaching triumph of India was a muddle (as we call it) a frustration of reason and form'. The aged Rajah is brought in and plays his appropriate part. He is dying and is carried out quickly to some less sacred place. The clock strikes midnight and the buffooning of the little military state becomes confused with the celebrations of the birth. The prose, already throbbing with vivid life, increases in tempo. Rosy powder is thrown into the air, the clanging and the shouting increases: 'All sorrow was annihilated, not only for Indians, but for foreigners, birds, caves, railways and the stars; all became joy; all laughter; there had never been disease, nor doubt, misunderstanding, cruelty, fear.'

Then comes the last long paragraph of the chapter, a sustained climax in a prose triumph. More buffooning. 'There is fun in heaven...By sacrificing good taste this worship achieved what Christianity has shirked: the inclusion of merriment.' Perhaps, if we forget the Middle Ages. Then the great black jar which they struck at with their sticks: 'It cracked, broke, and a mass of greasy rice and milk poured on to their faces. They ate and smeared one another's mouths, and dived between each other's legs for what had been pashed upon the carpet.' Connoisseurs compare this description with those in Lowes Dickinson's *Appearances* and Ackerley's *Hindoo Holiday*.

The clamour turns to the silence of thought as Professor Godbole remembers Mrs Moore again:

> and round her faintly clinging forms of trouble. He was a Brahman, she Christian, but it made no difference whether she was a trick of his memory or a telepathic appeal. It was his duty, as it was his desire, to place himself in the position of the God and to love her.

What then had he achieved in this festival?

> 'One old Englishwoman and one little, little wasp', he thought, as he stepped out of the temple into the grey of a pouring wet morning. 'It does not seem much, still it is more than I am myself.'

One theme in the novel has found completion.

We have already learned in the swirl of the festival that Aziz is State Doctor and now we learn that Fielding is visiting the State as an Inspector of Education. He has come to see Professor Godbole's college which we have heard about before. Unfortunately, the college has not been a success and at the moment it is being used as a granary. It will require all Godbole's brahminical skill to keep Fielding from discovering that, and in the end he is defeated by Aziz who tells Fielding by chance and Fielding sensibly ignored the misfortune.

We turn to Aziz and at once the atmosphere of the final chapter of the Edwardian novel enfolds us. He had escaped from the English and if he had not quite married again he had made a suitable arrangement. His children are with him. We find him playing with them, as we found Stephen Wonham playing with his little daughter. He has overcome his old troubles so thoroughly that when he comes across Fielding and his brother-in-law while walking he is able to meet them. He had not called at the Guest House as he had heard that Mrs Fielding was there and he never wanted to meet Miss Quested again. He quickly learns his mistake. Fielding had married Stella Moore and this young man is her brother. He still repels them: 'I wish no Englishman or Englishwoman to be my friend.' Is the theme of friendship to fail finally?

Not quite. First, Aziz must meet Ralph Moore and, when they

talk, Aziz calls him an oriental and then remembers with a shudder
that this is what he had called Mrs Moore. In time, the heart of
Aziz warms again and it is now that he says: 'This is our monsoon,
the best weather...Now is the time when all things are happy,
young and old!' The spring of the Indian year, the time of re-
awakening. Aziz is able to behave towards the boy as a friend, but
'the two nations cannot be friends' and he has for simple answer
from the boy: 'I know. Not yet.'

The story tangles with the festival again, which ends in a jumble
of noise and commotion: 'no man could say where was the emotional
centre of it, any more than he could locate the heart of a cloud.'
Last scene of all, Aziz and Fielding together again. 'Now they rode
through jolly bushes and rocks'—we are seeing through the eyes of
the Edwardian Fielding—'Presently, the ground opened into full
sunlight and they saw a grassy slope bright with butterflies.' Aziz
produces a letter he has written to Miss Quested, thanking her for
behaving so well two years ago. Something makes him add a sentence
that is more warm, more gracious. The influence of the season and
of the festival are at work. Then Aziz has his own mystical moment:

> When he had finished, the mirror of the scenery was shattered,
> the meadow disintegrated into butterflies. A poem about
> Mecca—the Caaba of Union—the thorn-bushes where pilgrims
> die before they have seen the Friend—they flitted next; he
> thought of his wife; and then the whole semi-mystic, semi-
> sensuous overturn, so characteristic of his spiritual life, came to
> end like a landslip and rested in its due place, and he found
> himself riding in the jungle with his dear Cyril.

The theme closes after a flurry of political prophecy: 'Until
England is in difficulties we keep silent, but in the next European
war—aha, aha! Then is our time', and Fielding retorts: 'Who do
you want instead of the English? The Japanese?' Not bad for 1924.
And Aziz: 'We shall drive every Englishman into the sea, and then
...you and I shall be friends.' ' "Why can't we be friends now?"
said the other—But the horses didn't want it—they swerved apart;
the earth didn't want it' and all nature around them, 'No, not yet'.

Novels, like other artefacts, depend on what the workman can do, and the author of *A Passage to India* could write prose and discuss ideas. His plot was to discuss friendship and religion and he concocted a story accordingly. The love interest was minimal and it is cleared away before the triumphant third Part, where the only characters admitted are those who can help in expressing the great themes. The story does not matter very much. It allows the writer to embroider fine passages of natural description; to give us animated crowd scenes, the bridge party, the picnic, the trial, the religious festival; and, most valuable of all, those scenes in the inner mind of Mrs Moore and Adela, of Aziz and Godbole, in which the novelist rivals the dramatic poet. The value of *A Passage* is in its poetical quality, the natural descriptions, and the entry into the minds of the central characters when they were in a febrile state.

The rest is difficult. *Howards End* has made us think of Forster as a social historian or at any rate that special kind of historical novelist who has written what he saw and heard and in time it has become history. We accept his English pictures but we cannot accept his pictures of people in India. The descriptions of the Indian scene are probably the best we have in English and when he is inside his characters we feel we are touching universal truth. But the flaw in the character of Aziz, half boy, half professional man; in Dr Panna Lal, a clowning babu instead of a medical man; in Godbole, who is too naive for any brahmin trained in western ways and in daily contact with Englishmen; and the whole English professional group, paper people who would have been less than useless in India where their responsibilities were so great; all these flaws trouble the reader who is sympathetic to his author and the subject. It may not matter; the artist does not undertake to emulate a photographer, we say. What we must record is that our greatest novel about India and one of the great imaginative discussions of friendship and the quality of love in religion is conducted amongst imperfect characters. To fall back on Forster's own word, we could hardly have a better example of the novelist's ability to bounce us.

The case against the Indian characters has been put bluntly by Mr Nirad Chaudhari: '*A Passage to India* presents all the Indians in it as perverted, clownish, or queer characters. There are few delineations of the Indian character which are more insultingly

7

condescending to self-respecting Indians, Muslim or Hindu, than those of this book.'[1] Mr Chaudhari speaks emphatically when he speaks at all and his sweeping charge, which overlooks the extensive literature of the comic babu, makes us think by reaction of such charming characters in *A Passage* as the Nawab Bahadur and Hamidullah, who have the Muslim grace and poise, and those splendid compliments to a whole people which Forster offers in describing Muslim groups. But it will be admitted by any Englishman who worked among the professional services in India that he is inclined to a reaction as emphatic as Mr Chaudhari's to the English people in the novel. Such people could be found in India but not among the professional people and their wives. Professional life, in India, as elsewhere, was concerned with work, not race, and the normal courtesies of professional life were observed and respected. They were treasured on the English side, because our Indian colleagues had so much to offer us.

When we seek an explanation as to why Forster depicted his own people in India in this way, we may find a useful comparison in one of his contemporaries, another liberal mind who had as little experience of India, Lord Attlee. He withdrew all the professional English cadres from India. He saw, like Forster and Mahatma Gandhi, that it was time for them to go. The traders stayed and the dividends flow on. The political power, which is no more than heavy responsibility, was transferred along with all the heavy professional duties. Rightly so, for it has made all the difference to Indian efforts to bring their country into the modern world. In this great release of English professional people Forster's novel played its part. It was a nuisance to them because many Indians thought they found in the novel what the English really believed about them. Those who met the very few Englishmen about knew better, but it did not help our personal relations as long as we were there. But it helped to dig us out of a country where our ruling caste was no longer ruling with conviction and where, as a result, a great deal of our professional work was being wasted.

The novel was well timed to do this beneficent work. If it had been completed and published after Forster's first visit to India it

[1] *Continent of Circe*, p. 93.

would have been well before its time. It is worth looking at an Anglo-Indian novel published in Edwardian days. *Siri Ram— Revolutionist* was published in 1913, just before the war that sapped our imperial confidence. Like all novels about India, like *A Passage* itself, a good deal of it is about what happened in that strange country, reportage without much imaginative effort. There is a long description of an epidemic of plague in the Punjab, which was stamped out by two young Englishmen, an administrator and a doctor, who became one of the last victims of the epidemic. The atmosphere in which it is described is the Kipling atmosphere, 'it's all in the day's work'. When it comes to the question why the English are in India, Fielding in *A Passage,* talking to his Muslim friends is only able to say: 'I cannot tell you why England is here or whether she ought to be here. It's beyond me.' Whereas Skene, the college principal in *Siri Ram,* is able to harangue his students thus:

> 'Don't think I want you to believe that India is a distressful burden which we bow under from a sense of duty only. I hate cant. India is as much the property of the English as the estate of one of your zemindars is the property of the landlord whose ancestor won it by the sword, or was given it for service. Tell your zemindar he must divide his property among his tenants because they are becoming fit to manage it themselves, and hear what he will say...We are here because it is our country. Incidentally it happens to be our way to recognize our obligations to our tenants as no other rulers have done or are ever likely to do.'

In the next paragraph we learn that Skene is not very pleased with his effort and it ends with this astringent Forsterian touch: 'It would be so easy to put the case to them if they were not Indians.' It was just over thirty years before the English were out and the Indian landlords were handing over their land.

These humdrum novels—Edward Thompson's *An Indian Day* in 1927 is another good example—offered accurate descriptions of scenery, and people whose lives were spent in fighting plagues, floods and famines. They were mostly written by men, like Matthew Arnold's brother, who were working in India. When Forster wrote most of his novel he had been only a few weeks in the country, and it is astonishing not that he got so much wrong but that he got so much right. In the first two parts he has got the Muslim group scenes very neatly as well as the delightfully comic railway station scene before the picnic. He is adrift with the Hindus, the English and the Eurasians. The third part is quite different in impact, for the Hindu festival is imaginative interpretation of what had been observed and we have in *Devi* the text of the observations to compare with the imaginative reconstruction. Furthermore, Aziz has become a coherent character. Fielding no longer treats him like a student, and he behaves as one would expect a doctor to behave.

The visit to the caves and all that happened there has the quality of truth, for here again the imagination is at work, though this time it is constructing what—so far as we know—had not been observed. The validity of the experiences of Mrs Moore and Adela is confirmed by a description of a very similar experience in Kipling's *From Sea to Sea* (1889). In the eleventh chapter he describes how 'the Englishman' visited Chitor in the same silent intensity of heat as that visit to the caves. Outside a dark room in the palace 'he tripped and fell and, as he put out his hands, he felt that the stairs had been worn hollow and smooth by the tread of innumerable naked feet. Then he was afraid and came away very quickly.' He goes on to the Tower of Victory which had been 'raised by some pious Jain as a proof of conquest over things spiritual'. We recall that the Marabar Caves were Jain. In that second tower the Englishman notes 'the slippery sliminess of the walls always worn smooth by naked men' and we recall the smooth shining walls of the caves. The message of the tower is about power: 'To attain power, wrote the builder of old, in sentences of fine stone, it is necessary to pass through all sorts of close-packed horrors, treacheries, battles and insults, in darkness and without knowledge whether the road leads upwards or into a hopeless cul-de-sac.' It was a similar baffling darkness in the Marabar. Then the Englishman became really frightened of the place, 'the Genius of the place must be responsible for making it so', he became hysterical and dashed downhill, as Miss Quested did. He 'slipped and bumped on the rocks' and felt at the bottom that he had been led 'two thousand years away from his own century' and that he would be drowned in the tank 'or that some of the stone slabs would fall forwards and crush him flat'. The Englishman's final comment again echoes the experience of the ladies in the Marabar: 'there was something uncanny about it all. It was not exactly a feeling of danger or pain, but an apprehension of great evil.'

We may never know whether there was any personal experience of Forster's behind this study of disintegration, whether he ever had heat stroke or whatever it is that induces this condition, but we have Kipling's evidence that experiences of this order were not unknown. As a mood, it was common in England as an aftermath of war. Two years before *A Passage* was published, the *Waste Land* appeared:

What are the roots that clutch, what branches grow
Out of this stony rubbish? Son of man,
You cannot say, or guess, for you only know
A heap of broken images.

Twenty years after he published the novel Forster went to Glasgow to lecture about prose between the two wars and he notices an obvious characteristic: 'It is the product of people who have war on their mind.' He goes on to speak of Freud and Einstein and what he says helps us in understanding what happened to these two women in the caves and how it was possible to use such material. Of Freud, he says:

Man is beginning to understand himself better and to explore his own contradictions. This exploration is conveniently connected with the awful name of Freud, but it is not so much in Freud as in the air. It has brought a great enrichment to the art of fiction. It has given subtleties and depths to the portrayal of human nature. The presence in all of us of the subconscious, the occasional existence of the split personality, the persistence of the irrational especially in people who pride themselves on their reasonableness, the importance of dreams and the prevalence of day-dreaming—here are some of the points which novelists have seized on...

The phrase which ends that paragraph will help us: 'if you prefer the language of Freud...the conscious must be satisfactorily based on the subconscious.' Was that what was wrong with Mrs Moore and Miss Quested? There are hints in the developments of their characters that it was so. On the other hand, there are hints that Aziz, the poet, was satisfactorily based and in particular his own moment of mystical vision to show that he was. So he was untroubled by echoes.

The mention of Einstein which follows immediately in the lecture takes us into the realm Forster makes familiar to us in his discussion of Hindu thought and belief:

> the idea of relativity has got into the air and has favoured certain tendencies in novels. Absolute good and evil, as in Dickens, are seldom presented. A character becomes good or evil in relation to some other character or in a situation which may itself change. You can't measure people up because the yard-measure keeps altering its length.

The novel was planned long before these tendencies developed, after his first visit to India with Goldie, and if it had been completed then it would probably not have got much farther than Goldie got in his letter: 'We're in the real jungle, forest around us for miles and I'm so happy.' He describes the vivid natural life around him, especially the inescapable insect life, flies, wasps, spiders:

> What a thing nature is! How do the spiders feel? Let's hope they are unconscious! In the face of these things, most religious talk seems 'tosh'. If there's a God, or gods, they're beyond my ken. I think, perhaps, after all, the Hindus took in more of the facts in their religion than most people have done.

Between that end and the final writing of the novel the war had begun a spiritual earthquake and out of the ruins there came another tendency which Forster notes in his Glasgow lecture: 'to which I will attach the name esoteric; the desire on the part of writers— generally the most distinguished writers—to create something better than the bloodshed and dullness which have been creeping together over the world.'

There is another little discussion in that lecture which illuminates our thoughts about *A Passage*. It will have been noticed in the quotations from it that obsolescent words, old-fashioned turns of speech and rhythms which go back three hundred years are frequently used when the prose is heightened. It is in the tradition of all our heightened prose since the Authorized Version, which Forster here says: 'has constantly influenced our talk and writing for the past three hundred years. Its rhythm, its atmosphere, its turns of phrase, belonged to our people and flowed into our books.' Then he says all that is gone and 'there is now an unbridgeable gulf between ourselves and the Authorized Version as regards style, and the gulf widened about 1920.' Yet it appeared quite naturally and appropriately in the texture of *A Passage*. No one recently has used more easy, lively and vigorous English as his normal manner than Forster. But in his greatest novel, with the beliefs of man as his theme, he elevates his style and still retains its pace and vigour. We feel it in the ceremonial descriptions which open and close the parts and naturally we feel it most of all in the last part when sentences like these are trumpet-tongued: 'Some hundreds of miles westward of the Marabar Hills and two years later in time, Professor Narayan Godbole stands in the presence of God...he pressed forward from the back, already in full voice, that the chain of sacred sounds might be uninterrupted...Infinite Love took upon itself the form of Shri Krishna, and saved the world...He may think, if he chooses, that he has been with God, but as soon as he thinks it, it becomes history and falls under the rules of time.'

There is a Cambridge echo of the human dilemma which Forster faced in this novel in another lecture by a Cambridge man some years later. Sir Charles Sherrington, in the climax of his Gifford lectures in 1937–8, is speaking of altruism as man's unique contribution to natural evolution, man's best answer to the transitoriness of life and its lack of values. We find echoes of man's loneliness in a world which operates without any knowledge of values and which is antagonistic to man's mind.

> To look round at the world and find there nothing whose thought partakes his 'good' or his 'evil' excites in man a strange sense of loneliness. Laforgue turned from the stars and midnight sky saying 'comme nous sommes seuls pourtant sur notre terre.' He felt the pathos of that detached remoteness from even the nearest sky-comrade, unreachably afar. But that is not man's loneliness to the full. His crown of loneliness is his loneliness

'at home' within the compass and amid the community of his planet. The human mind is strangely placed there; no other mind its equal, let alone superior to it. All other mind its inferior, and almost uncompanionably so. His thinking is thus thrown utterly upon itself. Grappling with its newly found 'values', yet with no experience except its own, no judgement but its own, no counsel but its own...Man's spirit thus yearns for company. His medieval thought had judged him a thing apart, but never allotted to him a loneliness such as this he is now conscious of. Nothing at all outside himself with which he can commune on what is next his heart.

It is that dilemma which Forster deals with in *A Passage* to more than India and to which he suggests the Hindus may have found an answer.

Great skill is the name and nature of all Forster's novels. Novels are made of words, and words used skilfully become rhythms, and however they are used they become a mirror of the writer. The quality in all Forster's novels is intellectual power and nowhere is that power so concentrated and deployed as in the great rhythms of *A Passage*. The greatest novelists often give themselves vast land and sea spaces as background and Forster found India and Indians so sympathetic that he took their country for background when he wanted to deal with a universal theme. 'The sense of space which is the basis of all earthly beauty', as he says in *Howards End*. We have seen his development from witty comedy to the serious discussion in *The Longest Journey*. The prophetic note that failed to sound very certainly in the Cadbury Rings was heard in *Howards End*, when his preoccupation with the spirit of place reminded us that peace of mind comes most easily from the earth and houses which seem part of it.

But Forster was ambitious and had more to say and wanted to say it with greater force and resonance. He foresaw the troubles of the world and he wrote his last novel to offer a solution to some of them. Events have shown that as a human family we are as far away from that solution as ever we were, so his prophecies remain to be fulfilled. They were great themes, the theme of friendship and the theme of infinite love. There could have been others or farther expression of these themes. But he fell silent and no one has explained why, and Forster has been as shy about explaining things as Professor Godbole himself. That most sympathetic critic, Peter Burra, uses words by Forster to suggest 'that the organism, being perfectly adjusted, is silent'. Certainly there has been no more prophecy, but the great preaching did not fall silent. Anything but. A greater volume of material has been published since *A Passage* than before and the preacher has been hard at work, exhorting and illuminating deep into old age. He has even surprised himself by how much he has done: 'I am both surprised and glad to discover from this bibliography that I have written so much.'

We may find a clue to the creative silence in that Glasgow lecture in 1944. He is speaking about economic influences on our island society: 'It has meant the destruction of feudalism and relationship based on the land, it has meant the transference of power from the aristocrat to the bureaucrat and the manager and the technician. Perhaps it will mean democracy, but it has not meant it yet, and personally I hate it.' Not a mood for creative work. At the end of his lecture he mentions again the esoteric tendency, which 'tried to create through art something more valuable than monotony and bloodshed. The best work of the period has this esoteric tendency.'

A Passage, compact with that tendency, is recognized as one of the outstanding works of the period, the last in which a body of great creative work was written in England.

7*

The Short Stories

IF A WRITER begins with some short stories, we may expect to find themes he will develop later. Pan appears in the first story. The second is a study of old age. Later, the art of reading comes in, the idea of heaven, the oppressiveness of English philistinism, caricature curates, a lady novelist. There is never a strong story line but in all of them there is the enquiring mind, often postulating a situation that seems untenable so that he can amuse himself by making it acceptable; writing a parable in the Anglo–Saxon manner, domesticating a Greek legend. There is a lively and nimble fancy in them all and a surprising amount of strain and cruelty and violence. If we count the sudden deaths as Beveridge did in reviewing *The Longest Journey*, we shall find two characters killed to begin the story, five deaths and the destruction of the world.

He calls his stories fantasies: 'These fantasies were written at various dates previous to the first world war' and he reminds us that while fantasy today tends to become apocalyptic, in Edwardian days it 'functions for Hermes who used to do the smaller behests of the gods—messenger, machine-breaker, and conductor of souls to a not-too-terrible hereafter'. The first short story he wrote, 'The story of a Panic', came to him fantastically enough: 'it was in the May of 1902 that I took a walk near Ravello. I sat down in a valley, a few miles above the town, and suddenly the first chapter of the story rushed into my mind as if it had waited for me there.' A. E. Housman records similar experiences when he wrote verses and tells us how very often the missing and concluding stanza took a very long time to find and fashion. While Forster serenely enjoyed the intellectual exercise of developing the story he had received. He could have left the first chapter as a complete story and relied on his readers to use their intelligences.

The Story of a Panic

The story is told by the familiar Edwardian fiction figure, the narrator. He is a stuffy fellow but so precise and correct that we are bound to believe him, for he certainly could not have invented this Panic visitation. He is not at all the traditional storyteller, the Eastern bazaar figure, who charms us into listening, but 'a plain, simple man with no pretensions to literary style.' The story is about Eustace, a repellent boy of fourteen, a member of a party of tourists. He is going to be possessed by Pan, so to heighten the contrast he was lazy, found walking a bore, could not swim, and liked to lounge in an easy chair on the terrace. A very ordinary boy, and there is an ordinary artist, who gets very angry because some trees have been cut down and exclaims that it is because of such vulgarity that the classical creatures have left us and 'the woods no longer give shelter to Pan', to whom an ordinary curate responds: 'Pan is dead. That is why the woods do not shelter him.'

Then comes the pregnant silence and the shattering blast of Eustace's whistle and silence again. Pan possesses them and they rush downhill in a panic, ending with the ashamed admission: 'I had been afraid not as a man but as a beast.' Here, in his first creative moment, Forster is absorbed in these supernatural presences that recurrently haunted him; at Cadbury Rings and the Marabar Caves. The two chapters which follow are intellectual creation. Everything is made to seem likely and a willing suspension of disbelief is no longer expected of us. As Forster says in his Introduction: 'a fresh hemisphere has swung into action. All a writer's faculties, including the valuable faculty of faking, do conspire together thus for the creative act.' So the next youngest member of the party was very nearly possessed by Pan, and Eustace, who was, behaves in beastly fashion when he sees the goat's footmarks and 'lay down and rolled on them'.

We are told how it all happened. There is a 'carrier' or 'medium', the young Italian waiter. It has happened before, to a girl in his village and she died because she was shut in when possessed by Pan. Young Gennaro, the waiter, becomes alive as the other characters do not, just as Gino, in the first novel, has much more life than the suburbanites with whom he deals so aptly. But Gennaro gives his life for Eustace. It has been said that the inspiration of these later parts of the story is intellectual but within that ambience comes the first of those highly-wrought paragraphs which Forster achieves as a good Edwardian. It comes when Eustace escapes from the house at night and is possessed by speech: 'here was a boy, with no sense of beauty and a puerile command of words, attempting to tackle themes which the greatest poets have found almost beyond their power.' Then comes the description which the Edwardians so often made as if accepting a challenge: 'He spoke first of night and the stars and planets...He spoke of the rivers and waterfalls...And then he spoke of the rain and the wind by which all things are changed, of the air through which all things live, and of the woods in which all things can be hidden.'

The Road from Colonus

Forster received his next story—'sitting down on the theme as if it were an anthill' he calls it—in Greece, 'where the whole of The Road from Colonus hung ready for me in a hollow tree not far from Olympia'. It is the story of an ageing man who has nothing to live for being suddenly reconciled to life, understanding and accepting it and in that moment instinctively putting himself into a position to end it. This appropriate move is prevented by a daughter who officiously preserves him from his perfect ending. It becomes the favourite Edwardian theme of being tied to the wheel of life and we watch the inevitable disintegration of the old man and recall the similar disintegration of Mrs Moore in *A Passage* after her experiences in the cave.

A second reading brings the famous echoes for the first time. The old man's experience is associated with the water running from the tree: 'he lay motionless, conscious only of the stream below his feet, and that all things were a stream, in which he was moving.' It was his moment of reconciliation: 'something unimagined, indefinable, had passed over all things, and made them intelligible and good.' The echo comes angrily in the second chapter when the old man cries out peevishly after a bad night in his own home: 'there's nothing I dislike more than running water.' It is the first of many studies of querulous old age, and there is irony too, that the old man, wrapped up in his complaints, should have completely forgotten his moment of reconciliation with life. When, by an ingenious bit of machinery he learns that the great tree had fallen during the night he would have been there, he waves it all away. He is absorbed in present irritations: 'the children next door are intolerable, and I cannot stand the noise of running water.'

The Other Side of the Hedge

There was a third story that year, and it was Anglo-Saxon rather than Greek. It would have done for a sermon to simple folk and if it were treated by critics as scripture it would yield a volume of parallels, cross-references and exegesis. It is a parable on the vanity of the active life, an exhortation to the life of contemplation amid gracious natural surroundings: a monkish apology. The speaker has got everything wrong. 'Give me life', he cries, 'with its struggles and victories, with its failures and hatreds, with its deep moral meaning and its unknown goal!' We meet him when he was beginning to fail in the race, and he thinks he is going to be like his brother, who failed earlier: 'He had wasted his breath on singing, and his strength on helping others. But I had travelled more wisely.' He escapes through a gap in the hedge and does not realize he is out of the race. When he walks with the man who pulled him out of the water he finds it difficult, for instinctively 'I was always trying to outdistance my companions'. He has escaped from the rat race into a William Morris heaven where everyone was content, 'engaged in gardening, hay-making, or other rudimentary industries' while he declares: 'Science and the spirit of emulation – those are the forces that have made us what we are.' The whole situation is strangely modern. He is 'bewildered at the waste in production' and asks what it all means. When he is told it means nothing but itself, he cannot agree, for 'every achievement is worthless unless it is a link in the chain of development'. So the narrator reproduces all the arguments for Progress, but in the end he drinks symbolically and sinks into oblivion as he recognizes beauty, and the man whose drink has given him oblivion as his brother. A Pre-Raphaelite effect.

The Eternal Moment

In the following year he published 'The Eternal Moment' in three instalments, in *The Independent Review*, a magazine founded by Goldie and other friends. So far as we are concerned they did so to set Forster on his way, for the previous stories were published there also. This story is entirely different in treatment and mood. Much nearer D. H. Lawrence. This is the year in which he published his first novel and this piece is almost a novella. The supernatural does not appear. The storyteller and not the preacher or the scholar is in charge. With the result that this story has faded more than the others. The notions on decorum and class on which the story depends are those from which we have broken away.

Miss Raby, the central character, is established in the opening as a novelist of good sense and ample intelligence. 'She was not enthusiastic over the progress of civilization, knowing by Eastern experiences that civilization rarely puts her best foot foremost, and is apt to make the barbarians immoral and vicious before her compensating qualities arrive.' She had written a novel, *The Eternal Moment*, early in her career: 'she had written it when she was feeling young and happy and that, rather than maturity, is the hour in which to formulate a creed.' The novel was set in a tiny village in the Alps and was such a great success that the place had become a popular resort. Now, twenty years later, she was going back rather apprehensively to see what had happened. As soon as she walked through the village again she sensed 'the indefinable corruption which is produced by the passage of a large number of

people'. Was it said that the preacher was not in charge? Here is a
sermon against the tourist trade, the gist of it in one splendid
paragraph: 'A village must have some trade; and this village had
always been full of virility and power...Civilization did not relax
these energies, but it had diverted them; and all the precious
qualities, which might have helped to heal the world, had been
destroyed. The family affection, the affection for the commune, the
sane pastoral virtues—all had perished...' And the people who had
done it were 'ladies and gentlemen, who were good and rich and
often clever' who 'thought they were conferring a benefit, moral as
well as commercial, on any place in which they chose to stop.'
What a sermon for the times, when we are all so busy vulgarizing
one another's countries.

Among those who had been harmed by the popularity of the
place was the old woman who owned the original hotel, a place as
unlike the garish new hotels as possible. It is a 'cleanly, gracious
dwelling' where the 'most trivial things—the sofa cushions, the
table cloths, the cases for the pillows—though they might be made
of poor materials and be aesthetically incorrect, inspired her with
reverence and humility'. Miss Raby is determined to help the old
lady and discovers that in the hotel run by the old lady's son, who
takes most of her trade away, there is a concierge who bribes every
contact and publicity outlet. She also learns that this concierge is
the guide who made passionate love to her on the hillside twenty
years ago. This leads to a dramatic scene in the lounge of the new
hotel and the third person in the scene is Colonel Leyland, with
whom she is travelling. It is here that we meet the old manners and
social rules. It was outrageous that a young peasant had offered her
flowers and declared his passion. It was thoroughly embarrassing
to the peasant to be reminded of it now. He thought she was trying
to ruin him, whereas she only wanted him to show mercy to the old
woman in the old hotel. As for Colonel Leyland, the retired soldier
and bachelor who had vague thoughts of settling down and suggesting marriage to the rich woman novelist, it completely finished him.
'She had exposed her thoughts and desires to a man of another
class' and in his manly way he discovered she had been in love with
this concierge and probably still was. Her own discovery was that

she was only just no longer in love with him. In a well-wrought
Edwardian paragraph, in that nostalgic tone we can hear in so many
of these writers, we hear what this unacknowledged love had done
for her: 'the incident upon the mountain had been one of the great
moments in her life—perhaps the greatest, certainly the most
enduring...A presumptuous boy had taken her to the gates of
heaven; and, though she would not enter with him, the eternal
remembrance of the vision had made life seem endurable and
good.'

What could be more Edwardian than that? A contemporary
reviewer could have been forgiven if he saw here the first blos-
somings of a great popular novelist. She even wishes to adopt one
of the peasant's children, and then we drop back into reality as we
see him calculating as Gino calculated the bribe against love. In the
end, she escapes the scene she has made without further tragic
gesture and goes out to face old age alone, while the men recover as
men of the world do. If the reader requires a tonic reaction to this
story of the Swiss tourist trade at that time, he will probably turn to
Norman Douglas's agreeable outburst in *Siren Land* six years later:
'long may Switzerland with its sham honey, sham wine, sham
coffee, sham cigars, and sham Wilhelm Tell...continue to attract,
and wholly absorb, the superbly virile energies of our own upper-
better-middle classes.'

The Curate's Friend

It was a couple of years before another story was published and
the next was light-hearted mockery of fauns. 'Current literature did
not suffer from any lack of fauns' said Max Beerbohm and Forster
has his throw at them here. It was the other side of his preoccupation with the spiritual presences in nature. The narrator is a
curate, the traditional butt. 'Every Tuesday I gave what I called
"straight talks to my lads"—talks which led straight past anything
awkward. And every Thursday I addressed the Mothers' Union
on the duties of wives and widows, and gave them practical hints on
the management of a family of ten.' It is all good Sawston fun. He
goes on a picnic, as Edwardians always seemed to be doing, with his

fiancée, her mother and a pleasant youth. Unfortunately fauns are about and unfortunately he alone sees them. They tease him and he behaves with apparent foolishness. Then the faun, as fauns do, turned his attention to the boy and girl: 'They, who had only intended a little cultured flirtation, resisted him as long as they could, but were gradually urged into each other's arms, and embraced with passion.' Friendly faun! The curate is released from the threat of marital bondage and lives happily ever afterwards.

The Celestial Omnibus

'The Celestial Omnibus' was published four months later and could have been in response to the great liking of the Edwardian public for serious literary references, so amply satisfied for example by William J. Locke. We can be sure that Mr Bons, presumably a literary snob emigrant from Erewhon, was a reader of this kind. More probably, the story was in revolt from this sort of thing and Mr Bons's literary tastes are no better than those of Leonard Bast. But here it is not the sophisticated collegian who is the true reader, but the boy. Mr Bons comes a terrible cropper when he meets Dante, while the boy travels serenely with any of them, Dante or Sir Thomas Browne. We are in suburbia again, well-known Forsterian territory by 1908, and the boy is cruelly ridiculed by his parents in a suburban way. But he defies them, manages to get out of the house and finds his omnibus, in which he travels with Sir Thomas to a Wagnerian heaven. He is rescued from this heady experience by Jane Austen and is soundly beaten by his father for untruthfulness when he innocently talks about his journey. Mr Bons undertakes to prove to the boy that he has dreamed his journey by undertaking to go with him to the bus stop at the right time. Off they go and in their excited talk the boy confuses all writing, Dante and Dickens and Tom Jones. We recall the picture Forster drew twenty years later in the Clark Lectures of all the novelists at work together in one room. The boy faced the reality of literature innocently and happily. He stands on the shield of Achilles at the hero's bidding while that cultivated reader, Mr Bons, whimpers in terror. The fantasy ends with Dante telling Mr Bons: 'I cannot save

you. For poetry is a spirit; and they that would worship it must
worship in spirit and in truth.' Mr Bons fails, of course, and his
body is later 'found in a shockingly mutilated condition in the
vicinity of the Bermondsey gas-works'. The boy is crowned with
laurel leaves.

We note the literary references: Keats rather than Shelley,
Dante, one of Forster's three great writers, Jane Austen. But the
most interesting reference is the most oblique: the Erewhonian
name of Mr Bons—and we turn to Forster's essay on *Erewhon* to
have our story illumined. The story of 1908 is explained in 1944.
'He wanted to write a serious book not too seriously.' So he used
the fantasy technique: 'I like the idea of fantasy, of muddling up
the actual and the impossible until the reader isn't sure which is
which.' That is exactly what we are given, a mixture of suburbia
and Wagnerian heaven, which we absorb without difficulty. The
mixture is made to seem quite natural, we are easily 'bounced'. We
also learn in this essay what we see implied in the story about Mr
Bons, that he and his like will never really be able to read: 'I
suggest that the only books that influence us are those for which we
are ready, and which have gone a little further down our particular
path than we have yet got ourselves. I suggest, furthermore, that
when you feel that you could almost have written the book yourself
—that's the moment when it is influencing you.'

Other Kingdom

'Other Kingdom' brings further echoes. Here, the cultivated and
sensitive girl escapes in classical fashion from her coarse business
fiancé, for she is able to disappear among the trees, apparently by
becoming one. In *Howards End*, Helen escapes the crudities of
Henry Wilcox because her own intellectual intolerance and his
crudity are all mellowed by the influence of the house. The clash of
temperaments is the same as here. It is a similar clash as between
Soames Forsyte and his wife, and they illustrate the Edwardian
theme, the appearance of intellectual womanhood in our philistine
society. H. G. Wells deals with it in his own way and Shaw, in
Irish detachment, least painfully of all. Forster uses an echo. The

boy says the classics are full of tips: 'They teach you how to dodge things' and gives examples. 'You aren't particularly keen on Universal Nature, so you turn into a reed.' Miss Beaumont catches the allusion and when Midas is introduced she declares he will not touch her. Then her fiancé, Harcourt Worters, joins them and we recognize a lesser Henry Wilcox at once. He has bought the copse, which had 'always made an ugly notch in the rounded contours of the Worters estate'. The boy is silent at the news but he smiles to himself and reminds us of Eustace. These young boys in early Forster, so near nature. The girl makes postures like a tree while her lover smiles and tells her that the copse is hers. He tells her it is a second engagement ring but we know it is not another bond but an escape.

There is a little sketch of Worters' hypocrisy and then one of the boy Ford, who has dreams of a better society: 'robust dreams, which take him, not to heaven, but to another earth.' The approach to the improbable is made gradually. The wood bought on a lease is now bought outright. It is Miss Beaumont's for ever. We learn she has come from Ireland and she is still unformed. In Edwardian parlance: 'She has not yet developed her soul.' We recall what Forster said in the introduction to these stories: 'All a writer's faculties...conspire together thus for the creative act, and often do contrive an even surface, one putting in a word here, another there.' Our eye is attracted again and again to the boy, Ford, as if he had the clue all along to a mystery which will be unfolded to us. As the words are put one after another to develop Worters, we see he is partly another Bons, a man who reads quite in vain. 'She scarcely knows her Tennyson at all. Last night in the conservatory I read her that wonderful scene between Arthur and Guinevere.' Leonard Bast never did quite so badly as that.

Then the words develop the girl's unconscious instinct for freedom, never to be tied, never to be fenced in. He is going to 'develop' her wood with fences and asphalt paths. She tells him local rustic stories about cutting initials on trees and the section ends in sheer fantasy when to please her he cuts their initials: 'Harcourt! What's that? What! that red stuff on your finger and thumb?'

The section that follows, the third, is Meredithian in its speed

and allusivesness. Mr Worters discovered the boy's private notebook, with its many caricatures of his guardian. The tutor tries to
persuade him to apologize and Miss Beaumont overhears. She
refuses to believe that apology is necessary and to prove it she goes
to Worters. The boy knows that she is about to be disillusioned and
cries for her. She comes back in disarray, defeated and sends a
parting message to the boy who is being sent away: 'I am sorry I
called him a cry-baby. He was not crying like a baby. He was
crying like a grown-up person, and now I am grown-up too.'
Words and then words, for we are not allowed to pause at section-
ending on that pathetic note, but on one of horrid sycophancy.
The tutor is speaking: 'I judged it right to repeat this conversation
to my employer.'

We have come to the last section when the words have to carry us
into the Other Kingdom, the utterly fantastic. They have got to
'bounce' us. It opens on reality and fantasy and while we look at the
tutor and the staid sisters we are also aware of the wood and the
great wind calling to Evelyn Beaumont and we watch her responding
unawares. Soon Forster has to increase the speed and intensify the
rhythm as she dances one of her tree dances and cries: 'I have all
that there is in the world.' Once again, thus early, he displays his
great prose power. The chase follows, and she escapes him, for ever,
as Ford assures him grimly when Worters chases her to Ford's home
in the vulgar belief that he will find her there. 'She has escaped
you absolutely, for ever and ever.' This is fantasy turned to passion
as nowhere else in the short stories. The old theme of escape by
dying, in the classical fancy of not returning into the earth but
remaining on it.

The Machine Stops

The play of fancy returns to intellectual amusement in 'The
Machine Stops', 'a reaction to one of the earlier heavens of H. G.
Wells', published later in 1909, when Wells had left scientific
fantasies far behind and published *Tono-Bungay* and one of his
pieces on the emancipation of women, *Ann Veronica*. We have to
remind ourselves as we read the plain, bare expository style of this

short story that Forster had already published three of his
novels. (Or was it written even earlier? Once again the puzzling
problem of the dates of writing comes up.) The lucid, colourless
exposition continues through two chapters in which we learn all
about the new world in which everyone lives alone in a space
capsule, isolated from the earth and the atmosphere. It was so easy
for the Edwardians to foresee the lunacies of our day. Life is
entirely managed by the Machine (our computers, presumably)
and men are cut off from the air and the earth and the sea. Radio
and television are foreseen and when the telephone is used the caller
appears on the screen. Not bad for 1909. The sanction is Homelessness and that means being cast out into the atmosphere and that
means death. Kuno is threatened with Homelessness because he has
dared to visit the earth without an Egression-permit and he has
asked his mother, Vashti, to visit him so that he can tell her. The
Machine, unlike Big Brother, cannot overhear. The second chapter
provides a certain amount of sterilized fun about space fiction.
'Each infant was examined at birth, and all who promised undue
strength were destroyed.' Later, when Kuno describes his journey
to the earth's surface, his mother replies that he is brave and so:
'She knew he was fated. If he did not die today he would die
tomorrow.. On avatism the Machine can have no mercy.' *Fin de
siècle* space fiction? Forty years later, Orwell was pointing out that
machines would eventually make adventure impossible and courage
unnecessary. Man would become a drugged animal in a space ship.
What scientists do today imaginative men told us years and years ago.
Kuno had his adventure: 'I have seen the hills of Wessex as
Alfred saw them when he overthrew the Danes.' We are back in
the country of *The Longest Journey*, with all the strange attraction
of pre-history. 'I felt that those hills had called with incalculable
force to men in the past.' Part Three opens with a little amused
embroidery of the theme. A lecturer exhorts his audience to
'beware of first-hand ideas'. They seem to live on non-stop radio in
their capsules, though apparently not so inane as the real thing now.
'Let your ideas be second-hand, and if possible tenth-hand, for
then they will be far removed from that disturbing element — direct
observation. Do not learn anything about this subject of mine —

the French Revolution. Learn instead what I think Enicharmon thought Urizen thought Gotch thought Ho-Yung thought Chi-Bo-Sing thought Lafcadio Hearn thought Carlyle thought Mirabeau said about the French Revolution.' Forster has never been very far from scholarly problems. Things in the story then begin to go badly. Vashti receives a disturbing telephone call from Kuno. She is still with us only because the Machine had rejected her request for Euthanasia. The death rate was not allowed to exceed the birth rate and breeding stock was not in good supply. Kuno said 'The Machine stops' and the rest of the story describes that happening. Everything broke down, until an unexpected terror came—silence. It killed thousands of people, those who relied most on perpetual radio. Eventually, all the incapsuled people died, while Kuno prophesies that life will continue in Wessex among the mist and the ferns, and humanity will never again make the mistake of making machines. So, for an unexpected moment, Forster and Gandhi meet. But you can't get round the toothache, as Forster said elsewhere, and most of us are grateful for the machines that kill pain and do away with discomfort. We prefer comfort to courage if it is indeed true that the two are incompatible.

Mr Andrews

The next story, 'Mr Andrews', was published in the *Open Window* in April 1911. One of the wonders of Edwardian life was the number of journals in which short stories could be placed. Those were the bad old days when printers were paid less than writers. Once again the fantasy settles upon religion and plays round accepted belief. A Muslim and a Christian arrive in heaven together, the Muslim after fighting the infidel, the Christian after a life spent in the Board of Trade. Each receives the kind of heaven he expected. Each is dissatisfied as they learn from one another when they meet. Clearly it is true that anticipation is better than realization and generosity of mind better than both. 'Though he had all that he expected, he was conscious of no great happiness, no mystic contemplation of beauty, no mystic union with good. There was nothing to compare with that moment outside the gate, when he prayed that the Turk might enter and heard the Turk uttering the same prayer for him.' A moment later the Turk echoes these unexceptionable sentiments and they sensibly leave heaven together and become part of the world soul.

The Point of It

When Forster published 'The Point of It' later in 1911, his Bloomsbury friends did not like it. ' "What *is* the point of it?" they queried thinly, nor did I know how to reply.' Perhaps they did not know the wisdom of being cynical and so did not see the terror in the story. It seems to say that there is nothing in life or after it except the accumulating horror of memory. A strange example of young Forster's uncanny appreciation of the weariness of being old. In the story the good die young, with Forsterian suddenness, rowing against the tide, and they have fewer memories to disturb them. The rest live on uselessly, like Sir Michael, who had an exemplary life in the British Museum and in literature, and all that he had done was superseded before he died. He goes to hell, as everyone does, and hell is empty of everything but pain, the agonizing pain of things remembered and eventually the sickening pain of hope. Hope stirs him and he feels again the agony he endured when Harold rowed himself to death.

This is the only dangerous fantasy Forster wrote. Studied too much, it became corrosive, and it was written three years before his first visit to the country of Ancient Night, where, under the Indian sun, mind and all its values can so easily disintegrate, and where also the highest hopes of man can be evolved, his feet in the cloaca and his head amid the stars. There is a harsh streak in some of these fantasies, a preoccupation with old age and its disillusion, a recurring to the vanity of human wishes but never so concentrated as here. What possessed Forster to depict the old man lying paralysed, hearing his children and their children speak of the uselessness of anything he had ever done? In the end he rises out of hell to escape, it is suggested, by the efforts of Harold who rowed himself to death long ago. The ending is not nearly so powerful as the opening or these disintegrating descriptions in between.

Co-ordination

'Co-ordination' was published in June of the following year in *The English Review*, under the title of 'Co-operation'. It is all gaiety and nonsense, delightful fun, with every tinge of sadness turned to joy. It mocks greatness and the whole apparatus, so familiar to us now, of promoting popular reputations. Little girls at school play the Eroica as piano duets. Beethoven up in heaven is delighted to hear that his symphony is played so often but not more delighted than Napoleon, who regards this (and the reading of Wordsworth's sonnet 'Once did she hold') as homage to him. Each hero decrees that the performers shall be rewarded, and this all goes splendidly wrong and there is more joy in the girls' school than ever before. It is the gayest of romps culminating in another discomfiture of Mephistopheles. This, and not the frightening teller of the previous story, is the Forster we have known who leads to gaiety because it is hardly sensible in a pitiful world to lead anywhere else.

The Story of the Siren

The last story of all is scarcely gay. It was published by the Hogarth Press in 1920, but there is the usual teasing problem about when it was written, as Forster says in his Introduction: 'These fantasies were written at various dates previous to the first world-war, and represent all that I have accomplished in a particular line.' So this last story probably lay unpublished for many years, and he gave it to friends to help their publishing venture, as was his wont. It is a cruel little story, with much disagreeable ugliness, more suited to the world that had known the war. It is a Mediterranean story and goes naturally with all the stories about the men who knew that sea, from Norman Douglas's *Siren Land* to Maugham's 'Salvatore'. There are the usual tourists, the Colonel and the clergyman and the ladies, and there are the Italians. Sicilians this time, who know all about their siren. Giuseppe saw her and was possessed by her. 'When a child was born he would cover his face with his hands. If anyone married — he was terrible then.' The narrator reacts to the story of Giuseppe by being filled with desire to help others, which produces the familiar Forster comment on that aberration: 'the greatest of all our desires, I suppose, and the most fruitless'. The story continues, cruelly as a Mediterranean community can contrive. Giuseppe marries and his wife conceives. The rumour goes about that she will bear Antichrist. 'The whole village was in tumult, and the hotelkeepers became alarmed, for the tourist season was just beginning.' The village subscribes to pay her to go away and before she goes she climbs the cliffs to have a last look at the sea. She is pushed over the cliffs and Giuseppe prevents his younger brother avenging her by spraining his wrists. Giuseppe dies while searching for the Siren and the younger brother confidently expects her coming, when she will destroy silence and save the world.

There are two kinds of story, one in which what happens is what matters and the other in which what happens is only interesting because it affects a character or promotes reflection and speculation in the reader. In this collection of twelve there is only one normal short story, *The Eternal Moment*, and it is of the second kind. The story element in Forster's work is never strong. It is the play of intellect through the medium of well-managed prose that attracts us. The eleven fantasies are embroideries on amusing ideas. Believe in fauns and see what happens, or that a girl can turn into a tree or that Pan still lives. Go one further than H. G. Wells in science fiction and demonstrate that the world is shattered. Meditate, as some young people do, on old age and see how disillusioned you can become about ourselves and our society. Take the Christian and Muslim idea of heaven and see how it stands up to examination. Embroider playfully the idea of recording angels and great souls in heaven and an English girls' school and enjoy the gaiety of pure extravagance. Be driven by Dante to a Wagnerian empyrean and see if you survive not to tell the tale. Postulate the extraordinary and bring it within the ambience of the ordinary. By this test the fantasies are successful. One after another, oddities of thought that the Edwardians cherished are brought up for treatment, and very successful it all is. The only surprise is that there is so much cruelty and violence. In that, quite classical and so modern.

Abinger Harvest

ABINGER HARVEST is a collection of short pieces written between 1903 and 1935. They are mostly journalism, beginning with his earliest pieces, published in the Edwardian decade, when some Cambridge friends founded *The Independent Review* and printed his first essays as well as his first short stories. There is no elaborate design in the book, no cumulative impact, but only a rather perfunctory grouping of the pieces into four parts, The Present, Books, The Past, The East, followed by the text for a country pageant. The parts themselves do not cohere to achieve unified impact. The writer is a humanist who was never attached to a great sect whose gospel he must preach consistently. What we have here is the periodical journalism of a scholarly and imaginative young man of independent means who only wrote when he was interested, developing into the journalism of a distinguished writer in middle age. Most of it still gives pleasure and some of it is important for our understanding of the writer.

Take the first part. It begins with 'Notes on the English Character' and ends with a speech delivered in Paris on 'Liberty in England'. The 'Notes' can be compared amusingly with Orwell's findings twenty years later and the piece on 'Liberty' goes naturally with the essay 'What I Believe' which appeared in 1938, three years later and is reprinted in *Two Cheers*. The other pieces are shorter and may be considered first. The general impression is of an intense concern with values, a writer challenging those who have other values or none at all. 'Our Diversions' range from a note on a concert party in Egypt in 1917, an astringent reminder of what the English soldier expects as entertainment, to a facetious note on his own centenary and a perceptive analysis of the character of Mickey Mouse. 'Happiness', in 1920, is a review of a picture book on Macao and inspires reflections on magic islands which are 'the outcome of our sadness, and of our disgust with the world that we have made'.

'Gallipoli' in 1922 is a savage dialogue between two graves at a time when war threatened in the Middle East. It attacks the war leaders Lloyd George and Churchill and represents a general opinion not often heard. 'Me, Them and You' in 1925 is a further attack on war in response to a picture of gassed soldiers in the Royal Academy. 'Them' are the rich who go to the private view and 'You' are the soldiers whose sufferings are idealized in the picture, sterilized, so that it can hang in the fashionable exhibition. Literature has often noticed English soldiers returning from French battlefields to the cosy unawareness of home. Here, it is not only war but the social order that is pilloried: 'For what would we do without you? What would become of our incomes and activities if you declined to exist? You are the slush and dirt on which our civilization rests.' At the end there is a rhetorical note of hope: 'far away from the snobbery and glitter in which our souls and bodies have been entangled, is forged the instrument of the new dawn.' Which in due course turned out to be Hitler. The next piece—we are taking them by date and not by order of appearance in the book, and when the date in the book differs from the date in the bibliography, the bibliography is preferred—is about 'My Wood'. What effect does ownership have on us? He watches himself with genial amusement, it is all great fun and there are echoes of the short story 'Other Kingdom' if we care to hear them. In 1932 'Mrs Grundy at the Parkers' made a contribution to the literature on hypocrisy and interference. It ends with a throw at one of his familiar targets, committees: 'And as soon as they meet on committees...yes, I think we shall survive after all' says Mr Nosey Parker smugly.

The piece on Roger Fry after his death in 1934 is of a different calibre altogether and leads to the major essays in this part. It is an obituary celebration of the kind which adorns the second collection of essays. In these notices the subject represents some sorely needed virtue too little known today. In Fry's case, a belief in reason as against authority and intuition. 'Authority attracts our dictators and our serfs, because it seems to promise a stable society. Intuition attracts those who wish to be spiritual without any bother, because it promises a heaven where the intuition of others can be ignored.' He presses home the attack on intuition: 'the man who believes a thing is true because he feels it in his bones, is not really very far removed from the man who believes it on the authority of a police-man's truncheon.' He has always been willing to argue for the use of what brains we have. At the end he emphasizes the belief 'which underlies [Fry's] aesthetics' and all his activity: 'the belief that man is, or rather can be, rational, and that the mind can and should guide the passions towards civilization.' Once again, it is the intel-ligence which will carry us through 'the sinister corridor of our age'.

He is already in the deep shadows of the thirties but we can return now to 1926, when his 'Notes on the English Character' appeared in *The Atlantic Monthly*. He begins from the position that 'the character of the English is essentially middle-class' and names the common middle-class characteristics: 'Solidity, caution, integrity, efficiency. Lack of imagination, hypocrisy.' Orwell, who published his essay on 'The English People' in 1947, lists 'the salient charac-teristics of the English common people': 'artistic insensibility, gentleness, respect for legality, suspicion of foreigners, sentimen-tality about animals, hypocrisy, exaggerated class distinctions, and an obsession with sport.'

The virtues that Forster mentions as middle-class forty years ago, 'Solidity, caution, integrity' are in temporary short supply. The middle classes have decayed all over Europe and these virtues have to be fought for if Europe is to recover its tone. The gentleness which Orwell mentions is still there and well noted. He had lived where anger was sudden and turmoil habitual and noted the contrast when he returned to the 'deep, deep peace of England'. Today, we would mention acquisitiveness, because we have been corrupted by the extraordinary prosperity which has overtaken western nations. The most serious social aspect of acquisitiveness in England is obsessive gambling. The moral aspect is the loss of values either in behaviour or taste. English pleasure is normally dull vulgarity. The middle classes used to stand for individuality, which meant at one extreme eccentricity and at the other leadership which meant efficiency and integrity. So many now work in huge organizations that these virtues flourish uneasily. Neither Forster nor Orwell mention the political ineptitude of the English, nor the chronic addiction to amateurism in public affairs. The first is surprising as both had a developed political sense. Forster is first class on eastern affairs and Orwell was one of these rare Englishmen who could apply his intelligence clearly to politics.

We shall see in the next collection of essays how powerfully Forster spoke for freedom in the war years, but he could not foresee how busily we would make our own political and economic chains afterwards. Now, in the happy twenties, we find him enjoying himself at what is 'at the heart of the middle classes—the public schools'. Things have changed since he wrote and today it would seem desirable to send every boy to a residential school in the hope of making a clean break with the class obsessions of the workpeople and producing what has so consistently eluded the English, an educated people. Forster could not be expected to see this in 1926 and he is content to note, as so often before and after, that some men get no farther than being 'old boys', schoolboys at heart, all their lives. This seems very bad to him but it is a fact in nature and it is a merciful dispensation that they can do useful work in trade and industry at an early mental age. Quite a number of people, we might add, worship their college and their university all their lives and yet seem contented and useful.

Forster proceeds to what he believes is a public school weakness, 'the undeveloped heart', and in so far as this is a dislike of showing emotion, it is a form of social behaviour common to all classes of Englishmen and could fairly be described as good manners, an aspect of Orwell's 'gentleness'. Forster is now in a dilemma, for if the Englishman is emotionally slow and cool, how is it that he has produced so much great poetry? It is because the English heart in general is not really cold, there are 'hidden springs of fire'. And there is a social inhibition about revealing them. He turns to religion, another aspect of things of the spirit. Here the innate English decency comes out and religion encourages the habit of thinking of others instead of selfishly. 'Right conduct is his aim. He asks of his religion that it shall make him a better man in daily life: that he shall be more kind, more just, more merciful, more desirous to fight what is evil and to protect what is good.' As he says: 'No one could call this a low conception' and in the restless turmoil of acquisitiveness which we now endure, we could wish that these religious ideals still prevailed. He goes on to note that we have produced no prophets and few saints. Our religious norm has been 'a steady level of piety, a fixed determination to live decently'. Would that we had this piety today when acquisitiveness has fragmented society.

He comes to the traditional charge against the Englishman—he is a hypocrite. But self-deceit is a universal human complaint and quite unconscious, so he comes energetically to his own habitual charge: 'Muddleheadedness? Of this I believe them to be guilty. When an Englishman has been led to a course of wrong action, he has nearly always begun by muddling himself.' It is an early discussion of doublethink before Orwell gave us the word. It all comes into *Howards End* in the Wilcox family. He retails a long example, Jane Austen's Dashwoods in *Sense and Sensibility* when he might have referred to the discussion of the note Ruth Wilcox wrote just before she died.

When we compare Forster's essay generally with Orwell's, it would seem that the English have not improved noticeably in twenty years. They had not been easy years. The slowness which in Forster is incompleteness becomes gentleness in Orwell. The public schools, representing class distinctions, are still there. Hypocrisy is still an obvious trait and even in Orwell has not yet become doublethink. Twenty years on there is still no dramatic improvement to report. The English still think that cheating one another is the natural way in which a human society works. The economic marvel which has brought such affluence to Western Europe has changed the stresses a little but the Englishman remains much the same, gentle and stupid, politically inept, chronically addicted to amateurism in the conduct of public affairs, averse to showing emotion, without much feeling for beauty, a chronic gambler and prominent among the doublethinkers. It would be a pity while enjoying the pleasure of denigrating ourselves, to forget entirely that a generation is growing around us that shows the high promise of every generation and which only requires leadership that has vision and is selfless to transform English life and make the acquisitive agglomerations in this island a human society.

He touched on social questions when he spoke in Paris in 1935 to the Congress of Writers. In that place of Latin oratory, he pursued his English fashion of plain, lively speech, keeping to what was real and even running into a mass of detail about a particular case, a serious book by James Hanley called *Boy*, which had been prosecuted as an obscene libel. He begins by asserting our cultural tradition of free speech and admits that we did not mean freedom for Indians and Africans, or that freedom meant much to the unemployed. 'The hungry and the homeless don't care about liberty any more than they care about cultural heritage. To pretend that they do care is cant.'

He admits his bourgeois upbringing and admits that he might have been a communist 'if I was a younger and a braver man, for in Communism I see hope. It does many things which I think evil, but I know that it intends good.' He offers a perceptive phrase which we would do well to remember today, 'Fabio-Fascism', which is 'the dictator-spirit working quietly away behind the façade of constitutional forms...it is the traditional method by which liberty has been attacked in England.' He goes on to speak for positive things, more freedom of expression for writers and critics, which to him means revision of the libel laws and the laws on writing about sex. He wants more publicity for all sorts of comment and notes government control of broadcasting as a difficulty. Today, when we see what freedom offers, we cannot be so sure. Freedom of comment was common among the Edwardians but they did not pay their printer well and that is surely the main reason why we have so little comment now; it has been priced out of the market.

He raises his voice as he comes to the end of his address. He is conscious of ideological opposition from his English colleagues at the Congress. It was the days of silken intellectual communism, a gesture and a pose that was very soon to be abandoned when the war came. He says he speaks individually and probably his English colleagues at the Congress 'may feel that it is a waste of time to talk about freedom and tradition when the economic structure of society is unsatisfactory'. He pursues the thoughts of his fellow-delegates: 'They may say that if there is another war writers of the individualistic and liberalizing type, like myself and Mr Aldous Huxley, will be swept away. I am sure that we shall be swept away.' Wrong. It was the silken communist conference-haunters who were heard of no more. He has come to the end and rises to eloquence: 'I am worried by thoughts of a war oftener than by thoughts of my own death.' It is one of his most eloquent outcries about the coming catastrophe and the prospect haunted his writing all through the thirties. His last word is an exhortation to courage: 'If a writer is courageous and sensitive he has to my mind fulfilled his public calling. He has helped to rally humanity in the presence of catastrophe.'

It is the Stoic attitude, trying to make man invulnerable, able to achieve tranquillity. But Forster, like the rest of us, was torn two ways. He has the Stoic idea of detachment, of peace within the general worldly agitation. But he has always been involved, committed to speaking out, as English writers have always done, for freedom of speech, freedom from the fear of tyranny. Yet he would probably subscribe to Arnold's idea of independent men:

> *Bounded by themselves, and unobservant*
> *In what state God's other works may be*
> *In their own tasks all their powers pouring.*
> ('Self-Dependence')

The Stoic is apt to bear on his shoulders all the weight of a weary world, and Forster has avoided that by his insistence on gaiety and by fighting for the freedom that writers require without dissipating his energies on a more general crusade. It is that concentration of his power on his own tasks, which has made his great literary reputation during the decades when he has produced no imaginative work.

We find this modified Stoicism expressed three years later in his essay 'What I believe'. He speaks for 'tolerance, good temper and sympathy' which is a warmer Stoicism. He says: 'I have to keep my end up' in an Age of Faith and starts with personal relations. Elsewhere there is no certainty. There is 'something incalculable in each of us, which may at any moment rise to the surface and destroy our normal balance.' People let him down at times, so he must be reliable himself, and that involves warmth: 'reliability is impossible unless there is natural warmth.' Most men, he says '*want* to keep faith'. Then comes the Stoical indifference to outward things: 'I hate the idea of causes, and if I had to choose between betraying my country and betraying my friend, I hope I should have the guts to betray my country.' He expresses the Stoic view of the nature of things: 'there lies at the back of every creed something terrible and hard for which the worshipper may one day be required to suffer.' It is a hard way of saying that we must stand upon principle, and belief so far has taken us no further than the conservation of friendship.

This is a basis for social relationships and he turns to public relationships by declaring for democracy. Not because it is very good but because it is better than the alternative. 'It does start from the assumption that the individual is important and that all types are needed to make a civilization.' The second cheer for democracy comes because it allows criticism. There is still one place where an Englishman can speak freely if he can catch the Speaker's eye. There is always the possibility that a scandal, great or small, will be taken up in the newspapers or on television.

He turns to consider force and violence. In the thirties they could not be ignored. We felt them pressing on us from Europe. 'I realize that all society rests upon force. But all the great creative actions, all the decent human relations, occur during the intervals when force has not managed to come to the front.' These intervals he calls 'civilization'. As he goes on we feel the pressure of the times upon him: 'I look the other way until fate strikes me...I know that if men

8

had not looked the other way in the past, nothing of any value would survive.' Then at once there is an echo from the speech on Liberty in England, when he said in the heightened peroration: 'One must behave as if one is immortal, and as if civilization is eternal. Both statements are false—I shall not survive, no more will the great globe itself—both of them must be assumed to be true if we are to go on eating and working and travelling, and keep open a few breathing holes for the human spirit.' To us now it may seem a little extravagant to have to say anything that is so obviously the condition of human life, but in that time of the breaking of Europe he repeats it in this second declaration of faith: 'The people I respect most behave as if they were immortal and as if society was eternal. Both assumptions are false: both of them must be accepted as true if we are to go on eating and working and loving, and are to keep open a few breathing holes for the human spirit.' A following phrase shows again how much the burden of the times lay upon him, however much he looked the other way: 'men have always insisted on behaving creatively under the shadow of the sword.' It comes again, a little further on: 'This is such a difficult moment to live in, one cannot help getting gloomy and also a bit rattled, and perhaps short-sighted.' Some day someone will analyse the reactions in our writing during that decade to the sense of imminent catastrophe.

Meanwhile, he has acknowledged the possibility of a more opti-mistic view. 'Others, with more vision or courage than myself, see the salvation of humanity ahead...Certainly it is presumptuous to say that we *cannot* improve' and at once we think of another con-temporary humanist, Julian Huxley, who also has written about Belief. In a lecture delivered in 1954, when Europe was recovering rapidly from the thirties and forties, Huxley looks forward as scientists do, instead of backwards like those who are only concerned to conserve. For the scientist, the possibility of a brilliant future lies before mankind. Like Forster, Huxley is against force, especially the forcing of beliefs, and notes that 'the largest advances have taken place when there has been the greatest outbursts of free, creative activity of the human mind and spirit'. Those periods which Forster says come in between and which he calls civilization. Huxley says we can bring better things into existence and elsewhere he stresses that the one possibility of further natural evolution is the human brain. Other evolution has reached its limits but the human brain can become more efficient. As he says here: 'Man is the agent or instrument of further evolution.' Our most creative belief must be in human possibilities. Faith will move the mountains of ignorance and prejudice and inertia. We may see it as the problem of turning neoliths into modern man, a problem successfully tackled in Russia and which we could all struggle with usefully, as our social aim no longer admits an elect living among the unconscious proles, but requires a healthy ambience in which all can react upon one another towards healthy progress.

The classical European view, to which Forster subscribes, is stated by Jung when he is writing about 'The Spiritual Problems of Modern Man'. He sees the truly modern man as solitary because he has risen so far beyond his fellows. 'Every step forward means an act of tearing himself loose from that all-embracing, pristine consciousness which claims the bulk of mankind almost entirely. Even in our civilization the people form, psychologically speaking, the lowest stratum, live almost unconsciously as primitive races.' We have not got away from that, as anyone who has met a 'D' stream in one of our Modern Secondaries knows. Jung, writing also in the thirties, can be even more depressing. He looks on twentieth century European man as the culminating achievement of twenty centuries and describes him as 'the worst conceivable disappoint-ment of the hopes of mankind'. For him, the man of the thirties 'has suffered an almost fatal shock, psychologically speaking, and as a result has fallen into profound uncertainty'. This is Forster's state in his essay as he looks, apparently in vain, for firm foundations. Nor is he able to see, like Jung, the best as well as the worst. Jung can speak of modern man, the one who is ahead of his fellows, making the way along which they will follow, in the old ecstatic words: 'the man who stands upon a peak, or at the very edge of the world, the abyss of the future before him, above him the heavens, and below him the whole of mankind, with a history that disappears in primeval murk.' It is this modern man, or Huxley's man with the increasingly better brain, who will dip into the future far as mortal eye can scan.

It is a fine conception, but when we return to Forster we find him, as usual, taking the very ordinary view. His head is never in the clouds and here he is discussing the aristocracy which keeps democracy sweet, the 'aristocracy of the sensitive, the considerate and the plucky...They represent the true human tradition, the one permanent victory of our queer race over cruelty and chaos.' These, for Forster, are the salt of the earth and their temple, as Keats said: 'is the Holiness of the Heart's Affection, and their kingdom, though they never possess it, is the wide-open world.'

Why is it never possible for such men to lead the nation? That, he says, is our tragedy: 'that no device can be found by which these private decencies can be transmitted to public affairs.' Forster, it seems, is more happily placed than his scientific brother humanists. He does not have to wait for a modern man to evolve, whose better brain will look after us, as it were a new scientific version of the theory of the elite so dear to Fascism. The saviour of the future, Forster is certain, 'will merely utilize my aristocracy, he will make effective the goodwill and the good temper which are already existing'. Under this aristocracy we will enjoy sensible economics which will banish poverty and in morals and politics: 'Not by becoming better, but by ordering and distributing his native goodness, will Man shut up Force in its box, and so gain time to explore the universe and to set his mark upon it worthily.'

It is not in his nature to hold these heights for long, so he speaks of failures, of the failure of Christianity, and he speaks again of insecurity and felt there was no shame in that 'since other people, whatever they felt, were equally insecure'. He even falls back on death as he did elsewhere, to give us hope. He has the preacher's instinct to know that his last word must be of immediate help in the situation which presses now, and the dread which pressed on England then was the dictator and the totalitarian. Human beings 'are obliged to be born separately, and to die separately, and, owing to these unavoidable termini, will always be running off the totalitarian rails. The memory of birth and the expectation of death always lurk within the human being, making him separate from his fellows and consequently capable of intercourse with them.'

We who have survived that decade and the catastrophe which followed and who have seen what a little mark, if any, it has left on the generation born in the forties, look upon this human resilience as a miracle and probably the miracle that will always save mankind. Human memory is one generation long, and this simple truth will help to evolve that fortunate society which will live beneficently under an aristocracy of the 'sensitive, the considerate and the plucky'.

Books

When we come to the next group of essays, on books, we do not at once leave these pressing topics. 'We are passing through... perhaps the roughest time that has ever been.' It is 1934 and we are discussing what books can do for us in time of general emergency. That an author tells us about himself when he writes of other authors is a commonplace that shine in these essays on books, as well as in the note which opens the part. He speaks in that 'Note on the Way' quite personally about what solace he finds in books in time of trouble. He speaks of the need for stoicism: 'Life as a retreat is rightly discredited; it is both selfish and foolish to bury one's head in the flowers. But herbs grow in the garden too, and share in its magics, and from them is distilled the stoicism which we badly need today.'

He mentions 'the early T. S. Eliot' as one of the writers he clung to in the worst days of the first war, and later he wrote three short pieces on Eliot's work, the first in 1928 the others in 1949 and 1950. Forster and Eliot are intellectual writers who do not address 'the lazy, the stupid, or the gross'. After that, the differences between them are obvious. The one is quintessentially English, the other would have liked to be. The one rises out of the tradition of English writing, the other could only long to be of it. The one is a humanist, the other in his search for acceptance into English traditionalism, was a High Anglican. The one is a master of the easy English writing way, the other a master of the high American way. We could not imagine Eliot in country tweeds. 'Literature to him is a serious affair' and one felt that life was altogether as serious to him as a part played on a stage, a place where you would never catch Forster.

With differences so obvious, it was natural that Forster should begin with compliment and he excels himself. He is writing of *Prufrock,* the book which had helped him in Alexandria: 'Here was a protest, and a feeble one, and the more congenial for being feeble. For what, in that world of gigantic horror, was tolerable except the slighter gestures of dissent?...he who could turn aside to complain of ladies and drawing-rooms preserved a tiny drop of our self-respect, he carried on the human heritage.'

The quotation is as well known as the later one on tradition. In the previous year, in *Aspects,* Forster had invited us to see all the novelists together at one time in the same room, so he could hardly subscribe to Eliot's thoughts on tradition. The final comment is a little unmerciful: 'one has a feeling at moments that the Muses are connected not so much with Apollo as with the older county families.' He is equally sharp over Eliot's love of the cryptogram-matic. It is no way for a writer to use his intelligence, to amuse himself setting traps for his reader. In the end: 'The verse always sounds beautiful, but often conveys nothing. The prose always conveys something, but is often occupied in tracing the boundaries of the unsaid.'

Over twenty years later Forster once again noticed two pieces by T. S. Eliot. Of the *Notes towards the Definition of Culture* he briefly says: 'But what cumbersome English.' And later, there is the same nimble way with the great American: 'There is much that is subtle and profound, much that is provocative, and we are bound to admit at the end that culture is even more important than we guessed.' The final notice is on *The Cocktail Party.* Forster clearly did not like it and to show his feeling about it he simply describes the story in short sentences of simple words. The effect is devastating. There is one generous touch at the end: 'It is most beautifully and lucidly written. T. S. Eliot can do whatever he likes with the English language.' But the final word is: 'On the stage, such diction may well carry all before it, and, reinforced by sound stage-craft, may place affairs in a less puzzling perspective.' Eliot's greatness lies elsewhere, but for once Forster permitted himself to point out weaknesses because the integrity of the intellect in writing is all-important and Eliot's reputation had got out of scale.

The essay on Ibsen was written in the same year as the first piece on T. S. Eliot and it is the most interesting piece we have on one of Forster's own special gifts, the power to raise prose writing to poetry. Ibsen does it in the drama as Forster does it in his novels. In general, the essay, like the one on Proust, reminds us how badly humanity comes off in the hands of great writers in fairly recent times. Ibsen took 'a harsh or a depressing view of human relationships...he found personal intercourse sordid. Sooner or later his characters draw their little knives, they rip up the present and the past, and the closer their intimacy the better their opportunities for exchanging pain.' The same morbid theory of 'only connect' is attributed to Proust. How they stressed that tragic dilemma in the human condition. This was not Forster's way but Virginia Woolf in her essay on him finds an affinity between him and Ibsen. 'Ibsen has the same realistic power. A room to him is a room, a writing table a writing table, and a waste paper basket a waste paper basket.' Earlier she has said that Forster has 'the impulses of a poet. The neat surface is always being thrown into disarray by an outburst of lyrical poetry.' But there is no comparison made with Ibsen there, while Forster finds that Ibsen 'was a poet during the earlier part of his life...He was a poet at sixty also...At some date previous to his Italian journey he must have had experiences of passionate intensity among the mountains' as Forster had had among the ancient Wiltshire Rings. Forster's poetry is the poetry of age, people of great age and the earth associated with ancient men in the rings and the caves.

Proust, like Ibsen, is a writer with whose work we shall welcome help. Forster's first piece is an appreciation of the Scott Moncrieff translation and in it he puts down what is essential in the long novel. The book 'is an adventure in the modern mode, when the nerves and brain as well as the blood take part, and the whole man moves forward to encounter he does not know what'. Europe as he wrote was enduring the first agonies of the decay she was to endure before rebirth. It was the cycle we meet in *A Passage to India*, the decay in the caves and the rebirth in the Temple. 'Avoiding tragic horror, which perhaps he mistrusted, and pity, which he could seldom supply, he has achieved a new view of the impermanence of the human race...But his actual belief in decay—that lies deeper than any fancy or theory, that rests direct upon his equipment of despair. Despair underlies all his view of personal relationships.' And Forster follows that with a note on the evil we come up against whenever we are tempted into optimism. Back of all hope is 'the element of gratuitous cruelty that exists in us' and which these writers in the twenties so clearly saw. Some day someone will write an essay on that decade in literary Europe. It will be an exercise in pessimism and it will dwell on the work of Proust, whose 'general theory of human intercourse is that the fonder we are of people the less we understand them—the theory of the complete pessimist'.

Towards the end he says that Proust 'exploring both the realms of social conduct and the realms of art' thought that 'on the whole art is best' which connects with the later piece, written in very different times. In the twenties we could afford despair. In the early forties, during the war, we looked everywhere for hope and for stable things. The second piece was a broadcast to India. It has a good word to say for Jewish blood and one or two other propaganda murmurs. The prose texture and the plan of the little essay have the simplicity required by the disembodied voice which is radio. The joy of the piece is that it tells us so much about Forster. He was always ready to speak openly to Indians. Here, for instance, is the *locus* on the famous echo. He says of Proust's novel: 'it is full of echoes, exquisite reminders, intelligent parallels, which delight the attentive reader' just like all Forster's novels. And Forster's readers will do well to take the advice he gives for reading Proust: 'It is important when tackling Proust to be patient and to be intelligent. He makes no concessions to stupidity...He expects a constant awareness, both from the mind and from the senses.'

There is one more theme in this essay we shall wish to remember, for it echoes all through his work; it is the Bloomsbury one, art. He says that Proust 'raised that rather tiresome word "art" to an importance and a sublimity which we cannot neglect' and he ends this wartime piece by saying that it is art which gives us hope: 'I do not believe that this art business can be swept aside. No violence can destroy it, no sneering can belittle it. Based on an integrity in man's nature which lies deeper than moral integrity, it rises to heights of triumph which give us cause to hope.' In another place it was the integrity of art, something that was whole and complete in a time of chaos.

It is natural in this Bloomsbury atmosphere to turn to the pieces on Virginia Woolf. They are apt to leave us a little uneasy, because Forster is always uncompromisingly honest (as she was when she wrote about him) and there is a sense of struggle in these pieces. Virginia Woolf loved writing and could write like an angel. She was trying for something very fine, a breakthrough in the technique of the novel, and it is possible to claim that she had some success. But when he is writing about her we feel that she was unable to give him the necessary help. It suggests the generalization that Forster is at his best only with the greatest writers. He has all the equipment to interpret them, just as we noticed in *Alexandria* that he has all the equipment to interpret the great ones in history. But here, as in the Forrest Reid pieces, his material does not give him the basis he needs.

The essay on Virginia Woolf's early novels appeared in the *New Criterion* in 1925 and is a model for the critic who seeks to distinguish a writer's special quality. The novel in the twenties tried to break out of the bonds of the old techniques and begin again. The novelist's material is words ('pen-marks on paper') and in the twenties, while Forster was using all the traditional power of words with the colour they had accumulated from the Authorized Version onwards to give us a great novel, Virginia Woolf and James Joyce were making original experiments with language patterns. The experiments were successful in themselves but not in establishing a technique which the next generation of novelists could develop. 'English fiction', says Forster in this essay, 'despite the variety of its content, has made little innovation in form between the days of Fielding and those of Arnold Bennett.' Despite experiment it continues in that condition.

Forster traces the development of Virginia Woolf's work with sensitive interest. Her style acquires its unique quality first in *Kew Gardens*: 'Her style trails after her, catching up grass and dust

8*

in its folds, and instead of the precision of the earlier writing we have something more elusive than has yet been achieved in English.' (He approves that so much he repeats it in the Rede lecture.) He quotes a long sample and suggests that the apparent objection to this kind of writing is that: 'it cannot say much or be sure of saying anything.' Then: 'So at least one would suppose, and that is why the novel of *Jacob's Room* (1922) comes as a tremendous surprise. The impossible has occurred. The style closely resembles that of *Kew Gardens*. The blobs of colour continue to drift past; but in their midst, interrupting their course like a closely sealed jar, rises the solid figure of a young man.' He defines the achievement: 'The coherence of the book is even more amazing than its beauty. In the stream of glittering similes, unfinished sentences, hectic catalogues, unanchored proper names, we seem to be going nowhere. Yet the goal comes, the method and the matter prove to have been one, and looking back from the pathos of the closing scene we see for a moment the airy drifting atoms piled into a colonnade.'

The magic is at work again. At the end, when the test comes that Forster always uses, the reverberations may be almost inaudible, but here we can only go on enjoying his skill. In the second part of the essay he distinguishes the subject matter she treats in this way. It starts with the first gift, 'visual sensitiveness', which 'becomes in her case a productive force...Yet vision is only the frontier of the kingdom. Behind it lie other treasures; in particular the mind.' That is her chosen subject matter: 'What thrills her—for it starts as a thrill—is the actual working of the brain, especially of a youthful brain, and there are passages in *Jacob's Room* where the process becomes as physical as the raising of the hand.' He develops the point: 'It is easy for a novelist to describe what a character thinks of; look at Mrs Humphry Ward. But to convey the actual process of thinking is a creative feat, and I know of no one except Virginia Woolf who has accomplished it.' (Poor Mrs Humphry Ward, why is he so unkind to her so frequently?)

The business of the novelist has always been to let us know what his characters are thinking, that private world which we reveal and conceal as we can in real life. Here, in the middle of that wonderful decade, Forster says this of characters in the novel: 'to capture their inner life presents a different problem to each generation of novelists; the great Victorians solved it in their way; the Edwardians shelved it by looking outwards at relations and houses; the Georgians must solve it anew, and if they succeed a new age of fiction will begin.' Two years later, in *Aspects,* he reminds us that people in a novel can be quite exposed if the novelist wishes: 'we have been told all about them that can be told; even if they are imperfect or unreal they do not contain any secrets, whereas our friends do and must, mutual secrecy being one of the conditions of life on this globe.' The Edwardian is speaking very soon after the publication of his last novel, when so many secrets were withheld between the characters and between writer and reader. He did not then know that he was to fall silent and that the Georgians were eventually to fail. He ends with the admission that Virginia Woolf's experiments are not all completely successful. Her characters are not alive all the time. He puts it in a way that recalls our feeling about *A Passage to India.* He says that her problem is to 'allow her readers to inhabit each character with Victorian thoroughness'. And he goes on: 'Think how difficult this is. If you work in a storm of atoms and seconds, if your highest joy is "life; London; this moment in June" and your deepest mystery "here is one room; there another", then how can you construct your human beings so that each will be not a movable monument but an abiding home, how can you build between them any permanent roads of love and hate?' It reads to us as a summary of the problem he set himself as a novelist, from the amusing juxtapositions in the early comedies to the character clashes against an Indian background. He indicates that the new technique had failed so far to solve it altogether, but: 'She herself believes it can be done, and, with the exception of Joyce, she is the only writer of genius who is trying.'

Between this piece and the lecture in 1941, Virginia Woolf wrote an article on Forster's novels which was as sympathetic and generous as his own. She notes that the 'social historian will find his books full of illuminating information' about the bicycle, the motor car and the domestic habits of Sawston. She notes the balance of stress in the novels: 'Sawston implies Italy; timidity, wildness; convention, freedom; unreality, reality.' She sees the poetry in the novels:

'he is also the most persistent devotee of the soul...it is reality; it is truth; it is poetry; it is love.' She notes, as we noted, that Forster insists on fighting: 'He believes that a novel must take sides in the human conflict.' She speaks of the poetry again: 'The neat surface is always being thrown into disarray by an outburst of lyric poetry.' She is describing her own gifts in describing his and now she comes to one which Forster stressed in the Rede lecture: 'Yet if there is one gift more essential to a novelist than another it is the power of combination...the single vision...the immense persuasiveness of a mind which has completely mastered its perspective.' This is what they were both seeking. She confirms the view that Forster is a preacher while she divides novelists into teachers and preachers and says that Forster 'has a strong impulse to belong to both camps at once.' He teaches us to connect the prose and the passion. Ibsen is brought in and our impression is confirmed that Forster was drawn to Ibsen because he gives us the effects of ordinary life and illuminates them with poetry, as Forster instinctively does himself. The analysis continues with feminine honesty, a troubled honesty, for neither *Howards End* nor *A Passage to India* achieves unity of vision, and perhaps Forster is most at home in comedy. He had immortal tragic longings in him. In her view, they have not been successful, and she ends in the hope that he will attempt something more.

In the Rede lecture he is able to cover all her work and there are modifications of the earlier view. He begins at the beginning, which was that she loved writing, turning sensations into words 'until out of the interactions, something, one thing, one, arose'. Has the idea of composition ever been better conveyed? This one thing, he says, is itself 'analogous to a sensation. Although it was so complex and intellectual, although it might be large and heavy with facts, it was akin to the very simple things which had started it off, to the sights, sounds, tastes. It could be best described as we describe them. For it was not about something. It was something.' She is an aesthete with no great cause at heart and that is the great distinction between her work and his. Forster always had a cause to fight for and usually to balance that a gay sense of comedy. Virginia Woolf lived in a middle region and had 'all the aesthete's characteristics;

selects and manipulates her impressions; is not a great creator of character; enforces patterns on her books; has no great cause at heart.'

When he comes to analysing the novels one by one he lifts whole sentences from the earlier essay. He analyses the novels with zest and the other writings dutifully and, having finished his survey, he states her problem: 'She is a poet, who wants to write something as near to a novel as possible', just as Forster found himself trying to transmute the novel form into poetry. It is at that point that we expect the lecturer to follow the essay and tell us that her unique contribution was 'to convey the actual process of thinking' but nothing of the kind. He tells his audience (in those days of food shortages) how good she is at describing food. 'She had an enlightened greediness which gentlemen...might envy.' Having tantalized his audience with her description of making a Boeuf en Daube (in 1944 he wrote a short story for *Wine and Food*) he gracefully proceeds to her intellectual qualities and her feminism. The world was man's mess and she would not be responsible for it. The valedictory note is triumphant: 'she pushed the light of the English language a little further against darkness.'

The other pieces in the section require only brief notice. When in 1920, he writes about Conrad, we see that long before the cult had grown, Forster is sceptical. 'Is there not also a central obscurity, something noble, heroic, beautiful, inspiring half a dozen books; but obscure, obscure?' It is easier for us to understand Conrad's difficulty now that it has been shown how much he depended on Maupassant when he wanted to explore emotion. Forster distinguished his greatness: 'what a noble artist is here, what an austere character, by whose side most of our contemporary writers appear obsequious.' But he is reviewing the *Notes on Life and Letters* and he diagnoses the weakness at the heart of Conrad's work with clinical finality: 'These essays do suggest that he is misty in the middle as well as at the edges, that the secret casket of his genius contains a vapour rather than a jewel; and that we need not try to write him down philosophically, because there is, in this particular direction, nothing to write.'

Forster had no difficulty in getting at the core of a character however much he 'bounced' us when it came to creating them. As we see in two pieces on minor Americans. One is on Sturgis: 'a foreigner in a front seat. His friend Henry James, equally well placed, fidgets in the seat slightly, and registers at moments a gratified awe as the procession passes, but Sturgis sits very quiet.' The piece is one of those delicious sketches of an Edwardian by an Edwardian, the kind of life, as Forster says, that was only possible at that particular stage in our civilization. 'His life wore away in quiet occupations, and in hospitality to interesting people and to the young, family servants looked after him or grew old in his service, invalid dogs tottered about, he lost much of his money, he became ill, and at the age of sixty-five he died in his own house.' He had taken to embroidery when he failed as a writer, which suggests the possibility of a massive export trade if others followed his example now. It was on the embroidery that the special incident depended: The revealing nonsense appears again:

> After lunch I made a little slip. My host led me up to the fire-place, to show me a finished specimen of his embroidery. Unluckily there were two fabrics near the fireplace, and my eye hesitated for an instant between them. There was a demi-semi-quaver of a pause. Then graciously did he indicate which his embroidery was, and then did I see that the rival fabric was a cloth kettle-holder, which could only have been mistaken for embroidery by a lout. Simultaneously I received the impression that my novels contained me rather than I them. He was very kind and courteous, but we did not meet again.

So much for the author of *Belchamber*. Sinclair Lewis receives less feline treatment and he was probably included because 'he is against dullness, heartiness and intolerance, a trinity of evils most closely intertwined'. The essay develops the contrast between the photographer and the artist and Sinclair Lewis was at best an efficient photographer.

Two more slight pieces should be noticed, one on T. E. Lawrence and one on Ronald Firbank. The writings of the ebullient twenties would be incomplete without fantasy and one of the strangest fantasists of them all, Ronald Firbank, appeared then, though, like so much of the twenties, he was a survivor from a former world.

'He is *fin de siècle*, as it used to be called; he belongs to the nineties and the *Yellow Book;* his mind inherits the furniture and his prose the cadences of Aubrey Beardsley's *Under the Hill.*' He seriously devoted himself to unseriousness and would go to great trouble and expense to display a pose. To the delicious stories in Osbert Sitwell this one may be added. At one time, when he dined every evening in a Roman restaurant, a fresh bunch of the best available grapes was put on his table. He raised the bunch delicately in front of him as he drank his wine and stared at them but never ate them. But: 'What charms us in him is his taste, his choice of words, the rhythm both of his narrative and of his conversation, his wit, and—in his later work—an opulence of gathered fruit and enamelled skies.' It is the mark of a great critic that he can place his contemporaries as well as those who come later, and Forster exerts here as so often that other quality of critical greatness: the work has additional vitality for us when we have read him.

For contrast we turn to a piece on *Seven Pillars of Wisdom*. Forster first met T. E. Lawrence in 1924 when he advised on the first draft of the book. In 1935 Forster reviewed it and three years later he wrote a short sketch on Clouds Hill, T. E.'s cottage near Bovington Camp. As usual, he gets to the heart of the matter. In the review he says: 'If we take compassion as a lodestar, it may lead us through the psychology of the *Seven Pillars* as surely as Damascus led us northward through the geography. Here is a young man describing himself as he was when still younger.' The young man who could 'lead an Arab army, fight, bluff, and spy, be hard and disciplinary' had an inner life which 'runs contrary. That course is turbid, slow, weighted by remorse for victory, and by disgust against the body.' He sums up by seeing what we would expect him to see: 'there is a latent unselfishness, a constant goodwill which are fundamental, and which the fires of his own suffering fuse into compassion.'

The later piece, in *Two Cheers*, reads like the more casual prose of broadcasting and the same ideas are suggested in a different way. We are among the daily details to which Forster loves to bring us back: 'T. E.'s kindness and consideration over trifles were endless, and after he had returned from camp one would find a hot water bottle in the bed, which he put there in case his precious visitor's feet should be cold. That was so like him.' This second piece, by being so casual in its happy nature, admits the nonsense: 'There were no fixed hours for meals and no one sat down. If you felt hungry you opened a tin and drifted about with it. It's a grand way to feed.' Then there was the nightjar that would call to keep Forster awake and the familiar cry about silence: 'Silence scarcely exists now...it is a lost luxury.' The ending is about the love of the countryside. Both T. E. and Forster had lived long enough under burning suns in barren lands to enjoy the deep, deep peace of the English countryside. 'T. E. cared intensely for the English country-side; he was hoping to explore it quietly upon a pushbike when the end came.'

We are left with the Jane Austen pieces, in which scholarship and critical faculty are lucidly combined. There are three pieces and they celebrate the work of R. W. Chapman, his great edition of the novels in 1924, of Sanditon in 1925 and of the letters in 1932. 'She is my favourite author! I read and re-read, the mouth open and the mind closed. Shut up in measureless content, I greet her by the name of most kind hostess, while criticism slumbers.' We recall that he prudently keeps three sets of the novels here and there in his rooms. The only thing of importance in the first piece is the recommen-dation, long since followed, that the shorter pieces should be reprinted.

The brief Sanditon piece is full of points. 'She writes out of what she has written, and anyone who has himself tried to write when feeling out of sorts will realize her state. The pen always finds life difficult to record; left to itself, it records the pen.' He notes that Sanditon exists 'as a geographic and economic force' and we imagine what a splendid romp Jane Austen would have given us if she had retailed all the economics of founding a watering place. But there was something else in her mind then. She has looked out of the window 'weary of civility and auntish fun' and Forster's ear catches a new cadence when from the window we see 'the road and all the Paths across the Down'. We have indeed a pentameter, a serious symptom in a prose writer. But we may also recall the time when Forster determined to desert comedy and was tempted out of doors in England by the Cadbury Rings.

In the piece about the letters, Forster gives his rather perplexed admiration to the scholar who can remain absorbed in uncovering little secrets, some 'almost peculiar to the hens' while the world is getting ready to crash about our ears: 'we can look on with admiration, our hands folded uselessly before us.' The letters are not very good letters. 'They do not draw distant ages together, like the letters which were written at the same time by Keats. They were temporary and local in their appeal, and their essential meaning went down with her into the grave.' They are about little things, they must be: 'She has not enough subject-matter on which to exercise her pen' and little things only have charm 'when it is the charm of Cowper'. But the little things must hold out their little hands to one another; and here there is a scrappiness which prevents even tartness from telling.' He is writing with an extraordinary intimate knowledge of this woman: 'perhaps she is one of the few country writers whom wider experience and consort with the literary would not have ruined.' He shows us that these rather dull letters tell us the central and essential thing. She was part of a family and: 'The accidents of birth and relationship were more sacred to her than anything else in the world, and she introduced this faith as the groundwork of her six great novels.' No mere male has understood our women writers better.

In this section on books there is no criticism in the grand manner. The writer's nature has not changed. He prefers to stay with the facts and celebrate the glory in simple things. It is not philosophical criticism but it has his magic, the ability to bring alive books and the people who wrote them.

The Past

The third part collects journalism from many places over the years from 1903 to 1935. He opens with a piece on 'The Consolations of History', from *The Athenaeum* of 1920, which was the place and time of his best journalism. He was back from Alexandria, where he had been using his leisure in the war years to read history and write his *Guide* and journalism for a local paper. He sums it up in this astringent essay. Writing history is attractive because we can snub the dead. We mix only with the top people. He shows an interest in curious Indian history and a petulant contempt for historians. 'With existence as it threatens today—a draggled mass of elderly people and barbed wire—it is agreeable to glance back at these enchanted carnages, and to croon over conditions that we now subscribe to exterminate. Tight little faces from Oxford, fish-shaped faces from Cambridge—we cannot help having our dreams.' He had been living in the Mediterranean harmony, among the cosmopolitans. But in the end, he says, the historian 'returns to the finer pleasures of morality' and awards marks. 'Sweet then is dalliance, censure sweeter. Yet sweetest of all is pity...To pity the dead because they are dead is to experience an exquisite pleasure.' The preacher wrings the last bitter drop from his theme. 'Pity wraps the student of the past in an ambrosial cloud, and washes his limbs with eternal youth...not "I feel chilly and grown old". That comes with the awakening.' He had not yet recovered from the war and we happily slip back to a 1903 piece about a trifle of Etruscan jewellery.

The theme of Friendship appears for the first time, beautiful men leaning on their spears, who have just been through another trial together. It includes the first defence of the humanist outlook as against the Christian: 'It declares that when the body is feeble the soul is feeble: cherish the body and you will cherish the soul. That was the belief of the Greeks; the belief in wearing away the body by penance, in order that the quivering soul may be exposed had not yet entered the world.' It ends for the first time in a way that is going to become familiar, a retreat into the ordinary from an O Altitudo. The woman who bought the trifle would have nothing to do with these brave interpretations of the engraved figures: 'I bought the thing because it was pretty, and stood nicely on the chest of drawers.'

In the next piece, on a visit to Cnidus, there is another reference to the wretched physique of so many people around this young Edwardian, the preoccupation that echoes in the novels: 'they are so weak-chested and anaemic and feeble-kneed.' The joy of the piece is the accomplished travel prose:

The rain hammered down on our umbrellas, and filled our ears with fictitious uproar. It was only when we put the umbrellas down to speak or listen to each other, that we heard what was really happening. There were sounds then from the black and illimitable grey—the bark of a dog, a sheep coughing in the wet, and the most certainly the sound of human voices. We put up our umbrellas again and hurried on; for human voices are alarming when they cease to be imaginary. It is not pleasant to meet new people in the dark.

We cannot be too grateful to the Cambridge men, Goldie among them, who first brought Forster into print. They published his first short stories, and these charming little essays which have something of the nature of short stories, so naturally do the subjects come alive. When Goldie and H. O. Meredith edited a series of Greek and Latin classics, they brought Forster in to introduce the Virgil, which gives us the first rather meagre sketches of great Roman figures and scarcely hint at the accomplished portraits he was to make in Alexandria a decade or so later. Just how much 'editing' there was of the young writer's efforts, just how detailed the encouragement they gave him, we are never likely to know, nor does it greatly matter. The work has the precocity which is frequently seen in brilliant young writers; already he has the golden pen, as was quickly recognized by that skilful authoress, Elizabeth. In 1905 Forster was living for a few months as tutor in the household of her husband, Baron von Arnim. A copy of the *Independent Review* arrived with his piece on Cardan. She took it away to read, warning him that she was a very severe critic. 'She brought it back in a highly chastened mood, saying, "You've simply got to go on and win, I've no more to say." ' The Cardan piece has all the Edwardian sophistication; it has the kind of good thing that Forster was to give us for the next fifty years and more and they ring as true as anything he has offered in all that long time. There is no trace of weakness anywhere, not a single hesitation in the rhythm, no youthful flaw.

'Gemistus Pletho' is a most learned account of a minor Renaissance figure who wanted to revive the ancient religion of Greece as most likely to be benefit western man. This is very much in the vein of Forster's humanist leanings. There is a touch of a theme that was to recur: ancients, good; medievals, bad, as here: 'He saw in it a rule of temperate life, a possible escape from the asceticism which medievalism had professed, and from the sensuality which it had practised.' As contrasted with the Greek gods: 'their radiant visible beauty, their wonderful adventures, their capacity for happiness and laughter.' The piece may be read as the apology for the classical fantasies in the short stories.

Now we take a leap in time. In 1931 Forster had a brief flirtation with the *New York Herald Tribune* and contributed a number of gay articles on unexpected topics. There are two hilarious articles on Voltaire as a scientist, which are unclouded by serious relevance to current affairs until the end, when two Cambridge scientists are mentioned, Eddington and Jeans, because certain unorthodox people have been disquieted by their discoveries, 'because of the support for Christianity that may be extracted from it'. The Gibbon and Coleridge pieces were published in the same American news-paper and the only person on record as objecting to this 'lofty whimsicality' as a fault that 'becomes really bad' in the Coleridge piece and the earlier Keats piece, is the American critic, Professor Trilling. Which seems to show again that humour travels un-certainly. If Forster has to defend himself, we shall remember his saying that the nonsense must not be left out if we want life in our pictures. Shall we anywhere find young Mr Gibbon more alive, better quoted: 'But what I value most, is the knowledge it [his three wasted years in the militia] has given me of mankind in general, and of my own country in particular.' Or more cogent comment: 'This is the summary not so much of a philosopher as of a historian who realizes that it is impossible, through reading alone, to interpret the past. Nor is emotion enough. The historian must have a third quality as well: some conception of how men who are not historians behave. Otherwise he will move in a world of the dead.'

The Coleridge also consists of some little-remembered incidents which in Forster's hands acquire that strange quality we call life. The trick of concealing who is being written about works only once if at all, but if it does it gives sudden liveliness. Without that, we still see that the trivial incidents and quotations so neatly garnered and arranged give us a glimpse of a living, foolish man.

The piece about Keats is managed in the same way. To the uninitiated the secret is out only in the last quotation, but again something real, poignantly alive is offered; the meticulous rehearsal of a grave domestic injustice. As in the Coleridge, a fellow being is described in a situation that is too much for him. The fact that he was a poet is mentioned quietly at the end without any fuss about the verses and letters which have rung through the writer's mind all his life. The shocking little story, told here so quietly, would have started Dickens on a full-length novel.

It was at about the same time that Forster undertook an introduction to George Crabbe's life of his father and here he is completely traditional in his approach. This makes no difference to his uncanny power of bringing his subjects alive. We shall find clues to this secret when we read what he says about this biographer: 'Nothing kills like reverence; it is the cruellest tribute one can pay to the deceased, and the reputation of Tennyson, for instance, is only just recovering from the crushing "Life" deposited on him by his son.' We recall 'one of those Lives that might be called Deaths' in *Marianne*. Very soon we hear another familiar argument again: 'he had a taste for triviality. The lives of the great are usually unreadable because everything is on an enormous scale...George and his father cared about little things.' The third mention is for the biographer, George the son was himself a person: 'he could write at moments passages of independent interest, which show he had his own attitude to life and was not merely recording.' There, there is the secret of biographical writing. Forster in turn finds the magic to evoke the East Anglian coast and the spirit of Crabbe's stories again. 'He hated Aldborough [it has become 'Aldeburgh' in his later lecture] "where guilt and famine reign", where his queer rough father had made him roll casks on the quay, [in the lecture they are casks of butter and he still hated them] where, later on, he had practised as an unqualified surgeon and an unwelcomed curate...Yet Aldborough dominates his work...Into the work of Crabbe there steals again and again the sea, the flat coast, the local meannesses, and an odour of brine and dirt—tempered occasionally with the scent of flowers.' Could anything be further from the aridity of criticism or nearer the secret heart of a living man? The magic comes again in the opening of his Aldeburgh lecture sixteen years later.

The remaining pieces in the third part, to which we now return, adumbrate *Marianne Thornton*, for the first is about her godmother, Hannah More, and the next is about her home in Clapham. They can be taken along with the pieces on Henry Thornton and 'Snow Wedgwood' in *Two Cheers*. They all give us direct glimpses of Victorian days. It is a delicious sudden glimpse of Marianne's godmother to see her 'able to move into the country and practise philanthropy upon a commanding scale'. To see her as one of five old maids: 'Five, all attaining the age of seventy, all lively, hospitable and jabbering, all suppressing the Slave Trade and elevating the poor.' Some essayists merely inform us, Forster braces the mind and encourages thought. 'She taught the poor to read and wash, observe Sunday, and honour the King, and before her day nobody had taught them anything...Unless her pupils were farmers' sons she did not allow them to write, and she was horrified at the suggestion they should acquire history or science.' There is that wonderful glimpse of the perils of childhood in the early nineteenth century, culled from Miss Patty's correspondence. One of their teachers had died and Forster quotes what he calls 'one of the great masterpieces of macabre literature'. 'I said a great deal to them afterwards, and wrung their little hearts; for I knew but too well that the world and young blood would make an excellent sponge to wipe out, full soon, the awful lessons of that day.' The piece ends with a reminder of the interconnectedness of these Claphamite families. Zachary Macaulay goes down to say goodbye before freeing some slaves in Sierra Leone and Miss Mills is hidden away but he hears her sobbing and finds her and they marry and beget Tom, the historian, who comes down as a child and recites verses as they breakfast: 'Thus do the generations touch.'

In 1934 he reviews a book by Miss Pym on Battersea Rise. She also is a great-grandchild of Henry Thornton the elder. Forster waits another twenty-two years to use the family papers himself to give us *Marianne Thornton*. Meantime, he notices the virtues in her writing and quotes, as he will again, the description of the gardeners rolling up the snow into great balls: 'my aunt's words seem to me to have much beauty, and to call up a lovely picture of that lost house and garden.' The curious will note that she was born in 1797 and says she was three years old when she watched this wintry scene, yet Forster puts the date 'about 1842'. His knowledge of the family papers is so great that he shimmers about the century and sees it all at once.

Five years later he sees an exhibition down in Clapham and he writes a notice of it in *The New Statesman* which is a pen-portrait of his great-grandfather. In it we find the word 'aroma' which is so apposite to Forster's feeling for the century. He is writing about Henry Thornton's published prayers and he says we get from them 'no meaning, but an aroma, the aroma of a vanished society, the sense of well-to-do people on their knees, the old chairs into which the elbows dig, the antimacassared backs against which the fore-heads rest'. We are given a glimpse of teasing problems in family life at that time: 'For three generations it was a problem to religious Englishmen whether the breakfast dishes should come in before the prayers and so get cold, or should come in after, which meant a wait, and an unpleasant sense of hanging in a void between two worlds.' It is the nonsense which tells us so much as in this glimpse of Marianne, which we are not permitted in the later Life; reading 'the same passage out of the Bible again and again, because she was para-lysed by the sight of the cat eating the ham, and felt unable to stop either the cat or herself'.

The East

The fourth part is made up of journalism about India with one or two pieces about the Middle East which did not fit into *Pharos and Pharillon*. He opens with one of them 'Salute to the Orient', which is his most considerable individual piece about the contemporary Middle East. At the end, a weighty consideration of the Indian States and a very early piece on the *Gita*. The section divides by date roughly into two parts, those written after the first visit to India and those written after the second. The piece on the *Gita*, 'Hymn before Action' appeared before the first visit and showed how he prepared for it. The humanist notes that the Hindus have answers to questions about war which the Christians have not found. Another piece, on Marco Polo, is separated from the others in time, being published in 1931. It has the usual merits of a Forster performance, giving life to its subject and correcting mistaken values put on that classic. At the end it refers to the Emperor Babur, who had attracted Forster's interest ten years earlier. Always seeking connections, he begins each of these pieces with a cross date to a known reference. Marco Polo wrote while Dante was writing his *Vita Nuova* and Babur was 'a robber boy, sorely in need of advice...scuttling over the highlands of Central Asia' while Machiavelli 'was collecting materials for *The Prince*' and we are intrigued by the thought of the difference it would have made if Machiavelli had been able to watch Babur instead of Cesare Borgia. Somehow, these references make our western world seem very young.

No one wrote literary journalism more professionally—the later pieces that used to appear in *The Listener* in Joe Ackerley's time, were an unfailing delights—but he retained the amateur advantage that he wrote only about books and people that interested him. At this time, his interests were in the East, from Alexandria to Calcutta and he wrote about Tagore, Blunt, Hickey, and little descriptions which have the precision and gaiety of Moghul miniatures, as this one about preparing a 'pan':

> Her first labour is to find a perfect leaf. One after another she rejects, fantastically disdainful, and seeking that which grew not upon any earthly stem. Pursing up her lips, she takes the best available, trims it with a pair of scissors, lays it upon the palm of her hand, which it more than covers, and seems to think, 'This is a disgraceful leaf, a humiliating leaf; can I possibly proceed?'...As she proceeds, her movements grow quicker and her spirits improve, she forgets her disappointment and becomes all anticipation, she is every inch a hostess, and doing up the difficult fastening like lightning, she bends forward and presents a gift. Little gestures and a little gift.

It is in work like this that Forster and D. H. Lawrence are so near one another. The quotation is a perfect example of his natural sympathy with Indian manners. It comes from a later piece written in the same mood as four 1914 sketches which remind us that

Forster knew British India only as a tourist. But what an observant tourist and how quickly he caught the spirit of the places he saw. Here is agricultural India, the land of a million villages: 'The track we were following wavered and blurred, and offered alternatives; it had no earnestness of purpose like the tracks in England. And the crops were haphazard too—flung this way and that on the enormous earth, with patches of brown between them. There was no place for anything, and nothing was in its place.'

In the fourth of these sketches when he was 'adrift in India' we meet a Muslim friend, and we may find a clue to the mixed character of Aziz. Here is a pleasant young Muslim with natural dignity playing the buffoon and slipping occasionally into babu talk. He recovered at the end, and those who knew him may think it is a glimpse of Ross Masood. The Hickey piece brings the man alive and places him accurately. The precise placing seems important, Forster sorts everyone out like an oriental. There is a phrase which reminds us how much these great professionals in our time have been absorbed in their craft: 'that strange excrescence, the power to write.' The two short pieces on Tagore were written in 1914 and 1919. The earlier was written when Tagore's writing was the current London fashion and Forster, as usual, seeks to correct unbalanced enthusiasm. The second has a tribute to Bengalis, a great artistic and intellectual people, and it gives us a phrase which some would apply to *A Passage:* 'the writer has been experimenting with matter whose properties he does not quite understand.' Forster would have been happier with Tagore if he had seen the humour in the plays but that unhappily evaporates in translation.

In the piece on Wilfrid Blunt we find a phrase which describes one of Forster's most endearing gifts: 'It is a wonderful gift, this of writing about one's fellow creatures as if they were alive; and so rare.' There is another worth noting, of greatness: 'Blunt wasn't great. One must make that reservation. He was sensitive, enthusiastic, and sincere, but he had not within him the fiery whirlwind that transcends a man's attitude, and sweeps him, whatever his opinions, into the region where acts and words become eternal.' Are phrases all that are left alive in these pieces? Most of them are of vanished interests, but there are a few more considerable pieces which are still lively. They all appeared in the *Athenaeum*, where he placed his more serious material in the early twenties.

The piece on Museums kindles thought about a practice which still troubles, the organized acquisitiveness of beautiful things and rubbish which another generation thought valuable. These old objects, he says: 'breathe their dead words into too dead an ear. It was different in the Renaissance, which did get some stimulus. It was important that the Laocoon should be found.' The description of the robbery of the Papyrus of Ani for the British Museum and the more extensive pilfering in Mesopotamia by the same operator Sir Wallis Budge, is first-rate crime reporting.

The long piece 'Salute to the Orient' is Forster's most considerable statement on Egypt. It shows at once the difference between the Middle East and India. The contemporary Middle East seems to have no connexion with its ancient and magnificent civilizations. Too many peoples have mixed and mingled for any continuity to be apparent. But in India we are constantly reminded of the continuity of a culture as long as recorded history. Forster approaches Egypt here through popular fiction, English and French, and particularly through Pickthall, whose name is as forgotten as his books. He is uneasily conscious of political and social movement, of the presence of nationalism and the threat of communism. He has the usual sense of responsibility about a country in which he has lived for some time—much longer than he ever lived in India—a reponsibility for knowing and understanding what is happening and he knows perfectly well also that hardly anybody in England cared. He was making a contribution to the earnest debate at that time about empire, when nationalism had been strengthened so much in the East by the weakness of Europe after her war. He was entirely liberal but he sought to steady the discussion from his firsthand observation.

He must have written the long piece about the Indian Native States immediately after his return from Dewas. When a governing people gives a nation independence it betrays its friends and supporters in that country. It is morally bad to betray one's friends, like the Indian Princes, and morally good to give India independence. It would require a Hindu explanation of good-and-evil to reconcile the moral dilemma. Forster is writing from the point of view of the Native State, for his only lengthy stay in India was in one of the tiniest of them. He saw the Delhi administration as an alien and impudent tyranny, here as all through *The Hill of Devi,* and it is as a commentary on that book that this essay is valuable. For, as we all know, the Native States have been absorbed into the general Indian struggle for the better conditions of the modern world. His paper has much of the root of the matter in it. All through the final section of *Abinger Harvest* we feel, as we feel all through Forster's writings, that there is an intellect of unusual power and concentration behind what is often apparently casual writing on casual subjects.

There is an appendix to the book, the text of a village play he wrote for Abinger, his home for so many years. It celebrates the tradition of rural life in England. There are echoes, as always, echoes of the spirit of Thomas Hardy, to whose company Forster pledged himself, echo of the tulip tree in Battersea Rise which we hear of in *Marianne.* The hint of prophecy is there again, for Abinger was soon to be drowned in a new town: 'Look into your hearts and look into the past, and remember that all this beauty is a gift which you can never replace, which no money can buy, which no cleverness can refashion.' It is a celebration of the 'lovely provincialism' in England which he spoke of a year earlier in his essay on Hannah More. And we now know it was also a farewell. It is the spirit which presides over much of this harvest of essays: 'The lovely provincialism of England takes shape, detaches itself from our suburbanism, smiles, says "I like my books, I like my garden, I like elevating the lower orders" and manages not to be absurd.'

Two Cheers for Democracy

If *Abinger Harvest* is mostly journalism, *Two Cheers for Democracy* is mostly broadcasts and lectures. Forster, like Lowes Dickinson before him, discovered a gift for putting across the disembodied voice. The four lectures are outstanding and the broadcasts fuse into an unusual picture of a human mind during a crisis in human affairs, with the result that *Two Cheers* has a greater impact than *Abinger*. It is the work of his maturity, which gave him his great reputation and influence as a man of letters after his creative work was done. It divides into two parts, the first concerned with the 1939 War and the freedom which was being fought for then, the second about Forster's enjoyment of that freedom. The war pieces, including some about our state of mind before the war, give us what is not easy to find anywhere, an idea of the mental anguish of intelligent Europeans as 'The Second Darkness' approached with the inevitability of tragedy. The second part, 'What I Believe', is about the human heritage as Forster enjoyed it. It is much the longer part and it has the atmosphere of the essay, personal and natural, while the first part is preaching. Conflicting themes emerge, both powerfully, the war and the contrasting theme of freedom.

There are a few pieces which may be quickly disposed of as having little relevance to the main themes. The opening piece is on the Paris Exhibition of 1937: 'Oh the French! Why are they so good at organizing these light happinesses?' And he carries us back to his Wembley piece by saying: 'The English admire them, and themselves produce the suety dreariness, the puffed pretentiousness, of Wembley.' We are seeing an Exhibition through the eyes of a man who could not be expected to be particularly happy in this show for the populace, but he has his moments, as in this comment while he is in the Soviet pavilion. He is speaking of money and here, if anywhere, is an argument for his theoretical preference for communism. We could not have chosen a subject on which there is a greater divergence of view between the ideologies. The Russians can never understand why we are so enslaved to the stuff. Forster sees the weakness of our view thus: 'One of the evils of money is that it tempts us to look at it rather than at the thing it buys. They are dimmed because of the metal and the paper through which we receive them. That is the fundamental deceitfulness of riches, which kept worrying Christ. This is the treachery of the purse, the wallet and the bank-balance, even from the capitalist point of view. They were invented as a convenience to the flesh, they have become a chain for the spirit. Surely they can be cut out, like some sorts of pain.' So right at the beginning of this collection on war themes he puts his finger on the acquisitiveness which affects our society so deeply. It was probably much in his mind because he was at that time thinking of writing a book about Samuel Butler. For contrast, he states the Russian view, as usual quite unabashed at stating useful truth in an opposing system and in these Stalinist days it was not easy to look at Russia equably: 'Even if he is scared at Marxism he ought to realize that Russia has tried to put men into touch with things. She has come along with a handkerchief and wiped. And she has wiped close to the exhibition turnstiles and amid the chaos and carnage of international finance.' He was always in rebellion against his banking ancestors.

There are two pieces which appeared in the weeklies in 1939 about the Jews and racial tolerance. The piece called 'Jew-Consciousness' is an example of his exasperated tolerance, for he sometimes gives the impression that he preached it because he found it difficult, and there is an echo from *Pharos* of what he thought of Jews in Alexandrian days. 'Racial Exercise', the second piece, is written as a duty on a matter of growing public concern. In another slight piece, 'Our Deputation', we see words used to make a caricature picture of the uselessness of real men with a mission attempting to fire or even singe the villagers of Whitehall and Westminster with their zeal. The last slight piece, a review of Gerald Heard's *Pain, Sex and Time,* brings us nearer the main themes. The book is a contribution to the problem of ordering human affairs sanely and effectively. The review gives us another glimpse of Forster's natural awareness of the scientific point of view, for he states a variation of the view on which Sir Julian Huxley is so often eloquent, the hope in the last possible evolution, the development of the human brain: 'Man's physical evolution is at an end; his evolution through the psyche can, if he chooses, continue...If he can detonate his powers, he will blow away the economic and political horrors now surrounding him—horrors which do not merely destroy his body but work inward and destroy his power to understand.'

We come now to the series of documents which give us a remarkable picture of what intelligent men went through just before and during the 1939 War. First, the shame, the agony of apprehension about whether we should ever take a stand against totalitarianism and then the fear that we should never be able to defeat it. Our emotions then may never be fully described but we have glimpses of them here which make painful reading for anyone who lived through these shaming years. The series begins in 1935 with 'Menace to Freedom', another reasoned forerunner of the essay three years later, 'What I Believe'. The argument is that man has never been an individual. He was born in chains and remains part of the herd. 'Greece saw the first attempt' at individuality. The eighteenth and nineteenth centuries thought that freedom had to be recovered while now, after our history of war and tyranny, we feel that freedom has to be discovered. 'Man grew out of other forms of life; he has evolved among taboos; he has been a coward for centuries, afraid of the universe outside him and of the herd wherein he took refuge. So he cannot, even if he wishes it, be free today.' He proceeds towards an optimistic glimpse of a future in which:

'Perhaps, under the inrush of scientific inventions, the change will proceed still quicker. Perhaps, after the storms have swept by and the aeroplanes crashed into one another and wireless jammed wireless, a new creature may appear on this globe, a creature who, we pretend, is here already: the individual.'

The argument was continued by Ortega y Gasset, for these ideas were appearing all over western Europe then. Ortega argues that man can 'modify his environment to his own convenience' and so become an individual, creating an 'inner world for himself'. Then he emerges with a plan of campaign 'not to let himself be dominated by things, but to govern them himself, to impose his will and his design upon them, to realize his ideas in that outer world' and with a superb touch of Latin idealism 'to shape the planet after the preferences of his own being'. That was said in 1939 in his essay 'The Self and the Other'. In times of calamity men have their finest dreams and Forster's version of this shaping of the planet comes at the end of that brief *Spectator* piece: 'There is the Beloved Republic to dream about and to work for through our dreams; the better polity which once seemed to be approaching on greased wheels; the City of God.'

If we want a corrective to this effulgent vision, we can find it in the bitter and despairing words of Paul Valery in 1936 in an essay on 'Our Destiny and Literature'. Suppose, he says, 'that you have these objects of greatest luxury called leisure and silence and the right proportion of solitude and company which favours the pro-duction of the work of the mind' and Forster had all this, then, says Valery, 'I still do not know where you will find in this world, which drags us along and dissipates our energies, that presentiment of deep spiritual desire, those conditions of durable and unremitting attention, and even that sensation of a noble resistance, to conquer which would assure us of the value of our efforts.' And in reply to the visions of Forster and Ortega he sees that if 'we imprint the form of our mind on the human world, the world becomes all the more unforeseeable and assumes the mind's disorder'.

In the piece on 'Tolerance' in 1941 Forster corrected the idealist view on which he ended in 1935. We cannot love everybody but we can be tolerant. 'Love is a great force in private life; it is indeed the greatest of all things: but love in public affairs does not work...we can only love what we know personally. And we cannot know much.' So we must make do with tolerance, which 'is a very dull virtue. It is boring. Unlike love, it has always had a bad press. It is negative. It merely means putting up with people, being able to stand things.' It certainly can be dull and a good, cleansing hate has more attractions. It is, he repeats, 'a negative creed, but necessary for the salvation of this crowded, jostling modern world'. He recalls the names of men who have had this virtue, and the names echo back to 'What I Believe', Erasmus and Montaigne, 'who lived in his country house and wrote essays which still delight and confirm the civilized'. The tolerance of these great spirits is not weakness: 'Putting up with people does not mean giving in to them.' He began the essay insisting on strength. In 1941 everyone was talking of reconstruction, for by that time we had had a taste of destruction, and he reminds his readers that 'unless you have a sound attitude of mind, a right psychology, you cannot construct or reconstruct anything that will endure'. The essay ends, as we should expect, with an accent on love: 'Perhaps, when the house is completed, love will enter in, and the greatest force in our private lives will also rule in public life.'

Perhaps. But his outlook is steady, we feel it in the texture of the prose, and we do not feel that he is merely putting a calm face on it for his Indian listeners. We can look now by contrast at two pieces written for the weeklies in 1939 when he was anything but calm. The texture of the writing is phrenetic and when he repeats his phrases it is like cries of anguish heard again. Every paragraph carries phrases of horror: 'all the private miseries may be a prelude to an incalculable catastrophe, in which the whole of western civilization and half oriental civilization may go down': 'The pillars of the twenty-thousand-year-old house are crumbling, the human experiment totters, other forms of life watch': 'He will be half-frightened and half-thinking about something else.' Again and again the divided mind, that particular horror of the intelligent man who always sought the Stoic steadiness. 'The state of being half-frightened and half-thinking about something else at the same time is the state of many English people today': and again, 'the spirit of

1939, the spirit which is half-afraid and half-thinking about something else.'

He heard the news of Munich in London and saw that: 'Peace flapped from the posters, and not upon the wings of angels.' So what did he do? He turned to simple, practical things: 'On the Thursday I returned to the country, and found satisfaction there in a chicken run which I had helped build earlier in the week.' Practical things help but they cannot satisfy completely: 'All is lost if the totalitarians destroy us. But all is equally lost if we have nothing left to lose.' He states the dilemma again: 'if Fascism wins we are done for and...we must become Fascist to win.' He has been jolted out of his usual stoicism: 'We are worried rather than frantic. But worry is terribly insidious; besides taking the joy out of life, it prevents the victim from being detached and from observing what is happening to the human experiment.'

That was his message to *New Statesman* readers in April and in September they received this further help, in an article called 'They Hold Their Tongues'. 'Some day, some intellectual day, when Satire revisits our madhouse, an entertaining book could be written around this war...Enter the Science of Psychology. Officially installed in a cellar, it abolishes the art of knowing what people are like, and ensures that they are incomprehensible to themselves as well as to others.' Later, the phrases have an Old Testament quality: '...never before has the spirit of man been so menaced and insulted...Blood used to get warm before it was shed. Now— coldness, depression, suspicion, loneliness...Those of us who were brought up in the old order, when Fate advanced slowly, and tragedies were manageable, and human dignity possible, know that that order has vanished from the earth...those who chronicle this age and its silliness, and look back from their intellectual day upon us, the tongue-holders, will accord us not only pity, which we fully deserve, but disdain.' We turn back to the family tables which record the union of preachers and Claphamites, which produced these formidable utterances that mirrored our state so accurately.

He was quieter in the next year when he delivered 'Three Anti-Nazi Broadcasts'. They appeared later as a Macmillan War Pamphlet. The years were rich with pamphlets then. In the first

9

broadcast he has a brief passage on English culture which is like a bird-song in spring and echoes back to the essay in *Abinger* on the English character and to so much in the novels.

> In England our culture is not governmental. It is national: it springs naturally out of our way of looking at things, and out of the way we have looked at things in the past. It has developed slowly, easily, lazily; the English love of freedom, the English countryside, English prudishness and hypocrisy, English freakishness, our mild idealism and good-humoured reasonableness have all combined to make something which is certainly not perfect, but which may claim to be unusual.

His main theme is defence of freedom once again, the burden of all these war writings is the defence of freedom. The writer must feel free, he must be free to tell other people what he is feeling and the people must be free to listen: 'when their public is allowed to receive their communications, there is a chance of the general level of civilization rising.' These were the regular themes for pamphleteers then and we have all this in extended form in George Orwell's *The Lion and the Unicorn* a couple of years later.

Freedom must be for some good purpose, and Forster foresees the good purpose which should now be our concern, when the dust and heat are gone: 'When a culture is genuinely national, it is capable, when the hour strikes, of becoming super-national, and contributing to the general good of humanity. It gives and takes. It wants to give and take.' It is an argument apposite to our present situation in this small world, when we sometimes feel that it would contribute so much if we all concentrated on putting our own houses in order instead of escaping with missionary zeal to interfere with others. Let anyone take from our culture when we have made it worth taking again. Then, as Forster says, along with France, we were all for sharing, and we found ourselves against nationalist states who were out for themselves alone and we could not avoid the clash. 'Hitler's Germany is the villain, it is she who, when the hour struck, ruined the golden moment and ordered an age of bloodshed.' Germany had her war and Italy and part of Germany were freed from totalitarianism as a result and precious little else that pleases us.

The second broadcast was purely propaganda, fighting for freedom by talking of the suppression of truth and the third looks forward to another stiff and endless fight: 'as soon as the war is won people who care about civilization in England will have to begin another war, for the restoration and extension of cultural freedom.' That is a war that goes on all the time and we have so much still to win. At the end of this third broadcast is a passage which shows how propaganda can corner the liberal mind. It is a reasoned defence of the war, demonstrating that it had to be fought. He ends as a preacher should, with a suggestion of hope: 'Violence has so far never worked. Even when it seems to conquer, it fails in the long run. This failure may be due to the Divine Will. It can also be ascribed to the strange nature of Man, who refuses to live by bread alone, and is the only animal who has attempted to understand his surroundings.' The glory and the riddle of the world.

There are three pieces in this part of the collection which, like many later, are celebrations of individuals. The Gerald Heard has been mentioned, the George Orwell was written much later, and the third is about Ronald Kidd, one of the founders of the Council for Civil Liberties. It was an address delivered at his funeral and it celebrates a man much in the English tradition of individuals dedicated obsessively to an ideal which they work to make true. Forster speaks again of freedom: 'I know the political and philosophical difficulties inherent in this idea of freedom: freedom for what: freedom to do what: freedom at whose expense, and so on. As a conception it is negative: but as a faith it is positive, and Ronald Kidd upheld it till his dying day.' He reminds us that it is of the nature of freedom that unless all are free, none are free: 'he knew that freedom is not the perquisite of any one section of the community: neither the employing classes nor the working classes nor the artistic and literary classes can be truly free unless all are free.' Nowadays we are more likely to remember that social freedom depends on responsibility and interdependence, and we recall phrases by an essentially simple mind, Albert Einstein's, uttered away back in 1931: 'A hundred times a day I remind myself that my inner and outer life are based on the labours of other men living and dead, and that I must exert myself in order to give in the same measure as I have received and am still receiving.' Three years later Einstein offered this variation of the theme: 'The individual, if left alone from birth, would remain primitive and beastlike in his thoughts and feelings to a degree that we can hardly conceive. The individual is what he is and has the significance that he has not so much in virtue of his individuality, but rather as a member of a great human community, which directs his material and spiritual existence from the cradle to the grave.' That is what lies back of the idea that if any are free all must be free to help one another.

The theme of the pursuit of freedom is continued in a broadcast in the Home Service of the BBC in celebration of the tercentenary of Milton's *Areopagitica*. It was 1944 and still wartime, so the inevitable line was that Milton was demanding freedom in time of war and if we applaud the *Areopagitica* we must stand for freedom of speech in time of war, which boils down to the question at the end of the talk: 'Is there as much freedom of expression and publication in this country as there might be?' The answer in 1944 was that war censorship in the press and on radio was a necessary evil which had to be vigilantly watched all the time. The censoring of books was by paper rationing. These things have gone but we still have another restriction named here, the libel laws. And if we do not have censorship by paper rationing we have it economically, for publishers have to sell to stay in business and with wages and prices rising all the time and private libraries closing down, things get tighter and more difficult every year. Freedom of publishing today has been curtailed by acquisitiveness. We are forever defeating our finer selves.

Forster has a positive and warming passage in his talk, and some of the great Milton quotes, some of them with contemporary warmth: 'the flowering crop of knowledge, and new light.' But the strength of the talk for us now is the technical ability of this simple exposition of a great argument for listeners who may not even have heard of the book. He unfolds the argument with that judicious commentary which is so difficult to get right, especially in brief space. Reviewers can study this piece with advantage. 'Truth is a perpetual progression', Milton said here, and reviewers also serve in its unfolding, best without dust and heat.

There are two post-war broadcasts in this first part and they are here because they continue the argument. The first is from a broadcast series under the title, 'The Challenge of our Times'. Such series were popular then and Goldie had earlier appeared in them to advantage. They were a good illustration of the mutual support of print and radio, for the talks appeared as serials on a chosen subject in *The Listener,* helping to make it what it was at that time, the best cheap weekly stimulus to the intelligence.

Here, there is genuine debate. Professor Bernal had preceded him and Forster speaks for the humane intellectual against the scientists. He begins autobiographically with a description of the Victorian liberalism from which he sprang: 'In many ways it was an admirable age. It practised benevolence and philanthropy, was humane and intellectually curious, upheld free speech, had little colour-prejudice, believed that individuals are and should be different, and entertained a sincere faith in the progress of society.' It was also the golden age of dividends, and that is no longer with us. We live now, he says, in a new economy, which our planners tell us 'will evolve an appropriate morality' for 'when all the people are properly fed and housed, they will have an outlook which will be right'. It is a variation of Ortega's argument, which we have just heard. The argument which Forster doubts is that it will be all right 'because they are the people' and he replies, 'I can't swallow that. I have no mystic faith in the people.' Certainly not, he had lived in London and though we have no more Leonard Basts, our New Towns do not seem to be entirely heavens upon earth and those who work with the people know they do not help one another more than before. It all takes time and it would be comforting to see signs that time is on the side of moral progress.

Forster's answer is that we 'want the New Economy with the Old Morality' and presumably supposes that the Old Morality would extend its power. But he sees the difficulty. 'We want planning for the body and not for the spirit. But the difficulty is this: where does the body stop and the spirit start?' He explains what he means by demonstrating that if you want everyone in the world to be properly fed you soon land yourselves in a series of controls which soon includes population control, which is birth control, which is supervising parenthood and already: 'You are meddling with the realms of the spirit, of personal relationships.'

Clearly, he says, it is a collision of principles and loyalties, and tells us about his childhood home, at Howards End, which was drowned in the New Town of Stevenage. Good agricultural land gone, country lives doomed, the immemorial tilling of the soil gone forever and on the other hand 60,000 people well-housed and the possibility (with the Old Morality working) of a strong and healthy human community. He ends by going for the scientists again.

> Owing to the political needs of the moment, the scientist occupies an abnormal position, which he tends to forget. He is subsidised by the terrified governments who need his aid, pampered and sheltered as long as he is obedient, and prosecuted under Official Secrets Acts when he has been naughty. All this separates him from ordinary men and women and makes him unfit to enter into their feelings. It is high time he came out of his ivory laboratory. We want him to plan for our bodies. We do not want him to plan for our minds, and we cannot accept, so far, his assurance that he will not.

The two cultures jarred with a grating sound. Two decades later we do not fear the scientist or anyone intellectually trained. That rivalry and suspicion has gone, and the two sides must combine against the common enemy, the bureaucrat, who only thinks of us as units. Here, here, is the threat to the individual.

The last piece is about a man who was strong on these questions. It is a review of a posthumous collection of essays by George Orwell, for whom Forster did a good deal of overseas broadcasting during the war. The review becomes an obituary notice, a summing up of a life that was lived hard. It rounds off this section because it ends by associating George Orwell in a special way with the search for freedom. 'Liberty, he argues, is connected with prose, and bureaucrats who want to destroy liberty tend to write and speak badly, and to use pompous or woolly or portmanteau phrases in which their true meaning or any meaning disappears...Many critics besides Orwell are fighting for the purity of prose and deriding officialese, but they usually do so in a joking, off-hand way, and from the aesthetic standpoint. He is unique in being immensely serious, and in connecting good prose with liberty.' There was much in common between the two men. They each produced a comparatively small oeuvre, in which they preached and prophesied with a will, and exerted great influence. Each was involved in the way of the world, each tried to make people see and think so that they would insist on things becoming better. Each was spontaneously gay but that was not as evident as it might have been in their writings, for they lived in times of stress. Both were humanists, best seen in their delicate handling of prose, but Forster somehow knew more about science—he could catch it out of the Cambridge air—and was able to take a less gloomy view of its progress. The last word should be on prose, for they both saw and taught by example that, 'If we write and speak clearly, we are likelier to think clearly and to remain comparatively free.'

The second part of *Two Cheers for Democracy*, under the general title of 'What I Believe' is the treasure store of essays, broadcasts and lectures to which we go to enlighten us about the novels and biographies and to find the views in them confirmed. There is nothing very new in these pieces, the accents and the views are the same but, being spoken or written essays, they cumulate to give us a much more personal view of the writer. Let us begin by looking again at 'What I Believe' and see it in context.

As soon as we begin we hear again of tolerance, good temper and sympathy, the virtues preached because the speaker did not always find it easy to enjoy them. We hear again that the lawgivers are Erasmus and Montaigne, and that personal relationships are the solid things to cling to, although 'Psychology has split and shattered the idea of a "Person".' Then come the Two Cheers for Democracy, one 'because it admits variety' and another 'because it admits criticism'. It was written in a time of force and violence and the answer he finds to them has new meaning now: 'The people I respect most behave as if they were immortal and as if society was eternal.' It was the idea that society might not be eternal that shattered so many when they realized the possibilities of nuclear obliteration. Then comes the best argument for democracy, that its members should be aristocrats 'of the sensitive, the considerate and the plucky'. The ending reduces us all to equality: we are born and we die, in this we are separate and this we have in common. It is a macabre stoical performance, but it was written in the year of Munich.

The long piece 'Anonymity' goes back to 1925 and could have been included in *Abinger*. It antedated *Aspects of the Novel* and we have met it in discussing that book. The argument begins by stating the two functions of words: 'They give information and they create an atmosphere.' At the one end are Public Notices which give information and have no atmosphere and at the other end is lyric poetry which is all atmosphere and quite useless. Poetry generally is almost no use. Drama sometimes gives useful information and the novel is full of it. 'What a lot we learn from *Tom Jones* about the west countryside! And from *Northanger Abbey* about the same countryside fifty years later!' And how much we learn about Edwardian London and motor-cars and the position of women from *Howards End*! 'The social historian', Virginia Woolf noticed, 'will find his books full of illuminating information.'

Now he comes to his subject. Should writing be signed or not? He quickly demonstrates that information should be signed and anything else need not be. He is able, that decided, to go further. The term 'atmosphere' now requires strict definition. Partly it is style, the ordering of words to 'raise our emotions or quicken our blood'. There is something else and it is indefinable. It is the power to create a world more real than our own. While we read works in which this is achieved, like *The Ancient Mariner*, we forget the author. The piece becomes anonymous. He would support the thesis 'that all literature tends towards a condition of anonymity and that, so far as words are creative, a signature merely distracts us from their true significance'. He presses the point home: 'To forget its creator is one of the functions of a Creation.' We may put it thus: a perfectly achieved lyric tells us nothing about its author; it is the imperfect lyrics that tell us about Blake or Burns.

He comes to a fascinating glance at the nature of the creative power: 'each human mind has two personalities, one on the surface, one deeper down.' The one deeper down has to be used by the writer: 'because unless a man dips a bucket down into it occasionally, he cannot produce first-class work.' The theme connects with anonymity: 'It is in any case the force that makes for anonymity. As it came from the depths, so it soars to the heights, out of local questionings; as it is general to all men, so the works it inspires have something general about them, namely beauty.'

This recalls other statements on the unconscious in creation; the famous lecture by the mathematician Poincaré in 1908 on his eureka experience, of how he agitated the unconscious mind by mental concentration and how it threw up the answer; the famous passage in Conrad's *Personal Record* in 1912 when the general's daughter walked in—'I hope I am not interrupting?'—and smashed up a whole American seaboard and all its inhabitants: Somerset Maugham's pen, described in *The Summing Up* in 1938, which wrote down things the author had not been conscious of thinking. We shall pick up this bucket again.

Forster ends the paragraph with a reference to the reader: 'it transforms the man who reads it towards the condition of the man who writes' and that recalls the famous passage in A. E. Housman's *Name and Nature of Poetry,* in 1933, where he quotes Eliphaz the Temanite: 'A spirit passed before my face: the hair of my flesh stood up.' It also recalls things which Forster himself said, the passionate insistence in his lecture on Virginia Woolf that in the act of creation her novel became 'one thing, one', and the place in *Aspects* where he speaks of what happens to the listener when the Fifth Symphony has been played: 'we hear something that has never actually been played' and all the parts of the symphony 'enter into the mind at once, and extend one another into a common entity.' He relates that to the sensations the reader enjoys after finishing *War and Peace,* 'great chords begin to sound behind us'. Here, the statement of the reader's condition is more general and relates to the experience of beauty: 'What is so wonderful about great literature is that it transforms the man who reads it towards the condition of the man who wrote, and brings to birth in us also the creative impulse. Lost in the beauty where he was lost, we find more than we ever threw away, we reach what seems to be our spiritual home, and remember that it was not the speaker who was in the beginning but the Word.'

At the end, he returns to the two functions of words, to give information and to create. He appeals for the use of the imagination which 'is our only guide into the world created by words' and ends with the hope that the experts will be able to tell us more about the unconscious. The whole enquiry recalls that Anglo-Saxon swallow which flew into the banqueting hall from the darkness and out again into the darkness. In the fleeting moment of our lives we may, by taking thought, keep in touch with real existence of which this life is only an imitation.

Twenty-four years later he delivered an address on *Art for Art's Sake* in New York. It has echoes of the earlier pieces on Belief and Anonymity. In his usual way he reduces the art for art's sake cry to good sense: 'Many things, besides art, matter...Man lives, and ought to live in a complex world, full of conflicting claims, and if we simplified them down to the aesthetic he would be sterilized.' He then digresses to speak of order in daily life before speaking about it in art. We do not find it in daily life: 'Order...is an internal stability, a vital harmony, and in the social and political category it has never existed except for the convenience of historians.' Scientists are always changing our world and we cannot hope to keep in harmony with our surroundings.

He allows the mystic harmony and quotes Jacopone da Todi, as he had done eleven years before in *What I Believe*: 'Set love in order thou who lovest me' and admits that: 'The existence of a divine order, though it cannot be detected, has never been disproved.' It was the same admission inherent in the climax of *A Passage to India*.

He returns to his theme, aesthetic harmony. 'A work of art is unique...because it is the only material object in the universe which may possess internal harmony...The work of art stands up by itself, and nothing else does.' Art 'is the one orderly product which our muddling race has produced'. He returns sadly to the discussion of society in a way which recalls his definition of civilization as the brief spaces between disorder. And he stresses the pertinacity of art, providing 'little vantage grounds in the changing chaos'. He ends with his original claim: 'Works of art, in my opinion, are the only objects in the material universe to possess internal order.'

Three short pieces follow which do not add to the argument, one on 'The Duty of Society to the Artist' and two on 'Does Culture Matter'. The first is on the apparently insoluble question of how the artist should be supported and whether he should be supported at all. Forster in 1942 is gloomy about his prospects but time has demonstrated artistic buoyancy in the affluent society. In the two pieces about culture he is equally gloomy in 1940 and time has again proved him wrong. People listen to music and look at pictures enthusiastically and if not very many read things worth reading, very few ever did much reading in England. He states at the end his usual position about enjoying all works of art: 'Works of art do have this peculiar pushful quality: the excitement that attended their creation hangs about them, and makes minor artists out of those who have felt their power.'

It is in the next piece, 'The Raison d'Être of Criticism in the Arts' that he repeats in America in 1947 what he had to say about the nature of creative activity in the 'Anonymity' piece in 1925. He is lecturing about listening to music and he comes again to 'the gulf between artist on the one hand and critic on the other', to the place of criticism in artistic activity. Instead of enjoyment making minor artists of us, he says there is 'a basic difference between the critical and creative states of mind' and he proceeds again to describe the creative state. 'In it a man is taken out of himself. He lets down as it were a bucket into his subconscious, and draws up something which is normally beyond his reach'. And later he speaks of 'this stuff from the bucket, this subconscious stuff, which is not procurable on demand'. Once again we hear of Coleridge and the man from Porlock, and a parallel is drawn from the experience of Claudel, who writes: 'And having spoken I know what I have said' which is the old Platonic view of the artist as an instrument which is played and also impishly reminds us of the lady in *Aspects* who did not expect to know what she thought until she heard what she said.

Criticism, on the other hand, 'is grotesquely remote from the state responsible for the works it affects to expound. It does not let buckets down into the subconscious.' Criticism has two aims. It considers the work of art as a whole 'and tells us what it can about

9**

life'. That is aesthetic, and the other we may call scholarship, for it explains 'the relation of the object to the rest of the world'. There is 'no spiritual parity' between the two. Then comes the reconciliation with earlier statements about our approaching 'the condition of the person who created' the novel or the symphony. The critic is a third person, who tried to help to bring us together. Between artist and reader 'there has been an infection...Something has passed.' We feel the surprise the artist felt when he saw what he had created. At this stage criticism offers us no help, it has no part in it: 'she has to withdraw when reality approaches.' This reality is love: 'as in mysticism, we enter an unusual state, and we can only enter it through love.'

He goes on to speak of the freshness in art, what we have already distinguished as the quality of the classic, that it is always fresh and full of life. The critic, he says, works away, reading and re-reading, remembering and analysing and modifying his views: 'but he ought to remain startled, and this is usually beyond him.' But we know that a good critic can transform a dull reader and make him see a book freshly as Forster does again and again in this collection of essays. There is no third person then, critic and inspired reader are one, and anyone who overhears can share the experience.

He states, as often before, his experience in listening to music: 'I can conceive myself hearing a piece as it goes by and also when it is finished' and once again we can transfer this experience to the novel and acknowledge that the total impression of *A Passage to India* is greater than our enjoyment as we read. He goes on to another suggested function of the critic: 'It has been suggested that criticism can help an artist to improve his work.' He quotes Day-Lewis stating what Romain Rolland and many others have told us, that the artist is engaged in the next work when the critic speaks of the last and anything he says seems 'almost unreal' and the artist has 'a feeling of irrelevance'. Certainly the critic can help with the minutiae of style: 'The sort of trifling help which criticism can give the artist. She cannot help him in great matters.' His conclusion is as bleak as it is pontifical: 'My main conclusion on criticism therefore has to be unfavourable, nor have I succeeded in finding that it has given substantial help to the artists.' That is that and there is only one more thing to notice, that an adverse remark by a critic can rankle for years. He mentions Beveridge's remark about the high death rate in *The Longest Journey* and that was forty years before, which shows how an adverse criticism can rankle long after praise has been forgotten.

The section ends with three agreeable pieces on music and painting which need not detain us here as we hurry on to the great Aldeburgh lectures which adorn this book. The lecture on John Skelton is the later and livelier. It was delivered in 1950 at the Aldeburgh Festival, a small and intimate festival, more a gathering of like spirits than a public occasion and therefore *simpatico* to the speaker. There is no better example of his resurrecting power. It is a fitting opening to the long section called 'The Arts in Action', which includes the other Aldeburgh lecture on 'George Crabbe and Peter Grimes', the Rede Lecture on Virginia Woolf, and the W. P. Ker Memorial Lecture on 'English Prose between 1918 and 1939.' The rest is made up of broadcasts and reviews, many of them first broadcast to India during the war in that vestigial Third Programme of which George Orwell was the inspiration. When I reported to Orwell that the broadcasts did not have the listening figures they deserved, we arranged together the publication of some of them in pamphlets in India. We asked Forster if we could have six of his broadcasts to make a complete pamphlet but with all the good will in the world he could not give permission. Most of them were talks which he felt were not for appearance as prose. The difficulty is expressed in the introduction of *Two Cheers*: 'The broadcasts have been troublesome. There is something cajoling and ingratiating about them which cannot be exorcised by editing, and they have been the devil to reproduce.'

If critics, as Forster says, cannot help artists, they can help readers and he would be a poor reader who did not run to turn up the texts after reading the Aldeburgh Lectures. There seems to have been no teasing quandary here between talk and print. The naturalness of talk is contained in prose rhythms and the poets and their verses live again. There is also in each lecture a particular evocation of the spirit of place, the special gift in the novels seen again. He describes Aldeburgh in the opening of the Crabbe lecture just as he describes it in his Introduction to the Life. There is the same doomed sense of the land being at the mercy of the destructive waters: 'a couple of long streets against which the sea is making an implacable advance. There used to be as many as five streets—three of them have disappeared beneath the shallow but violent waters, the house where Crabbe was born is gone, the street that has been named after him is menaced, the Elizabethan moot hall, which used to be in the centre of the place, now stands on a desolate beach. During the past twelve months the attack has been frightening.' The Aldeburgh Festival is naturally dominated by Benjamin Britten and it was a charming idea to ask Forster to lecture on George Crabbe. He had written so well about Crabbe and Alde-burgh when introducing young George Crabbe's Life of his father, and he was very soon to collaborate with Britten by helping to write the libretto for his opera, *Billy Budd*. The earlier essay had evoked the spirit of place but the lecture is concerned with defending the existence of the place. In the opening, after the description of the erosion of Aldeburgh itself, he takes us down the estuary to Slaughden and gives us another pen picture of the bleak Anglian flats and another view of the plight of Aldeburgh: 'The prospect from Slaughden, despite desolation and menace, is romantic. At low tide the great mud flats stretch. At high tide the whole area is a swirl of many-coloured waters. At all times there are birds and low woodlands on the further bank, and, to the north, Aldeburgh sheltering among a few trees, and still just managing to dominate her fate.' In 1948 we were still slowly recovering from the *ennui* after the war. Very soon, further storms and coastline disasters roused us and more adequate defences have been built along the coast.

Crabbe is a poet of place, like Wordsworth, and 'I wanted to evoke these sombre and touching scenes as best I could, in order to give a local habitation and a name to what follows. Crabbe without Aldeburgh, Peter Grimes without the estuary of the Alde, would lose their savour and tang.' Like his contemporary Wordsworth, Crabbe was a regional poet: 'He had the great good luck to belong to a particular part of England and to belong to it all his life.' Then we come to the Peter Grimes story. At the end of a sensitive but tough analysis there is an interesting passage on dreams and the creative faculty. Crabbe's dreams may have been induced by opium. They all used it to alleviate the pains of the stomach disorders from the polluted water they drank. Crabbe recorded his: 'he kept a lamp and writing material by his bedside in order to record them before they were forgotten' and so by habit more dreams would be remembered when he returned to consciousness. Later, there is the only direct reference to Freud in these discussions of the unconscious and the creative faculty: 'The interpretations of Freud miss the values of art as infallibly as do those of Marx. They cannot explain values to us, they cannot show why a work of art is good or how it became good. But they have their subsidiary use: they can indicate the condition of the artist's mind while he is creating.' The lecture ends with a rich tribute to Britten's opera.

The Skelton lecture, which is even better and so the best that Forster ever gave, came two years later and is, of course, about another East Anglian. This time the place is Diss in Norfolk and the time is the uncertain one between the Middle Ages and the Renaissance: 'The solidity of the middle ages was giving way beneath his feet, and he did not know that the Elizabethan age was coming.' The place becomes at one point the interior of the church at Diss, where an 'ill-behaved curate, who took his hawk into the church, locked all the doors, and proceeded to train it with the help of two live pigeons and a cushion stuffed with feathers to imitate another pigeon. The noise, the mess, the scandal, was terrific.' The nave and choir of the church, being lofty, were 'suited to a sporting purpose'. The curate, excited by his sport, rushed up and down, 'uttering the cries of his craft, and even clambering on to the communion table. Feathers flew in all directions and the hawk was sick. At last Skelton found "a privy way in", and managed to stop him.' The lecture is delivered in that blithe spirit, telling next the story of how this Catholic Rector had his baby brought naked to church and exhibited to his gossiping, complaining parishioners: 'Is not this child as fair as any of yours? It is not like a pig or a calf, is it?' Skelton's obviously immense energies were given to fighting Wolsey, to quarrelling with his bishop, to satirizing the Scots, recently defeated at Flodden, to many escapades in London, where he spent prosperous years. It is all described with such *brio* that the scenes pass before our eyes. At the end he leaves us with the belchings of Elinor Rumming, after a great description of the poem:

> They get drunk, they tumble down in inelegant attitudes, they trip over the doorstep, they fight—Margery Milkduck, halting Joan, Maud Ruggy, drunken Alice, Bely and Sybil, in they come. Many of them are penniless and are obliged to pay in kind and they bring with them gifts often as unsavoury as the drink they hope to swallow—a rancid side of bacon for example —and they pawn everything they can lay their hands on, from their husband's clothes to the baby's cradle, from a frying pan to a side saddle.

It is certainly Forster's most vigorous platform performance—and he was seventy-one. The great advantage of the seventies is that so many inhibitions go. And if criticism can be as creative as this, what can Forster or anyone else possibly say against it?

The fourth lecture was second in order of delivery, three years after the Rede and so in 1944 when we were able to see ourselves through the war into some sort of future. Its subject was prose between the wars so he was not straying far from subjects already considered. The books with which he had to deal 'even when they were not directly about a war—like the works of Lytton Strachey or Joyce or Virginia Woolf—they still display unrest or disillusion or anxiety'. Writers, in Forster's judgement, are always involved: 'if they have any sensitiveness they must realize what a mess the world is in, and if they have no sensitiveness they will not be worth reading.'

The lecture is aloud with echoes. The great movements in these inter-war years were economic and scientific. When science became technology, it was changing things all the time and security was swept away. When it was relativity and psychology it extended notably the material available to the creative writer. 'Man is beginning to understand himself better and to explore his own contradictions. This exploration is conveniently connected with the awful name of Freud, but it is not so much in Freud as in the air.' Forster, we recall, gathered as much as anyone from the Cambridge air. Even relativity. 'Can literary men understand Einstein? Of course they cannot—even less than they can understand Freud. But the idea of relativity has got into the air.'

About the economic movement he is less enthusiastic. It would seem now that part of the cost of the Welfare State and our chronic inability to pay our way is at the expense of creative literature among other good things and that for the first time in four hundred years Englishmen are not writing very well. Everything costs too much for them to be able to give the time to it and there is no money to inherit as Forster did. Nor is it so easy to get good work published. Commercial material is turned out as much as ever but good writing is something we cannot afford. When Forster was lecturing, the economic revolution was the transfer of power: 'Perhaps it will mean democracy, but it has not meant it yet, and personally I hate it.' It looks now as if we shall wait a long time for anything like a democracy of aristocrats such as he approved.

When he turns to consider the special nature of prose we hear echoes from 'Anonymity' twenty years earlier. 'Prose, unlike poetry, does two things. It serves us in daily life and it creates works of art.' Good prose now wants to be informal and clear: 'Novelists too—they practise the friendly unpatronizing tone' which is an example of 'democratic good manners'. The references to the Authorized Version which follow have been found useful earlier in discussing *A Passage to India,* which is in the unbroken prose tradition of that unmatched translation, in which an old Mediterranean civilization has indeed been translated to the English countryside and made us feel one with the land of Israel and its prophets.

When he turns to the esoteric tendency in prose between the wars we see again into his own mind: 'It is an age that could not produce a Shakespeare or even a Madame de Sévigné or a Jane Austen: an age in which sensitive people could not feel comfortable, and were driven to seek inner compensation: an age similar in some ways to that which caused St Augustine to write *The City of God.* St Augustine, though he looked outside him, worked within. He too was esoteric.' Forster was never able to recreate his shattered world, even by recreating it within, 'temporarily sheltered from the pitiless blasts and the fog'. He takes Lytton Strachey as typical of the period and expresses a view of his *Queen Victoria* which is now everywhere accepted. D. H. Lawrence is mentioned at the end with the sensible view that *The White Peacock* and *Sons and Lovers* are his finest novels. He ends by looking back on the whole period and finding it good. With the barrenness which lies between us and the days of that lecture we find agreement with that judgement easy.

There is a reference to Samuel Butler in the lecture, saying that conscious knowledge of the subconscious 'comes at the beginning of the century in Samuel Butler's *Way of all Flesh*'. In the same year as the lecture he wrote an article in *The New Statesman* on 'Erewhon —A Book that Influenced me', and that is all we have of Forster's intention to write a book on its author. Butler, like Forster, instinctively rebelled against his Victorian forebears. But though a rebel, Butler was not a reformer and in his moments of dutiful feeling (and they are many) this is what Forster admires: 'Grace and graciousness, good temper, good looks, good health and good sense; tolerance, intelligence and willingness to abandon any moral standard at a pinch. That is what he admired.'

Why has the book influenced him? Butler was a master of the oblique, he slipped his opinions in sideways and Forster admits to liking that. Then *Erewhon* was just what he had been thinking about himself when he read it: 'the only books that influence us are those for which we are ready' and Forster thinks '(quite erroneously) that I could have turned out this little skit of Erewhon if the idea of it had occurred to me'. He had the same rebellious tough intelligence and the same love of fantasy: 'I like that idea of fantasy, of muddling up the actual and impossible' and he had never been able to exploit it since the short stories.

He has another confession of faith at the end. He wants to be good, but not in St Augustine's way; clever, in the way of Voltaire and not of Machiavelli; indignant like Butler, but not like Swift; and strong like Antigone but not like Carlyle's heroes. He had broadcast about Voltaire three years earlier, calling him 'one of the greatest men European civilization has produced'. Unlike the earlier pieces on Voltaire, this one is spoiled by being propaganda, which comes in obliquely as in Butler. The best things he had to say on Voltaire came later in his article on Ferney. In the broadcast it is Voltaire in the grip of the tyrant Frederick the Great: 'if a man believes in liberty and variety and tolerance and sympathy, he cannot breathe the air of the totalitarian state.'

The sketches and tributes to friends and other sympathetic characters are a feature of *Two Cheers*. The one on Edward Carpenter describes an idealist socialist with Orwell's disease, the desire to 'live and work with the manual labourers'. It is an upper class disease and appears in every generation. There is an acerbity in the comment which pleases today: 'He believed in Liberty, Fraternity and Equality—words now confined to platforms and perorations. He saw the New Jerusalem from afar, from the ignoble slough of his century, and there is no doubt that it does look more beautiful from a distance. When the armies of the down-trodden enter its gate, as thanks in part to his efforts they are doing today, the New Jerusalem becomes a more ordinary city, where the party leaders book the best rooms.' Carpenter became still more sympathetic by going to Ceylon and sitting at the feet of an Adept. He came back and worked 'for a socialism which should be non-industrial, unorganized and rooted in the soil'. A hopeless fellow, the salt of the English earth. 'Webb and Webb' is juxtaposed, a family portrait which sets our teeth on edge. Forster could hardly be easy with Beatrice Webb: 'what mattered in her view was work; have you worked? What is your work?' He was invited to lunch with the firm of Webb and Webb. The conversation was a series of pronouncements:

> I remember thinking when I visited them in their country home that if I could have confuted the pronouncement, it would have been instantly withdrawn. All I could do was babble, 'Well I don't somehow feel like that myself.' My remark was listened to, was dismissed, and the next pronouncement followed. I leant back in my deep arm-chair without any feeling that I had been snubbed. The atmosphere was authentic and noble. They were too serious to score.

It is a charming tribute to the remarkable pair, made after her death, but: 'I could never have been intimate with them: only those who worked with them could be that, and my own schemes for improving society run upon different lines.'

For contrast, he tells us of his friendship with Ross Masood, a kindred spirit: 'He woke me up out of my suburban and academic life, showed me new horizons and a new civilization and helped me towards the understanding of a continent.' And he confirms what this would make us think, that *A Passage to India* would never have been written without him. He is said to be partly the original of Dr Aziz and if we are to reconcile the half-grown buffoon and the skilled surgeon it is because Ross Masood had this touch of the buffoon in his otherwise serious make-up. He must have confirmed Forster's condescending view of English professional people in India: 'I pity the poor fellows from the bottom of my heart, and give them all the help I can.'

One of these poor fellows of an earlier time was William Arnold, brother of Matthew, who went to India as a soldier, changed over to the Civil Service and became Director of Education in the Punjab when he was twenty-five and four years before the Mutiny. He wrote a novel, *Oakfield, or Fellowship in the East,* which attracted Forster's attention. The novel is naturally autobiographical and, as usual, the Englishman's main interests continue to be about his homeland. Their tragedy was that not only were they not culturally and spiritually assimilated in India but they felt it necessary to resist assimilation if they were to do their professional work properly. In Arnold's novel: 'India is passed with a puzzled sigh, with a sense of ignorance and impotence.' The writer was invalided home and died on the way at the age of thirty-one. The broadcast ends with verses his brother Matthew wrote in his memory. The novel troubles Forster, for it had an evangelical, priggish uprightness (the Gordon spirit) and showed the gulf that so often existed between the peoples. It was not always easy for the rulers. Ruling meant getting work done for the ruled, to combat ignorance and famine and disease. With these difficulties Forster had nothing to do.

But he did have sympathy with both Hindu and Muslim thought, which was much more likely to endear him to Indians, so when the Punjabi poet, Mohammed Iqbal died, Forster was called on by the BBC to offer a tribute to his memory. We hear echoes of what he has been telling us since his Alexandrian days: the Muslim says: 'We shall see God perhaps. We shall never be God.' It is the Hindu who says that we shall be God. 'Iqbal dislikes the pantheism which he saw all around him in India—for instance, in Tagore—and he castigates those Muslim teachers who have infected Islam with it. It is weakening and wrong to seek unity with the divine. Vision—perhaps. Union—no.' It is the distinction between Godbole and Aziz, when each sees the vision.

It is time to go back to the beginning of this section of Part Two and discuss what is left. There is some care for juxtaposition in these pieces but the interests they cover are so wide that no thread runs through them. The general impression we get from these broadcasts and lectures and reviews is the impression we always get from a successful essayist, of an interesting person to whom we want to listen. It is Forster's substitute for not being a storyteller. He does not tell stories but he converses. As here at the beginning, about a performance of *Julius Caesar* given by the boys of a primary school—where some of us enjoy our Shakespeare most. We are in the school hall and for a little while we forget where we are and we hear about the play, the three explosions in it, and about the characters and then we are back in the schoolroom again. It was a broadcast to India, one of a series on the syllabus for Calcutta University, and so far no research worker has discovered how many more students passed that year.

The next piece is Shakespearian also, about a celebration at Stratford organized by Garrick in 1769. It is one of Forster's little triumphs in bringing a scene alive as he did thirty years earlier in these first pieces in *The Independent Review*. Any amount of exact detailed scholarship goes into it and it reads like a report of yesterday's gay occasion.

From Garrick we turn to Gibbon, and the allusions are made easier for us, as again we are overhearing a broadcast to India. We listen with care, for here is the historian Forster most resembled and who he just possibly could have rivalled if he had had the mind and found an adequate subject. He would not have escaped from the present like so many lesser historians. His view is rather that: 'it strengthens our outlook occasionally to glance into the past. 'He turns to the autobiography, for that is his subject, and offers a routine assessment and quotation, tainted as so often with the touch of propaganda: totalitarianism, bad; democracy, good. A few years later, in 1949, he was again broadcasting to India; about his library and at the end he names the three writers whose work he would like to have in every room and one of them is Gibbon: 'in a library one thinks of Gibbon most.'

The broadcast about the library is one of a group of personal confidences about himself and his family which supplement what we learn in *Marianne Thornton*. It takes us back to his great-grandfather's books and writings. It speaks of his own books and it is a joy to learn 'that my library, so far as I have created it, is rather a muddle'. Which is good support for many of us. Another flash of confidence brings us near him again:

'Do you ever lend books?' someone may say in a public-spirited tone of voice at this point. Yes, I do, and they are not returned, and still I lend books. Do I ever borrow books? I do, and I can see some of them unreturned around me. I favour reciprocal dishonesty. But the ownership of things does give me peculiar pleasure, which increases as I get older.

His three authors whose books should be in every room are Shakespeare, Gibbon and Jane Austen. 'And of course, I have some Tolstoy, but one scarcely wants Tolstoy in every room.'

The next piece is on the London Library, which was an extension of his own, and which he supported so munificently when the local authority threatened its existence by rating it. England needs many ombudsmen and mostly against local government enormities. The piece is a history and a celebration, an advertisement for a unique library. 'Knowledge will perish if we do not stand up for it, and testify. It is never safe, never harvested.' But what a pity he had to attack 'the crowd' in order to celebrate Carlyle and the Library he did so much to found. Local authorities supply the crowd with excellent libraries which are busily used and admirably run, not least in the district where the London Library stands.

One of the books in Forster's library is a folio-size notebook which was bought by Bishop Jebb and given to Forster's grandfather along with a pair of silver buckles in recognition of a lifetime's service to the bishop. Forster inherited the book almost blank and 'here I am scribbling notes about Marx in it, or copying extracts from Madame de Sévigné'. The next article, about Henry Thornton, parallels the main themes of *Marianne* very usefully. The reflections on the Clapham Sect are *loci* for all students of that excessively English group of banking evangelicals. When they used Henry Thornton's book of prayers (thirty-one editions and splendid royalties):

> The Clapham Sect listened, rose from its knees, ate, and then made money -- made as much as ever it could, and then gave away as much as it could. The activity in either direction was immense. Thanks to the economic condition of the times, wealth rushed down these worthy people's throats from morn to eve, and not being psychologists they thought it would have no effect upon their souls if they purged themselves promptly.

Then the comparison with the Quakers: 'to whom the Clapham Sect has sometimes been compared...they have what the Claphamites lacked: a touch of mysticism, a sense of the unseen, and a capacity for martyrdom.'

Little remains in the section. A short piece on William Barnes, which is not only a charming touch of the countryside which Forster loves so much but an expert discussion of some subtleties of prosody. The piece on three of Tolstoy's short stories connects, for 'They all teach that simple people are best'. It is a celebration of simplicity and it appears to be another broadcast to his Indian friends, more 'cajoling and ingratiating' than usual but free of propaganda. Our minds turn to Orwell's essay on Tolstoy as we read this acute analysis of his character and they turn to Orwell again when we read the piece called 'Mrs Miniver' for it is an analysis of the English class structure. This was 1939 when the class war was our favourite island conflict, which was left to smoulder during the war and burst out and partly burned out immediately afterwards. This piece is a useful little note of the social situation before things became fluid again.

The piece on Forrest Reid answers the earlier one in *Abinger Harvest* on this Belfast writer who is now so completely forgotten that we have to be assured by Rose Macaulay that he was a considerable novelist. Reid's special gift is named in the 'Abinger Notes' at the very end: 'He, better than any living author, can convey this atmosphere of baffled malevolence.' The remaining pieces are on French writers he will always enjoy, Proust, Gide and Romain Rolland. The Proust piece has been considered with the earlier pieces in *Abinger* and the piece on Gide is a check on what is said in *Aspects*. At the end of the Rolland piece, which is a celebration of *Jean Christophe*, which was especially sympathetic to Forster as the portrait of a Beethoven-like composer, Rolland is compared to Proust: 'a far bigger person than Proust from the social and moral point of view; he cared about other people and tried to help them, he fought for a better world constantly and passionately.' But he is forgotten. In his pamphlet *Above the Battle*, which was a call for internationalism, for some sort of League of Nations, Rolland speaks of his dream that men will 'build higher and stronger, dominating the injustice and hatred of nations, the walls of that city wherein the souls of the whole world may assemble'. It is another echo of the idea of the City of God which we hear again and again in the writings which Forster celebrates in this volume.

In the first piece on Gide there is an addendum on the German poet Stefan George which is almost pure propaganda, but this piece on Gide and the later obituary letter to *The Listener* are almost entirely free of base metal. He celebrates the humanist in Gide: 'curiosity, a free mind, belief in good taste, and belief in the human race.' He speaks here and in the brief later note about Gide's great oration at that writer's Congress in Paris in 1935 at which Forster delivered his speech on 'Liberty in England':

> His thesis was that the individual will never develop his individuality until he forms part of a world society. As his thought soared, his style became fluid, and sentimentality passed into affection. He denied that humanity would cease to be interesting if it ceased to be miserable, and imagined a social state where happiness will be accessible to all, and where men, because they are happy, will be great.

When he speaks of what Gide 'managed to transmit through his writing' in the obituary notice, we seem to hear a summary of what Forster has been doing in this collection:

> Not life's greatness—greatness is a nineteenth century per-

quisite, a Goethean job. But life's complexity, and the delight, the difficulty, the duty of registering that complexity and of conveying it...He has taught thousands of people to mistrust façades, to call the bluff, to be brave without bounce and inconsistent without frivolity. He is the humanist of our age—not of other ages, but of this one.

The last section of the book, 'Places', is in fact an almost total recall of his interests through a long life. It opens with a fantasy, different from the short stories because it is based on fact and instead of being a bright, hard surface it has sympathetic reverberations. It is a letter written in the London Library in 1931 to Madan Blanchard and it tells the sad reciprocal story of Prince Lee Boo who came to England and could not understand how anyone like Madan could elect to stay in the Pelew Islands. The poor fellow had no resistance to the tuberculosis which was then endemic in England and was quickly a victim. Forster has his own reaction to the Madan story of an escape to the innocence of South Sea life. In a famous passage he tells us again who are his heroes, the people who free themselves from social inhibitions:

> If it isn't one set of rules it's another, even for heroism. I ought to feel free myself, as I've health, strength and am middle-aged, yet I can't keep my hat on in church, for instance, even if no one's looking, and if I'm fighting never manage to hit below the belt. While not getting fussed over this, I can't but remember the people who managed better, and it's in order to meet them in the flesh that I study history. Here and there, as I rake between the importancies, I come across them—the people who carried whimsicality into action, the salt of my earth. Not the professional whimsies—their drill's dearer than anyone's—but the solid fellows who suddenly jib.

The next piece takes us back for the last time to his beloved India. 'I was back in the country I loved, after an absence of twenty-five years.' He is standing on the platform of the Great Mosque in Delhi, and in a mosque he felt the peace of Islam. Once again, he was able to look round at a social occasion and find he was the only Englishman in the company. Once again, he was completely among friends. Indians have that wonderful gift of friendship. He notices the changes since his earlier visits, particularly the emancipating of women. He goes to a PEN conference at Jaipur and listens to 'a moving address made by the Prime Minister of Jaipur, Sir Mirza Ismail. He described the atmosphere in which all modern writers must function, and held it to be their duty to keep in touch with the world, but not as politicians. Not much of the oratory was of his high order or struck the international note. But his concern with moral issues was typical of other speakers, and typical, too, his indifference to art for art's sake. Listening to him and to others, I felt that India had indeed changed.' He reports on writing, films, painting and sculpture. We feel that in twenty-five years he has got a little out of touch. He was in at the beginning of a new India, a rebuilding of India, complete with five year plans for health, work and food which seemed more important at that moment than writing and art because it was going to be the basis on which a new Mother India was going to be built so that all the things of the spirit might follow. We go back to his thoughts on death, which is the curse of the generations. Must I and my generation live and die without the joys of writing and painting and all the other arts so that another generation may be spiritually healthy? This has never happened in the world before and must it happen to us? He ends with the preacher's appeal for the virtue then most necessary, affection.

The next piece, 'Luncheon at Pretoria' is nonsense incarnate. His suit is ruined when a dish of hot food is spilt over it and the accident follows him right up Africa to Egypt. In a more interesting piece, he goes to America for the first time, at the age of sixty-eight. 'It was to provide me with scenery and individuals.' America has both in abundance. It is a broadcast, and it is propaganda again, exhorting us in 1947 not to nag at America. It was a time when all civilized Europe was afraid of America, of strength that might do anything and even destroy the world. It is followed by a piece on the American sect, the Shakers, which is hardly reassuring.

We return to Europe and see Voltaire's home, Ferney. We return to the ancient values of Europe, the natural values of Forster, who chose Voltaire as possessing the kind of cleverness he liked:

Civilization. Humanity. Enjoyment. That was what the

agreeable white building said to us, that was what we carried away...Voltaire felt that he saw too many people, and that the universe, though fortunately bounded by Russia, was upon too cumbrous a scale. He could just illuminate it, but only just, and he died without knowing that he was the last man who would ever perform such a feat, and that Goethe would die asking for more light.

Later in that paragraph we see unmistakably how Forster believed in the soil and the country life for human sanity, and in the horror which humanity becomes in the concrete living boxes of great cities. 'The boundaries of the universe were to extend bewilderingly, the common people were to neglect the pursuit of agriculture, and, worst of all, the human make-up was to reveal deadnesses and depths which no acuteness could penetrate and no benignity heal.' If this is truth, we are all doomed.

'Cloud's Hill', which follows, is T. E. Lawrence and his RAF friends, where Forster is easy, as he is amongst Indians. 'The little room opposite—that's now a bathroom containing a snowy and hygienic bath. Nothing of the sort in my time. I remember one of our party retiring into a corner with a coin, tossing it, and muttering to himself: "Heads I wash, tails I don't. Tails. I've won".' The spirit of the place was the spirit of the English countryside, 'where gentians can be found, and sundew'.

In the next piece, the echoes come from Cambridge. 'O spare Cambridge! Is not the city a little one? Is she not unparalleled? Oxford, her swollen sister, is so distended by endowments as to be unrecognizable...Cambridge still keeps her antique shape.' In the next piece he goes back to London and echoes are heard again. He is writing in a popular Sunday newspaper in 1937 and he stands above Billingsgate and describes the splendid confusion of architecture around him. He comes back to it full circle at the end, quoting T. S. Eliot's verses on the same scene. Between, he defends the muddles of so many of the London villages. He goes back to Moll Flanders and echoes what he said in *Aspects*: 'Give a thought to her when you are stifled with cant, for she is the goods.' He recalls how he hated London when he was young and echoes come from Stephen Wonham and Leonard Bast: 'I used to loathe London when I was young. Living an immense distance away (to be precise, in Hertford-shire), I used to denounce her for her pomp and vanity, and her inhabitants for their unmanliness and for their unhealthy skins.' Now, he celebrates London, 'the muddle which need not be un-pleasant'.

Last scene of all is Abinger, echoing the pageant which gave us the last scene in *Abinger Harvest*. He is returning to peace and he recalls, as before, the Mosque of Amr, even more wonderful to him than the Great Mosque in Delhi. Islam means peace. Whatever the creed may have done, the name means Peace, and its buildings can give a sense of arrival, which is unattainable in any Christian church.

> The tombs at Bidar give it, the Gol Gumbaz at Bijapur, the Shalimar Gardens at Lahore, the garden-houses at Aurunga-bad. But it came strongest from the Mosque of Amr, and I learnt afterwards, with superstitious joy, that others, besides myself, had noticed this; that the Mosque had been in early days the resort of the Companions of the Prophet; that the sanctity of their lives had perfumed it; that the perfume had never faded away.

Memories crowd and in the end he is standing with Old Empson, and all the echoes crowd in of what he has written of old age, for that, after all his desiccated description of it, is the supreme happi-ness. 'Old Empson and I are old and moderate friends, he regrets that I am going but did not say, he wanted to talk about fish. The loveliness of indifference! The restfulness! The happiness not mystic or intense! Nothing hanging on it.' This, this is the last best happiness, for which the first was made.

A Select Bibliography

(Place of publication London, unless stated otherwise.)

Bibliography:

A BIBLIOGRAPHY OF E. M. FORSTER, by B. J. Kirkpatrick (1965, revised 1968)

Collected Works:

THE UNIFORM POCKET EDITION (1947)
COLLECTED SHORT STORIES (1948)

Separate Works:

WHERE ANGELS FEAR TO TREAD (1905). *Novel*
THE LONGEST JOURNEY (1907). *Novel*
A ROOM WITH A VIEW (1908). *Novel*
HOWARDS END (1910). *Novel*
THE CELESTIAL OMNIBUS AND OTHER STORIES (1914). *Short Stories*
— contains: 'The Story of a Panic', 'The Other Side of the Hedge', 'The Celestial Omnibus', 'Other Kingdom', 'The Curate's Friend', 'The Road from Colonus'.
THE STORY OF THE SIREN (1920). *Short Story*
— hand-printed and published by Leonard and Virginia Woolf at the original Hogarth Press, Richmond, Surrey. Reprinted in

The Eternal Moment and Other Stories, 1928, and *Collected Short Stories*, 1948.

ALEXANDRIA: A HISTORY AND A GUIDE. Alexandria (1922). *History*
—second edition, enlarged, 1938. Reprinted, with a new introduction by the author, New York, 1961.

PHAROS AND PHARILLON (1923). *Essays*
—published by Leonard and Virginia Woolf at the original Hogarth Press, Richmond, Surrey.

A PASSAGE TO INDIA (1924). *Novel*

ASPECTS OF THE NOVEL (1927). *Criticism*
—the Clark Lectures at Cambridge, 1927.

THE ETERNAL MOMENT AND OTHER STORIES (1928). *Short Stories*
—contains: 'The Machine Stops', 'The Point of It', 'Mr Andrews', 'Co-ordination', 'The Story of the Siren', 'The Eternal Moment'. Reprinted in *Collected Short Stories*, 1948.

GOLDSWORTHY LOWES DICKINSON (1934). *Biography*

ABINGER HARVEST—A MISCELLANY (1936). *Essays*
—a collection of about eighty essays and articles contributed to English and American periodicals between the years 1903–34.

WHAT I BELIEVE (1939). *Essay*
—reprinted in *Two Cheers for Democracy*, 1951.

VIRGINIA WOOLF, Cambridge (1942). *Criticism*
—the Rede Lecture, at Cambridge, 1941. Reprinted in *Two Cheers for Democracy*, 1951.

THE DEVELOPMENT OF ENGLISH PROSE BETWEEN 1918 AND 1939, Glasgow (1945). *Criticism*
—the W. P. Ker Memorial Lecture, at Glasgow, 1944. Reprinted in *Two Cheers for Democracy*, 1951.

TWO CHEERS FOR DEMOCRACY (1951). *Essays, lectures and broadcasts*

THE HILL OF DEVI (1953). *Travel*

MARIANNE THORNTON (1956). *Biography*

Some Biographical and Critical Studies:

THE LAMP AND THE LUTE: STUDIES IN SIX MODERN AUTHORS, by B. Dobrée (1929)
—E. M. Forster is one of the six authors discussed.

'The Novels of E. M. Forster', by P. Burra
—published originally in *The Nineteenth Century and After*, November 1934, and reprinted as an Introduction to the Every-

man's Library edition of *A Passage to India*, 1942. A favourite study with Mr Forster and his readers.

THE WRITINGS OF E. M. FORSTER, by R. Macaulay (1938)

THE DEATH OF THE MOTH AND OTHER ESSAYS, by V. Woolf (1942)
—contains an essay on E. M. Forster and his work.

E. M. FORSTER, a study by L. Trilling (1944)

POETS AND STORY-TELLERS, by Lord D. Cecil (1949)
—contains a study of E. M. Forster which balances over-adulatory pieces.

THE COMMON PURSUIT, by F. R. Leavis (1952)
—contains an essay on E. M. Forster.

THE BLOOMSBURY GROUP, by J. K. Johnstone (1954)
—a study of E. M. Forster, Lytton Strachey, Virginia Woolf, and their world.

THE ACHIEVEMENT OF E. M. FORSTER, by J. B. Beer (1962)
—very readable and rewarding.

E. M. FORSTER: THE PERILS OF HUMANISM, by F. C. Crews, Princeton University Press (1962)

E. M. FORSTER, by K. W. Gransden. Edinburgh (1962)
—brilliantly concise and always profitable.

THE CAVE AND THE MOUNTAIN, by Wilfred Stone, Stanford University Press, (1966)
—a useful assembly of detailed and generally accurate information.

Index

288